Delivering Evidence-Based Therapeutic Support to Children and Families

Messages of Hope from an Inter-Agency Team
Working with Families Affected by Abuse

Edited by

Ann Catchpole

Russell House Publishing

Russell House Publishing
First published in 2006 by:
Russell House Publishing Ltd
4 St. George's House
Uplyme Road
Lyme Regis
Dorset DT7 3LS
Tel: 01297-443948
Fax: 01297-442722
e-mail: help@russellhouse.co.uk
www.russellhouse.co.uk

British Library Cataloguing-in-publication Data:

A catalogue record for this book is available from the British Library.

ISBN: 1-903855-85-3, 978-1-903855-85-0

Typeset by TW Typesetting, Plymouth, Devon
Printed by Cromwell Press, Trowbridge

About Russell House Publishing

RHP is a group of social work, probation, education and youth and community work
practitioners and academics working in collaboration with a professional publishing
team.

Our aim is to work closely with the field to produce innovative and valuable materials
to help managers, trainers, practitioners and students.

We are keen to receive feedback on publications and new ideas for future projects.

For details of our other publications please visit our website or ask us for a catalogue.
Contact details are on this page.

Contents

About the Editor and the Contributors

The Editor

Ann Catchpole is a qualified social worker with twenty years' experience of working with families where abuse has taken place. Before gaining a professional qualification she was for several years Director of the Lancaster branch of The Samaritans. She joined the Joint Agencies Child Abuse Team (JACAT) in 1989, soon after its inception (see page 2). Her early work with play groups gave her a liking for working with pre-school children, and she has written and published about working therapeutically with young children who have been abused. For the last ten years she has taken over the responsibility for running regular groups for mothers, and more recently for fathers, of children who have been abused.

The Contributors

Nick Booth is the only contributor to this book who has never been a member of JACAT. He works in the field of adult mental health and has a special interest in working with women and men who have been abused as children. Nick is Head of Psychotherapy Services, part of the Primary Care Trust in Plymouth.

Jo Bromley is a qualified family therapist. She specialises in working with sexual health and associated issues from a systemic perspective. Jo applies her working knowledge in various settings, including JACAT, Exeter Sexual Health Services and Adolescent Mental Health. She worked previously in a voluntary sector agency for HIV and AIDS support, and facilitated the Exeter HIV and AIDS Family Support Group. Until recently she chaired the local Forum for Domestic Violence.

Anna Flanigan qualified as an occupational therapist in 1986. Since then she has worked in child and adolescent family services in a variety of settings, specialising in therapeutic work with young people. This includes time spent working in an adolescent in-patient unit and the community Child and Adolescent Mental Health Service (CAMHS) team and as a counsellor at Exeter College. She spent eleven years at JACAT as a child therapist. She has done further training in drama therapy, family therapy and supervision, and is a clinical supervisor to both individuals and teams. She was for four years a tutor on the Diploma in Counselling Course at the University of Exeter. Anna left JACAT in 2004 and is now in private practice.

Juliet Gardner is a doctor who worked in general practice and chaired the social services' child protection meetings for Mid and East Devon over a number of years. She was instrumental in obtaining funding and getting JACAT started, and was its first co-ordinator. Juliet is now retired.

Sue Holt is an educational psychologist who has specialised in the needs of adopted and fostered children and other child care issues. She helped JACAT maintain good relationships with local schools. She was Co-ordinator of the JACAT team for a number of years' 1997–2001. She has written and published on the role of the educational psychologist from a systemic perspective and on childrens' and adults' self-esteem. Sue is currently in private practice.

Brian Johnson started working as a residential worker in 1979 and qualified as a social worker in 1983. He began working therapeutically with young males whilst still working in a residential setting. He has subsequently developed a specialism in working in the area of sexuality problems, gender dysphoria, and sexual behaviour which causes concern.

Richard L'Orme was a consultant paediatrician at the Royal Devon and Exeter Hospital, in whose grounds JACAT is based, and the paediatric advisor to JACAT for a number of years. He has published and lectured widely. He was one of the small team instrumental in getting JACAT started and as such provided useful background material to the chapter on JACAT's context. Richard is now retired.

Alex McCahearty was a psychology assistant when he wrote the chapter on *Research*. He is now a qualified psychologist working with adolescents in Taunton.

Paul O'Reilly is a consultant clinical psychologist and family therapist. He is a founder member of JACAT, and its current co-ordinator, and also works in the Child and Adolescent Mental Health Service. He is the director of the Family Therapy Centre, a registered charity. He has written and published in the fields of family therapy and child abuse as well as carrying out research on families and mental health problems.

Carole Town has been working as a clinical psychologist and family therapist in the Child and Adolescent Mental Health Services for the past twelve years and at JACAT for the past eight years. Having trained initially as a primary school teacher, Carole now specialises in working with younger children and families. She has published on children's understanding of illness, parenting issues in relation to childhood chronic illness, anxiety and stress management in relation to alcohol problems, and the development of family work within JACAT. Her direct work with children and adoptive families is informed in particular by attachment theory. Carole has also undertaken training in the diagnosis of and work with children with Autistic Spectrum Disorder.

Acknowledgements

This book has been several years in the writing and JACAT is nearer its twentieth anniversary than its tenth, which is when the idea for writing it first took root. Little did I know then what editing such a book would involve. All my colleagues who have contributed to it have done so on top of working full-time and I should like to pay tribute to their willingness to share in this project. That it has taken some time serves to illustrate the difficulty that practitioners have in recording their work and being able to share it with others.

As befits the work of a collaborative venture, which JACAT is, the book has been written co-operatively, so colleagues, and ex-colleagues, have had an input even into chapters which do not bear their name. Moreover much credit is due to newer members of JACAT who have supported the writing of the book without being able to participate in it, for they have covered for the times when the book has taken one or other of us away from other work. My thanks are due also to our two secretaries Linda Morgan and Helen Thomson who have helped with production of the book itself. I am also very grateful to Professor Mary John, formerly of the University of Exeter, who has long campaigned for children's rights and who encouraged us to persevere in writing it.

Two of the contributors to the book have subsequently left JACAT, Anna Flanigan and Sue Holt, and I am grateful for their continued co-operation in its production. Sue was originally co-editor and, as such, much involved in early planning.

Finally, I should like to acknowledge the inspiration I have gained from the women for whom I have run mothers' groups. Their courage and tenacity in the face of the potentially devastating effects of abuse on their families has been a great incentive to give a voice to victims on a wider stage.

We are greatly indebted to Russell House for publishing this book. As a first time editor I have found their ready availability to give professional advice and encouragement most helpful. My thanks in particular go to Geoffrey Mann, Martin Jones and Clive Newton as well as to Martin Calder the publisher's Reader.

We hope that all who read this book will be encouraged to continue their work with families and children where abuse has occurred and will appreciate the advantages of a holistic and joint agency approach.

Ann Catchpole

Foreword

Mary John
Professor Emeritus, University of Exeter

I am certain that I will not be alone in welcoming this carefully crafted work into the public domain. It is a truly remarkable book: in the inter-disciplinary work that it describes; in the bleak stories that it tells; in the quite exceptional level of belief in human possibility that it chronicles; in the individuals that form the substance of the 'evidence'; in the ingenuity of some interventions; in the multidimensional caring that provides the fabric of all encounters documented here.

Whilst we are all aware that all abuse of children fragments families, relationships, and self-confidence in so many ways, the work of JACAT with traumatised families and children provides a model of trust and support for human beings in all the shades and textures of life. 'Neither we nor our clients need be the victims of our history. But in order that our clients may free themselves as much as is possible from the vagaries of personal history, and yet live within the complexities of personal development, empowering assistance may be required.' (O'Reilly, p. 168) The 'empowering assistance' provided by JACAT is well illustrated here. Moreover, should arguments be needed for the importance of their work, this work is set in the context of working with adoptive families, with disabled children, with mothers' groups, with fathers' groups, with teenage boys, and also seen through the lens of the long term consequences of child sexual abuse as revealed in work with adults presenting with mental health problems in later life. Whilst it is indeed a very practical account, theoretical issues arising within family therapy with such a group and the challenges of collecting research data are skilfully addressed.

A multi-perspective insight is given into the operation of a system that has been developed over many years by a team of professionals from diverse disciplines and backgrounds. These individuals care about the issues, care for and about their clients, and care for and support each other in what must surely be the most demanding work with families and children. It provides a fine-grained detailed account of the Team's work. Professional activity in this area is fraught with pitfalls as many media frenzies, public inquiries and individual soul searching in recent years have revealed. The system described here details the ways in which thought, reflection, self-criticism and modification have played their part.

This is important, as systems intended to support children and families have often been found to have failed them lamentably. In the early work on the implementation of the United Nations Convention on the Rights of the Child, 'systems abuse' was identified as one of the ways in which activities designed to protect the child had often turned out to be themselves abusive. Significant amongst the reasons why such abuse occurred were found to be: lack of resources; lack of co-ordination; lack of skills and training; inadequate supervision and staff support; lack of voice for children (Cashmore, Dolby and Brennan, 1994). Whilst the issue of 'voice' has been a major preoccupation of mine over the years, I have been impressed by the trouble JACAT has taken to ensure that within the system they provide all such possible flaws have been addressed and provided for, and that provision has been made to ensure that their clients and their fellow workers are 'heard'. Of course, resources are never enough in this area but the team have been quite determined about what they regard as the minimum feasible provision and have worked accordingly. This is an impressive account of a team in operation over many years. This is what makes it such a valuable book – it brooks no compromise and gives a very detailed account of how the JACAT system operates.

It does indeed describe painstaking work. Work that literally takes on the burden of some of the pain of disclosure and also in its very painstaking nature makes it clear to the families and individuals that they matter. I have argued elsewhere (John, 2003) that to have any sense of agency and power to exercise one's rights an individual, whether child or adult, one has first to be treated as a person. Interacting with individuals, shunned, isolated and rendered powerless by their experiences, the Team take tremendous trouble with the details of the arrangements, the clients are treated with consummate courtesy and care. The importance of this is very much in evidence here. If any manager or funder of such a service were to query whether the service or intervention could be provided more quickly or more cheaply, having read this account they would be left in no doubt why the system must operate as it does.

Isolation and stigmatisation form the threadbare fabric of many of these children's 'family' lives. Here the Team dissect the nature of the problems and develop strategies for support amongst these families, and also recognise the potential costs to their own family lives and relationships of being involved at a professional level in such harrowing work. 'By taking responsibility for nurturing ourselves and others we hope to have the strength to keep the fact of abuse alive in our minds and also in the minds of others, and to continue to alleviate the suffering which abuse brings to whoever it touches.' (Catchpole, Holt and L'Orme, below, p. 14). In the intelligent and caring way they have interacted with their charges they provide a model of good practice. What I like about this book is that it makes so few assumptions, and from the way the whole operation runs makes evident the fundamental respect these individuals have for each other and their clients. Doing this sort of work well cannot be rushed or skimped and has to be deeply rooted in the professional team's philosophy.

Strange to say that I was exhilarated by reading this book. It recounts distressing experiences indeed, but whilst there are such professionals around who are prepared to harness their insight, energy, inventiveness, time and commitment to working in this way with such families it seems all is not lost. The Team have taken trouble for these families and in so doing have honoured them. Moreover, in the spare moments the Team have had for themselves over the years they have written about their work, about which they can be rightly proud, so that other concerned professionals working in this field can share the detailed programming. It does not provide tips for therapists but is the distillation of years of experience and practice. Many readers will be moved, as I was, and feel statistics, research evaluation, auditing, clinical rigour and so on, are all important but here we have the story of a journey jointly undertaken that reinstates the respectful *I and Thou* (Lincoln, 1993) in the arena of professional work with troubled children and families.

In the early nineties, following the ratification of the United Nations Convention on the Rights of the Child, when at the *World Conference: Research and Practice in Children's Rights* hosted in Exeter, we questioned the extent to which in those early days such research and practice was a matter of empowerment. Well over a decade later I am humbled by the dedication of JACAT, working with abused children, worried families and concerned professionals, which has continued to demonstrate how by working together tirelessly and incrementally over the years they have empowered many families and indeed each other. It is my hope that this publication will serve to honour the Team and the families who have shared some of their experiences here, and indeed enlighten other professionals working with damaged families in this important work. I urge anyone working in this field to read it.

Cashmore, J., Dolby, R. and Brennan, D. (1994) *Systems Abuse: Problems and Solutions.* Sydney, New South Wales Protection Council.

John, M. (2003) *Children's Rights and Power: Charging Up for a New Century.* London and New York, Jessica Kingsley Publishers.

Lincoln, Y. S. (1993) '"I and Thou": Method, voice and roles in research with the silenced'. In McLaughlin, D. M. and Tierney, W. (Eds.) *Naming Silences Lives. Personal narratives and Process in Educational Change.* New York & London, Routledge.

Preface

Dealing with the detrimental effects of abusive behaviour as a team

This book is a comprehensive account of how one group of professionals from diverse backgrounds, but whose work touched the field of child abuse either directly or tangentially, came together to work as a team. In the mid-1980s the Joint Agencies Child Abuse Team (JACAT) came into being as an attempt to tackle both the short- and long-term detrimental effects of abusive behaviour towards children and young people.

Child protection has been the subject of much debate, media focus and increased public awareness over the past twenty years, leading hopefully to better practice. At the time of JACAT's formation, practitioners in the field of child protection in the city of Exeter, and in the rural and often isolated settings of East Devon, were well-intentioned but ill-informed about the therapeutic needs of children who had been abused. Geographic distances and lack of funding, co-ordination, training and expertise proved crucial disincentives to the provision of therapy.

Joint working across professional boundaries

Aimed at practitioners, this book does not set out to offer itself as the only way forward: rather, it describes the methods of therapeutic intervention developed by individual therapists over a number of years, but under the umbrella of a team philosophy. What started as an experimental concept – namely joint working across professional boundaries – has been translated into an effective working pattern. This has stood the test of time due to the team's flexibility in tailoring its practice to keep pace with current needs as evidenced by research and their own practical experience.

How to use this book

This book will benefit from being read as a whole, but is one also for 'dipping into', being a description, chapter by chapter, of individual ways of working with different types of abuse, varying age groups, etc. The style, therefore, of each chapter, is distinctive according to the author and subject matter. This should not detract from its worth, as each clear, lucid account serves as a demonstration of what can be achieved by a well co-ordinated and financially secure group of professionals from originally diverse backgrounds.

The structure of the book

The first chapter, in Section One, sets out the context for the therapeutic work undertaken by the team. It describes the thinking behind the creation of the team: namely that close inter-agency co-operation should continue beyond the child protection process into the therapeutic arena, thus offering individual children the very best appropriate therapy available, regardless of the lead agency or speciality. It also provides a brief description of how JACAT sets about its work, the changes that have come about as a result of external pressures, usually caused by the impact of new legislation, and what it feels like to be part of a jointly funded and multi-disciplinary team. This chapter, too, shows how vital is good supervision, and illustrates the ways in which JACAT has sought to offset the potential damage done to practitioners who are constantly exposed to working with the after-effects of abuse.

The chapter on working with adolescents in Section Three is especially powerful, illustrating as it does, the necessary risk-taking and the cost to the therapist who tries to work in one of the hardest, but at the same time perhaps one of the most rewarding, areas of therapy.

Also in Section Three, the chapter on working with children with disabilities who have been abused, demonstrates the breadth of JACAT's therapeutic skill, while taking due account of the difficulties presented by this area of work, and the weaknesses that still exist in its practice. Hopefully, it will act as an incentive to others to offer this too often neglected but very needy group of young people support and understanding.

Group work was in its infancy when JACAT started and, despite the difficulties of convening such groups, has become a regular feature of the team's work. Much appreciated by professionals and carers alike, the chapters about it in Section Four clearly point to the obvious benefit to the participants. Chapter 4.3 on group work with the mothers of abused children provides an insight into what can be achieved with a group of adults, when their needs, so crucial to the future well-being of their children but hitherto not addressed, receive attention.

Two parts of the book illustrate particularly well the ability of JACAT to adapt its practice to the changing needs of its clientele. The emphasis of direct therapeutic work was in the early days centred on individual children, but Section Five on work with families shows how the pattern of working has been broadened to include all family members, when this is appropriate. Similarly, consultative work was only a small part of JACAT's work overall when it started, but Section Two on consultations shows how it has been possible to expand this work to the benefit of all concerned.

Finally, Section Six covers some of the research into the effectiveness of JACAT's services.

JACAT would never have got off the ground without the enthusiasm and perseverance of the small steering group. The willingness of the major agencies, namely the Health, Social Services, Education, Probation and the Police authorities to listen, support and contribute to the concept of close inter-agency collaboration was crucial to JACAT's success. For the then 'Exeter Health Authority' and East Devon Social Services who took a chance and agreed joint funding, which continues to this day, no praise is too high.

Hopefully, the sharing of the experience – the aim of this book – will give less experienced therapists working in this difficult field the confidence to work out their own ways of therapeutic intervention.

There are only two things we can offer our children: one of them is an understanding of their roots; and the other is wings. It is JACAT's hope that this book will aid increasing numbers of children to fly.

Juliet Gardner

Case Studies

1.1 **The Context**

Ann Catchpole, Susan Holt and Richard L'Orme

Introduction

The Joint Agencies Child Abuse Team (JACAT) was established in 1987 as a result of a clearly perceived gap in services for children who had been abused. Once the child protection system had been activated, and the children's safety assured, few therapeutic services were available for those children and families left damaged and struggling by the after effects of abuse. JACAT's composition and remit was heavily influenced by the impact of the events in Cleveland: both health and social services were aghast at the failure of the two agencies responsible for the safety of children to work together with trust and co-operation. Though JACAT was not to be a child protection agent it was recognised that it could have a significant influence on the prevailing atmosphere under which the principal agencies worked. Consequently a multi-agency and jointly-funded approach seemed by far the best option for the future. JACAT was asked to provide a consultation service to any professional working in the field of abuse, to offer individual work, preferably jointly with the referring agency where possible, to children or families suffering from the impact of abuse, to provide training on matters related to child abuse to professional or voluntary bodies where it was relevant, and to raise the general awareness, of professional and non-professional alike, of the issues raised by the experience of child abuse or of working with it.

At its inception it was envisaged that JACAT would cover East Devon from Axminster to Okehampton, and including Tiverton and Crediton in mid-Devon, following social service boundaries. This boundary was at the start coterminous with the boundary of the health authority, that being JACAT's other funding agency. The area is largely rural in nature, with most of the services based in the city of Exeter, by far its biggest town. Although Exeter was served better than any other towns there were still many outlying villages which were not on a direct bus or train route. This was a matter that had to be borne in mind when trying to establish a new service which would be available to all. In order to reach people in rural areas, and to engage in work with individuals or groups as well as to provide a 'drop in' service, JACAT came to use rooms in widely dispersed hospitals, surgeries, schools and health centres.

During the years that have passed since JACAT's inception, ways of working have evolved and emphases have shifted, while personnel have changed and increased in number. These changes have been driven by variations in the legal system, advances in research and the requirements of our funding agencies, but most of all by lessons we have learned from therapeutic work with our clients.

In the last few years in particular, services for children and young people have been a priority for government. There has been a number of important policy papers and proposals for provision by the major agencies as well as newly designed funding streams. The recently published Every Child Matters (2003) is the strongest plank in such policies. Together with the underpinning Children Act 2005 it was a direct response to the Victoria Climbié affair. These developments, along with the *National Service Framework for Children, Young People and Maternity Services* (2004), require major changes in how services are organised and delivered.

This book is an attempt to explain how we have learned to operate as a group when our origins and training are so diverse, and how we have used this diversity to the benefit of our clients. The key is to be found in the shared philosophy which underpins our work. The principles which evolved were arrived at in a series of discussions, and all team members subscribed to them. They are as follows:

1. We believe that our society, which affords little respect to children and sets out to mould and control them, creates an environment in which they are vulnerable to abuse of all kinds, and in which it is made very difficult for them to speak out about what happens to them.
2. We understand abuse as liable to interfere with development at all levels. A child's emotional wellbeing may be endangered, the capacity for spontaneity and intimacy may be distorted, the ability to learn may be disrupted, and the chance of forming sustaining relationships may be impaired. Since the adult world prefers to avoid those feelings of failure and guilt which often result from exposure to abuse, many children are left to deal with the trauma alone and unsupported. Thus the hope, the possibility of recovery, is reduced.
3. We believe that it is necessary to adopt a collaborative approach when facing the challenge of child abuse and its consequences. Therefore we work together with other professionals and those who care for children to listen to what children have to say and to offer support.

By taking responsibility for nurturing ourselves and others we hope to have the strength to keep the fact of abuse alive in our minds and also in the minds of others, and to continue to alleviate the suffering which abuse brings to whoever it touches.

Philosophy into Action

Three key factors have determined the ways in which JACAT has striven to translate the team philosophy into an organisational reality. The first is dealing with the psychological dynamics of working with child abuse. The second is a commitment to inter-agency working. The third is multi-disciplinary teamwork. The second and the third factors are, of course, closely related to the first. From a management point of view, it has always been acknowledged that the stresses and strains associated with dealing with child abuse must be taken into account in the way the team is structured and operates. Otherwise damaging splits and tensions might seep into the organisation and affect the work in a negative way.

Child abuse and its impact upon workers

Those who set up JACAT recognised that there were dangers inherent in creating a team dedicated to dealing with only child abuse. On the one hand, the costs to the individual worker were potentially damaging. On the other, there was the potential for organisational contagion from clients' powerful projections.

Writing about the impact on professional workers, Kate Kirk (1998) uses Finkelhor and Brown's model of 'four traumagenic dynamics' to illustrate how those who work with sexually abused clients can themselves be affected by trauma. She draws upon the growing literature on secondary traumatisation to explain the ways in which work with traumatised clients can impact on the workers themselves. Our understanding of this phenomenon means that we take it into account at all levels of the organisation. By way of illustration of this point, in the course of work with a lawyer specialising in compensation claims and who represented adults abused in care we became aware of how close to serious depression she had become. She found listening to repeated tales of sexual abuse unbearable, and she saw that they affected her in a way that no other work had ever done. In addition she found the on-going evidence of emotional and psychological damage particularly distressing and critically challenging to her view of the world's goodness and capacity for fairness. However, through the experience of sharing her distress with someone who understood the reasons for it, and through hearing about some of the positive outcomes for families who came for counselling, support or advice, she was able to value her work as a very important part of the whole picture and essential in the healing process for her clients. Thus she was able to continue her professional work despite the cost.

Whilst the Finkelhor-Brown model refers exclusively to child sexual abuse, it is possible to see how the dynamics of betrayal, stigmatisation and powerlessness are relevant to victims of child maltreatment in all its forms. As workers at JACAT we strive to remain alert to the ways in which projections from our clients' internal worlds can not only collide with individual unconscious processes but also begin to affect the way in which the organisation functions. The highest rate of referrals to JACAT is of children and young people who have been sexually abused, so it is important to consider how working with this client group can affect therapists and counsellors. Listening to accounts of sexual abuse on a regular basis may begin to influence how workers feel about their sexual selves and how they begin to experience sexuality within their own close relationships. Those of us who are parents have found ourselves questioning our values, motives and behaviours in relation to our children's emerging sexuality as well as expressing some anxieties and confusion about sexual boundaries. At JACAT we recognise that such themes may need to be discussed, either in the team as a whole or between individuals. However in all our discussions we also recognise the importance of preserving as carefully as possible the boundary between professional and personal matters.

As well as feeling these personal pressures, workers can also feel stigmatised. When we work with abused clients we become all too aware of a profound feeling of badness that pervades some children's and young people's sense of being. At times we find ourselves wondering if there is something wrong with us (in a perverted sense) for choosing to work in this area, and sometimes of course our clients will be wondering this about us too. Because the vast majority of abuse is perpetrated by males this is a particularly sensitive issue for our male colleagues. We always ensure that clients are offered a choice of male or female worker whenever possible, but as an organisation we are clear that men should not be stigmatised because of their maleness. They as individuals in their own right are not responsible for the destructive actions of other men.

The dynamic influences of betrayal and powerlessness can be hard to combat, and as individuals and as a group we can sometimes become despondent and suspicious. It is hard to hang on to hope in the face of people's determined belief in their own uselessness and in the knowledge that a childhood has been cruelly perverted and perhaps lost forever. We also have to accept the reality of our own impotence in preventing such abuse, without succumbing to the view that the work we do is ultimately only damage limitation. Suspicion can enter the organisation at quite a profound level and can be seen as mirroring the betrayal and lack of trust that characterise our clients' emotional world. This suspicion is usually expressed in terms of doubt about the genuineness of other organisations' or institutions' motives, and at such times the team meeting plays a vital part in allowing space for examination of our reactions. These dynamics also affect professional colleagues who come to us to consult about their work. Frequently the consultation process can be seen as a vehicle for exploring these dynamics with the consultee. We can use it to try and enable and empower them to act with purpose rather than remaining disabled.

Inter-agency working and the multi-disciplinary team

One of the most powerful tools in offsetting the tendency to criticise and be suspicious of other agencies is the closeness with which we work with other agencies, enabling us to see their difficulties and struggles at first hand and to recognise the limitations placed on their own room for manoeuvre. Moreover, we are ourselves correspondingly exposed to the scrutiny of other professionals. Even if we were so inclined – which we are not! – this makes it much more difficult for us to embrace the fiction of our own perfection. Similarly, because our team is made up of members from a number of different disciplines we have the constant opportunity to appreciate the talents and skills of others whose training is different from our own.

Although most team members, acting in a part-time capacity, have stayed at JACAT for longer than five years, the team has not been immune to the debilitating effects of constantly working in an area where clients and colleagues alike are subject to a sense of helplessness, faced with the effects of abuse upon children and families. When such feelings become too strong to allow the worker to operate effectively there has seemed little choice but to leave. The team attempts to offset this necessity by keeping an eye open for signs that a colleague is 'going under' and by suggesting ways of obtaining help. The Co-ordinator now sees every team member individually at least once a year to review their situation, including their feelings about the work, their workload and the variety of the work they have undertaken. The matter of each member being offered a sabbatical period after a certain number of years' work has been raised and is under review.

We also know that those who perpetrate abuse on children thrive in a climate of secrecy. At one level society colludes with this in the way it views children and in the ways in which it has been deaf and blind to abuse. It is only within the last ten years, for example, that there has been an acceptance and recognition of the dreadful abuse inflicted upon children in local authority children's homes. Abusers themselves frequently strive to create an atmosphere of secrecy through terror and aggression or, through trading on a child's naiveté and trust, to ensnare them in abusive activities. At JACAT we aim to serve our clients in an open manner, striving to engage with them and other professionals in a collaborative way. Although JACAT is not employed to do therapeutic work with abusers, or to assess formally any levels of danger, such men are often involved with us by virtue of being the father of the child with whom we are working therapeutically. Again, we are not immune to the difficulties created by these controlling men, particularly when they may be articulate, well-educated and even employed in a senior capacity in one of our two funding agencies.

In sum, our structure and our procedures are designed to minimise these dangers, firstly through the limitation of individual stresses deriving from work demands, secondly through openness in communication about the work, and thirdly through validation of the need to take care of our professional selves.

At this point we need to turn to another delicate issue. The conjunction of workers from two agencies, health and social services – the education service felt unable to contribute to JACAT in any substantive way – necessarily brings with it a tension in the intersection of different work cultures, expectations and experience. This tension has the potential to be at best creative, at worst destructive, and whilst there have been times when JACAT members have had to strive to understand each other and have had to face up to conflicts, on the whole the team's experience is of a supportive organisation which offers great benefits through its multi-disciplinary and multi-agency construction – an organisation which both nurtures and challenges.

What then are the factors that enable JACAT to regard itself as an organisation which both nurtures and challenges? For one thing, through the clarity of the aims expressed by our commissioning body, we have always been clear about the primary task. For another, our comparative freedom from interference on the part of both our funding bodies has enabled us to learn from the experience of being a joint-agency and multi-disciplinary group, and to adjust accordingly. By avoiding the pressures to be an investigative agency or to undertake risk assessments, JACAT has been able to hold its position as a supporter of post-abuse services as well as a provider of such services in its own right.

Rice (1963) defines the primary task of an organisation as the task it must perform if it is to survive. Roberts (1994) points out that different groups within an organisation may have different definitions of that primary task. The potential for this difference is magnified when team members come from different 'parent' organisations, perhaps feeling compelled to carry messages on behalf of their agency about what should be done. Roberts goes on to illustrate how problems in defining the primary task become greater in institutions that set out to change or help people, for they often have multiple tasks, every one of which is important. The temptation here is to avoid clear task definition, and thus to avoid dealing with conflicts in values and beliefs. In doing so the organisation ends up providing little guidance about the nature of the primary task or about how it should be done. For instance, as social services have become more and more restrictive in the definition of their own grounds for intervention within a family, or for remaining in touch with a family, so their workers request more and more frequently that we should undertake 'keeping safe' work with children, even children of a tender age. As social services is one of our two funding bodies the temptation to comply is great. However, again and again JACAT has to maintain its position that child protection and the safety of children is the responsibility of their service rather than ours and, moreover, that it is a prerequisite to the successful undertaking of post-abuse therapeutic work.

In terms of the multiple tasks that JACAT performs, we have always been clear that our overarching task is to ensure that abused children and young people, as well as those who care for them, have access to high quality therapy, help and support. All other activities serve to promote this, and we are careful not to allow other activities to take up a disproportionate amount of our time. For example, we are committed to providing training with and for other agencies but we keep a watchful eye and a careful check on how much of our time is devoted to this activity.

Personnel

Details of JACAT's personnel, and both the breadth of their professional experience and the range of their specialisms, provide a vital key to their collective work – indeed, to this book to which they are contributing – and these details can be found in About the Editors and Contributors. In a similar vein, and remembering that no organisation can function well without good administrative backup, JACAT is fortunate in having the services of two excellent part-time secretaries, Linda Morgan and Helen Thomson. Theirs is the voice that clients and professionals first hear on the phone, and they are the people who welcome them into the JACAT area. Their contribution as the 'face of JACAT' cannot be over emphasised.

All team members work for JACAT on a part-time basis, with no one team member — and that includes secretarial staff — working more than six sessions (the equivalent of three whole days) each week. All workers at JACAT have substantial experience of working therapeutically and are regarded as senior practitioners. From the outset it was deemed important to recognise that, as already described, this kind of work places particular stresses on workers and that it would be wrong for both workers and clients if they were to be exposed to this work on a full-time basis. Because all team members work the rest of the week in allied organisations there is the added advantage of ensuring that the needs of children and young people who have been abused have a high profile in those other contexts by virtue of the presence of JACAT workers.

It has to be conceded, however, that when the other half of the work, outside JACAT, also involves unmitigated involvement with abuse issues, the ameliorative effect is not great.

As well as the regular part-time staff, JACAT also has a number of secondees working with it at any one time. These are members of health or social services seconded to work part-time with us for a year. They are all people with therapeutic experience, and they work as an integral part of the team. They bring us the benefit of their up-to-date knowledge of their own agency, and also their scrutiny of our activities in the light of that knowledge, and they take back to their own teams an increased expertise in the area of abuse.

Roles and Responsibilities

JACAT is managed by a Co-ordinator. This role is based on the need for someone to ensure that business gets done and that it is done professionally. It emphatically does not derive from notions of hierarchy and control. All team members are accountable to themselves, their colleagues and their clients, the Co-ordinator included. In addition the Co-ordinator is responsible for ensuring that JACAT is seen and heard within the professional networks concerned with abuse work as well as in the wider professional arena.

The most essential aspect of the Co-ordinator's function is ensuring that the team is enabled to get on with the therapeutic work without undue interference from external influences. In this respect it is important that referrals are dealt with efficiently and that the Co-ordinator both protects the team from external pressures and passes on information and concerns from the team to the funding bodies and to other agencies. In this way the Co-ordinator protects the boundary around the system by regulating the input and output flows (Roberts, 1994) and acts as manager of the boundary rather than manager of people. The Management Committee, comprised of two members from each of the two funding bodies, the Co-ordinator and a team member, assists the Co-ordinator in this function. There is also an Advisory Group which meets twice yearly and is made up of representatives from a range of organisations working in the area of child abuse, including child psychiatry, paediatrics, the probation service, education, school health, the police, social services, trainers, connexions advisers and the legal profession. This group is a forum for the discussion of current cross-profession issues but it also provides advice and support for the work of JACAT. The advisory group is attended by all JACAT staff and is experienced as a supportive and stimulating group whose individual skills can be called upon when needed.

All team members offer therapeutic work, with a range of therapeutic interventions: individual counselling and therapy for children and young people; group work for young people who have been sexually abused; group work for mothers of abused children; group work for fathers of abused children; and family work.

The team meeting

The JACAT Team Meeting lies at the heart of the work. It embodies the philosophy of JACAT in respect of how it is thinking about abuse issues and its conviction about how the team should function. Attendance at the JACAT weekly Team Meeting is mandatory for all team members, including both team secretaries. The Team Meeting fulfils many functions and acts as a referral meeting where each new referral is discussed and action agreed upon; a meeting for tracking progress with cases; a consultation feedback meeting, where cases for consultation are discussed with the team, advice sought, and decisions about interventions agreed; a general business meeting where requests for training, staffing issues and so on are considered; a forum for exchange of information, where colleagues update each other on relevant professional issues; and finally, a space for team members to seek advice and support about various aspects of the work.

Consultation Services

Over the last four years the JACAT team has been extending and developing its consultation service. In general terms consultation offers the opportunity to think together about a case or a piece of work at a pre-referral stage. At this stage of a referral the responsibility for the work remains with the consultee. As our work has developed we have identified a number of different ways of offering consultation about child abuse. These include referral consultations; JACAT-initiated consultations; case consultations; family consultations; carer consultations; and telephone consultations.

All team members offer consultations, usually working in pairs. Details of this aspect of our work are set out in the chapter on consultations.

Training

Training is an integral part of the service we offer. All team members take part in it. It keeps us in touch with those who are service users, exposing us to their scrutiny and enabling us to learn from them. It raises awareness of issues relating to child abuse in a variety of places and enables us to use a variety of tools. Our two funding bodies have first call upon us, but we are open to requests from voluntary organisations, schools and other professional bodies who have no part in our funding. Seminars, workshops and conferences are all part of the repertoire. Many of these are run in conjunction with non-JACAT members or by other professionals on their own. Training often provides an opportunity to reach parts of the community that we might not normally meet. A full description of this further aspect of our work is set out in the chapter on training.

Conclusion

JACAT is a powerful example of partnership working in practice. The team reports to the Management Committee, which currently consists of senior representatives from health and social services as well as two representatives of service users (a recent innovation). The Co-ordinator and a team member also serve on the Management Committee. All team members report to the Co-ordinator with respect to their work for JACAT. It is, however, in the unique way in which team members have evolved a method of working with various clients and client groups, which highlight what is possible. There is a range of work with families, groups and individuals, and with carers, in which each team member can develop his or her own skills alongside others. The differences in terms of profession and agency of origin are celebrated, and the eclectic nature of much of the work is effective in the experience of young people and their carers. Barker and Price (2005) describe a smaller version of a similar model. In this case, however, there is only one person providing a service and the overall service is about the delivery of the therapeutic method. JACAT, on the other hand, is concerned to provide support to both the abused person and his or her family and those who work therewith, wherever the need arises in the geographical area of provision.

Anton Obholzer (1996) when talking about institutional functioning, observes that certain structures and approaches minimise defensive patterns of behaviour in staff groups and promote task-centredness. He names five key elements:

- Clarity of task.
- Clarity of organisational structure.
- Clarity of time boundaries.
- A staff venue to locate and work on the innate emotional difficulties arising from the work.
- An opportunity for ideas arising from point four to be transformed into institutional policy.

The current JACAT embodies these elements in its culture and organisation as a result of a process of adaptation and evolution. It is from this basis that we support the emotional health of the team. To quote Kirk (1998) 'It is in healthy and functioning workers that the future lies, and so too lies the healing of the thousands of known and unknown clients'.

1.2 Training and Other Related Matters

Ann Catchpole

Introduction

Training is an integral part of the service we offer, and all team members take part in it. When JACAT was established in 1987, those responsible had the foresight to include the training of others among its four main areas of responsibility. This imperative has brought with it a number of bonuses which may or may not have been predicted by them. Above all it has meant that we have not been able to detach ourselves from those who work in the field of child abuse and are not seen as carrying out our therapeutic work, in some mysterious way and never having to explain ourselves or be accountable to other professionals. We have, from the earliest days, had to stand up and explain the ways in which we work, the principles and beliefs upon which this work is based, and whether or not the work is proving effective. By holding seminars and conferences, workshops and 'drop ins', and by participating in the training of all the major groups whose work may involve contact with abused children, teachers, health visitors, social workers, mental health workers, play group leaders, and the police, we have held ourselves up to the scrutiny of others in a very public way. On the face of it, this does not seem to be an obvious attraction but rather a matter to strike terror into all but the most experienced and confident member. However, what it does do is make it possible for us to learn from others in the process, since most of our 'teaching sessions' have a healthy component of discussion and sharing of experience. Moreover, there is no more powerful an incentive to learning than the knowledge that it is going to be necessary to teach someone something!

Participation in the Training Schemes Initiated by Others

The teaching that we have done has fallen into two main groups:

- Training initiatives that we have ourselves taken, such as workshops, seminars and conferences.
- Participation in training schemes devised by others.

In addition to these there have been some requests for a major piece of training for a specific group. The involvement in such a piece of work has given us an insight into a world that would not otherwise have been accessible, and we, as well as the specific group, have been enriched by the experience. This is true to a greater or lesser extent of all our participation in the training schemes of others, particularly when they are not linked to our two funding bodies, health and social services, to one or the other of which areas most of the team members belong.

Training in Schools and Other Educative Bodies

Included within our training brief has always been the closely allied matter of consciousness-raising. When JACAT was established, child abuse still had a relatively low profile, and many professionals were ill informed about it, while the general public knew very little indeed. It was regarded as essential that these shortcomings be tackled if any worthwhile impact were to be made on the situation. To this end JACAT, whose initial membership numbered only five, all of them part-timers, set about making itself known by talking about the subject of abuse whenever and wherever it could usefully do so. Schools throughout our catchment area were one of the first targets, as it was recognised that teachers saw more of children than any other body, apart from parents. All schools in our catchment area, both public and private, were visited by a JACAT member, and out of this grew a most fruitful liaison which has lasted to this day. Changes in the funding of schools have, however, made it harder for them to participate in our training programmes, and competing demands on our time have sometimes stretched our human resources to near breaking point. Some schools requested the identification of a named JACAT person to whom they could refer for advice. Others requested a series of visits by a JACAT member, often to speak to the staff during a lunch-break, or to offer specific consultation.

Out of these early contacts came a JACAT initiative that in the first few years was warmly welcomed and supported by schools. This was the creation of a school workshop programme, in which we offered day workshops to schools on topics that seemed to us to be relevant, or which were suggested by them when we sought their advice. From 1993 till 1995 we ran five such workshops, all of which were very well attended, attracting between ten and fifteen teachers at a time. Many of those who came were head teachers or other staff with special responsibility for abused children, the so-called 'designated' teachers, for whom there was little else in the way of training at the time. The subjects covered were coping with children who had been emotionally abused, sexually abused or neglected; curriculum approaches to child protection; and the complementary contributions of home, school and therapy. Sadly our work with schools has been badly affected by the changes in school funding which has made it next to impossible for them to pay for the training which we could offer, on top of paying for someone to cover for absent teachers. Holding small workshops, of two hours duration, on JACAT premises, either during the day or in the evening, went some way towards solving the problem. Since we did not have to pay for the use of the premises, or supply food, we were, therefore, able to provide them free of charge. These workshops were at an hour when teachers did not require cover, only an enthusiasm to work late. Added urgency has been given by the withdrawal of educational professionals from multi-professional child protection training, a matter of extreme concern to the Area Child Protection Committee on which one of our members sits. However, our connections with schools remain strong through their use of our duty telephone system, which enables them to ring through with any problems they would like to discuss. Along with school nurses, teachers are the prime users of this service. Schools also continue to ask us to participate in training schemes which they initiate, or to lay on training which especially fits their needs. Recently we received a request for some training for the staff of a local secondary school whose pupils are all children with special needs and, therefore, particularly vulnerable to abuse.

Quite understandably, requests for training, just like requests for direct work or consultation and advice, focus more often on sexual abuse than on any other form of abuse. This seems to reflect both the general unease of professionals and non-professionals alike with the topic and a growing awareness of the prevalence of the problem. Still today, at JACAT, we sometimes have to remind people that there are other forms of abuse, such as emotional abuse, which are equally damaging to children and often even more difficult to prove and to heal. If asked about our own childhood experiences, it is likely that many of us would have a clearer and more painful memory of some slighting remark made by a parent or teacher, or of some sense of one's wishes or needs not being given sufficient weight in a family discussion, rather than of the time when we were smacked for some misdemeanour. This means that in our training we are often in a position of needing to challenge established thinking among parents, carers or professionals.

The definition of abuse which is principally used within JACAT training is that which is found in the multi-disciplinary handbook on Child Protection, to which all professionals working with children must look for guidance. Its definitions are now commonly accepted throughout England and Wales, both by local authorities and private sector agencies.

For some years now JACAT has been a keen participant in the training of BPhil and DipSW students and also probation service students, covering a number of different topics over the years. Similarly JACAT has had regular input into the training of PGCE (post-graduate teacher training) students. It has also participated in the training of educational psychologists. The presence of an educational psychologist within our team members from the beginning undoubtedly increased both our credibility with schools and also their readiness to use our services, as well as helping us to keep a foothold in the training of those who will work in schools.

Training for our Funding Agencies

Our two funding bodies, social services and health, have been the principal users of our training, as they have of our other services. Again some of this has been at their request and some at our initiative. On an annual basis we have taken part in the multi-agency training programme put on by Social Services, participating mainly at levels two and three, and covering such topics as therapeutic intervention for children who have suffered any form of abuse, helping children who have been emotionally abused, identifying risk, and the (much requested) recognising signs and symptoms of abuse. In Devon this multi-agency training scheme is the main plank in the child protection training given to all professionals who work with children, and as such is a very important component of our work. In addition each member of JACAT is in demand to undertake training on behalf of their own professional body which recognises that their advice will be supported by a thorough knowledge of the working conditions in which the trainees work.

Much of the training we have undertaken for social services has involved foster parents, for they, like teachers, find themselves bearing the brunt of the problems of children who have been abused. As many of the children who are fostered are likely to have been sexually abused, and often abused in other ways as well, it is not surprising that their surrogate families find themselves struggling to care for them, just as their natural families did. It is often helpful if foster carers can learn to differentiate behaviour that is normal for a child of a particular age from that which is attributable to the abuse suffered. Especially where teenagers are concerned this is a problem. Some of our training, therefore, will often include a component on child development.

When the effects of abuse, both long term and short term, are understood it becomes possible for the foster carer to shed the feeling of being personally under attack, as can be the case when children show tremendous hostility and aggression towards those very people who are doing their best to care for them. Similarly, it is helpful if a carer understands that a child or young person's inability to concentrate comes not from laziness or lack of ambition, still less from sheer bloody-mindedness, but rather from the presence of persistent disturbing thoughts and memories, worries and guilty feelings. These concerns occupy most of the space that is in their heads, making concentration on anything else extremely difficult. If the carer understands all that, then they may be more patient and seek appropriate help, rather than exacerbate the problem by heaping blame on the foster child. Few children are able to explain what is wrong as graphically as one seven-year-old, whose nights were being wrecked by persistent nightmares, and whose days were spoilt by constant anxiety. She was able to report: 'There is a man in my head whom I want to get out.'

Foster carers meet frequently in informal groups, usually in the evening, and JACAT members are often asked to speak to these groups on a variety of subjects. We are also regularly asked to participate in the training of new foster carers and in the advanced training of others. As many of the children who come to JACAT for therapy are in foster homes it is important that their carers understand the possible effects of therapy, opening up as it does memories of the abuse itself and of those responsible for it, upon the child for whom they care. Often the facing of difficult issues and dealing with unpleasant, frightening or distressing memories can lead to a child or young person becoming either withdrawn or, conversely, aggressive and hyperactive for a time. The benefits of therapy are not always felt immediately, and much patience is needed by the carers as well as support for the young person while it progresses. It is all too easy to give up in the early stages in the belief that, far from helping, it is making matters worse. If we are to work successfully with young people in care it is essential that foster carers understand the nature of that work and the possible implications for the young person's behaviour, and that the carers are themselves supported for the duration of the work. A clear indication of the importance of the foster carer's role is given by the fact that one of the earliest of our seminars, held in December 1988, was on the topic of foster carers who care for a child who has been sexually abused. The three speakers were a social worker, a member of the Foster Carers Association, and a foster carer. The use of other professionals highlights the principle of joint working which JACAT espouses. Similarly the involvement of service users who are non-professionals emphasises an inclusivity of approach.

Another group of people whose problems often overlap with those of foster carers are the adoptive parents. With the decrease in the number of babies, and even toddlers, available for adoption, many adopters find themselves taking on a child who has a considerable history, much of it abusive and potentially damaging. Sometimes, to add to the problem, this history is either unknown or only partially known, or occasionally has not been properly reported and documented. Sometimes the full extent of what has happened to the child only comes to light as they grow and exhibit behaviour of so worrying a kind that the adoptive parents are moved to seek professional help. More detail is set out in Chapter 2.2 on *A Consultation Service for Foster and Adoptive Parents*.

Some of the training JACAT does with adoptive parents is requested by Social Services and some by the other adoptive agencies. This may take the form of preparation for those who are about to adopt, or work with groups who have already adopted and are requesting help with difficult behaviour. For adoptive parents, even more than for foster carers, it is important to know that difficult behaviour springs from roots which are in the past rather than being an indication that the child does not love them or that they are not responding to them adequately as parents. Many adopted children and young people find the very goodness of the parenting they receive almost impossible to tolerate since it only serves to highlight the failures of their natural parents. Unless the adoptive parents understand this, they are liable to regard challenging and difficult behaviour as a personal insult and may be tempted to despair or react inappropriately. In recent years the demand for post-adoption support, sadly lacking in many cases through absence of funding, has risen dramatically, and this work of JACAT has involved the support of social workers and others who are struggling to understand how to cope with the seemingly insupportable problems which threaten placement breakdown. Such is the divisiveness of abuse and its after-affects on children that it can divide adoptive parent from adoptive parent and tear apart the fabric of marriage or partnership.

Seminars

Since JACAT began it has held regular seminars. These are held after work on a weekday evening, are all free of charge, and are open to anyone working with children. About forty to fifty people normally attend from all over Devon, representing the main groups from health, social services, the police, the law and education, and including some from the private and voluntary sectors. Seminars provide an excellent forum for the sharing of ideas and the spreading of knowledge as well as for making connections with workers throughout the region.

Some of the ideas for seminars come from our multi-disciplinary Advisory Group who, together with JACAT's own therapists, come from a wide background. This makes it uniquely positioned to pick up current anxieties and matters of moment, brought to its attention through its funding bodies and through connections with the wider professional world. Thus in 1988 JACAT members, in the company of a circuit judge, a solicitor and a magistrate, looked at the crisis of confidence experienced by many workers in the field of child abuse and its effect upon their practice, in a seminar entitled *After Cleveland*. The choice of topic reflected JACAT's perception that there was a very real danger of inaction, particularly among social workers and health workers, when working with families where they believed a child was at risk of abuse, because of their fear of being pilloried for removing a child unnecessarily. JACAT continues to deal with relevant and contemporary issues in its seminars. In 2004 the subjects of internet abuse and domestic violence were both scrutinised. As with the rest of our training, many of these seminars have been collaborative events and have reflected changes brought about by outside events or changes in legislation.

Although JACAT is a service for children, adults are not neglected either in its seminars or in other parts of its work. A growing awareness that the well-being of children is often best served, not by working directly with them, but rather with the adults most involved with them, has given rise to a number of seminars, of which those relating to foster and adoptive parents have been mentioned already. The interface between adult mental health and child protection is an area that causes grievous difficulties to our social work colleagues who work with those children who are at risk of abuse. This topic formed the subject of a seminar in 1999. The seminar highlighted the difficulty that even the best of adult mental health workers experience in keeping children in mind. One such worker confessed that 'Do you have children?' was a question that was seldom asked. Yet the welfare of children is so deeply intertwined with the welfare of their parents that, for a social worker working with children and families, it seems impossible that it is not routinely asked. If children are to be protected whilst the needs and rights of parents are not overlooked, it is essential that a dialogue be established between adult mental health workers and those who work with children and their families.

Seminars have a very important secondary function: they provide a channel for the exchange of ideas between JACAT and the professionals who use its service and upon whose help we rely in promoting conditions in which families can engage with us. Thus a JACAT-led seminar looked at ways of working with abused children. Specifically, it covered contra-indications for therapy (an effort to help those who make referrals to us and who struggle with the concept that therapy has to happen at the right place, at the right time, and when the child or young person is both ready and safe), and issues of engagement in therapy (an attempt to make clear the part played by all professionals in the preparation, support and follow up of children and families who wish to take part in therapeutic work).

National Conference

A natural progression from these seminars, a progression that reflects the growth in JACAT's confidence in its role as educator, was the introduction of a national conference, which we hoped would take place every two years.

The first such conference was held in 1997. Entitled *Prevention in Practice*, it brought together four keynote speakers from all over the country, as well as a number of more local practitioners, including some JACAT members, who ran workshops. It attracted a range of professionals from both the private and the public sectors, and the survey we conducted at the end indicated that it had been well received. Subsequent conferences covered topics relating to therapeutic interventions, the impact of abuse on adolescence, the impact of childhood trauma on the way in which a child's brain develops and the implications of this for therapy, and the detrimental effects of substance abuse.

In our second conference we broke away from normal conference approaches by using a theatre group, Wolf and Water, who work in prisons and elsewhere to promote understanding of child abuse and to offset its effects. As well as running a workshop about the work they do with offenders, they produced a dramatic rendition of the events and themes of the conference. There were also four other workshops:

- One exploring the work of art therapy in the recovery of adult victims of abuse.
- One exploring the role of family therapy in 'working to re-create connections between children and parents where abuse has taken place'.
- One looking at the role of a play therapist in the recovery of children from child abuse.
- One looking at the impact on abused children of setting up groups for mothers of children who have been sexually abused.

Our third conference considered the particular problems faced by adolescents who have been abused and by those who work with them. We used young people from the local college drama department to illustrate the impact of abuse on families. In doing so we were able to help these young people explore the effects of abuse in a way which was acceptable to them.

Conferences have been more difficult to run recently, and in 2004 we had to cancel one through lack of support. Further investigation revealed that it was the absence of available funding that was keeping people away. Accordingly we offered what was essentially the same conference over one day rather than two, thus cutting costs by over a third. This, together with reduced prices for voluntary bodies and students, which we were able to afford through the provision of some sponsorship, enabled us to attract full attendance in 2005. The main casualties were the workshops which were still available but whose time was cut by half. It looks as if we shall have to put more effort into obtaining sponsorship if we are to be able to run two-day conferences in the future.

Over the years JACAT has not restricted its training to its funding bodies, nor to the public sector, but has been willing to respond to requests from other sources when these seem to be in line with our general remit. Thus we have run preparation groups for pre-school workers from a number of different agencies, sometimes providing a specialist component for their training and sometimes responding to particular problems that they are experiencing. Some of these requests take us all over our catchment area and so involve a good deal of travel. Again JACAT benefits from its involvement in the wider world of work with children, often at the grass roots level.

Similarly invitations to work with staff at special schools, both local authority and privately funded, are doubly welcome. They increase our knowledge of the special problems associated with working in such a setting, and give us the opportunity of influencing practice in places where there is a population which is particularly vulnerable to abuse.

Clergy Training

Perhaps the biggest piece of training participated in by JACAT has been the training of all the Anglican clergy in Devon, both stipendiary and non-stipendiary, in child protection and child abuse issues. The Diocese of Exeter, in accordance with an initiative taken by the Church of England House of Bishops, produced a booklet for the various parishes setting out the policies and procedures which should be followed in child protection matters, entitled *Policy on Child Protection*. Wisely it did not rely on that alone for making sure that each individual church was led in such a way as to make the children within its setting as safe from abuse as they could be. Those at the forefront of the training recognised that the Church, with its emphasis upon forgiveness, sometimes to the point of naiveté, and its hierarchical and still largely male-centred tradition, could offer the appearance of a safe haven to those who had been guilty of an offence against children, or a golden opportunity for someone who is planning to commit such an offence. The *Introduction to the Diocese of Exeter Child Protection Policy and Procedures* (1997) makes this very point when it states: 'It is a sad fact of life that the abuse of children occurs in every area of society and yet, because the subject is so emotive and disturbing, it is easy for us to believe that it happens "everywhere but here".' Such a belief is delusory, but assuredly it can be found in church communities. Trust and acceptance are rightly seen as hallmarks of any Christian fellowship, but uncritical acceptance and naive trust have left children vulnerable, and the resulting incidence of abuse is considerable. Research among convicted abusers reveals that some have deliberately targeted churches because of the opportunity offered by the open and welcoming nature of the church community. When you add to this a desperate shortage of people willing to work with children in a voluntary capacity, and the trust with which such church workers are normally regarded by parents, the attractions of such a setting to the wrong kind of person, and the temptation to take up an offer of help without proper scrutiny, are only too obvious. It was JACAT's brief to heighten the alertness of the clergy to these issues, and to encourage them to look at their practice closely in the light of what is known about the needs of children and the profile of offenders, especially sex offenders. We undertook to work closely with other trainers from the church, among whom was an ex-social worker, to prepare the material we each would use. They covered child protection issues, the policy and procedures as covered by the diocesan booklet, and matters relating to forgiveness and confidentiality within church circles. In a series of nine day-sessions, held at venues throughout Devon, we covered all 360 of the clergy, only a few escaping this first trawl, and those being picked up at a follow-up session some months later. We worked in pairs, as did our counterparts from the church.

There followed a request that one of us should speak to the clergy wives from North Devon, as they are often the people who actually carry the brunt of the work with children and young people in a parish. Later still, we responded to a request for an advanced two-day programme covering some of the issues in greater depth. Out of this venture sprang a healthy respect for the work each of us was doing and an agreement to work together to promote understanding of the issues whenever this was appropriate. The first result of this agreement was a seminar held in 2001 at which the idea and importance of forgiveness in therapeutic terms was explored thoroughly. Two of the speakers came from the church, one of them the Assistant Chaplain at HM Prison Channings Wood, a woman priest whose job involved her in working with both sex offenders and the victims of sexual and other abuse. The third speaker was one of our psychologists at JACAT.

This work with the clergy demonstrates a number of things that are true of most of our training at JACAT. It illustrates clearly a cascade model of teaching: namely, educating the people who are at the head of any undertaking, in this case the parochial clergy, and relying on them to pass the message on to the wider community, in this case the parishioners. JACAT has always been a tiny team, only five part-time members at its inception and only double that number now, with a hugely demanding brief to cover within a large geographical area, so it has had little choice but to follow this method. It also illustrates one of JACAT's more unusual ways of working: to use two or more trainers on all but the smallest or most informal occasions. This practice probably grew from our early consultations that involved all or most team members, thus providing a truly multi-disciplinary approach to any problem. Now the demands of the workload make the involvement of so many team members impossible, but an effort is still made to provide two workers with different backgrounds and experience, both in consultations and in training.

As a result of using the cascade method of teaching and consciousness-raising JACAT personnel, though numerically few, have managed over the years to reach a larger number of people throughout Devon than any other teaching method would have made possible. The use of more than one leader or facilitator at most training events has not only enabled inexperienced members, secondees and trainees to participate in training and to learn from it, it has also had the additional enormous benefit of creating strong bonds of trust between one member of the team and the other. It has never been our policy to pair off in any particular way, but rather to pair off according to our specialities and experience, so we have each worked with all team members at one time or another, which has greatly increased our confidence in each other's ability.

For JACAT, as for others who are involved in training, there is always the difficulty of keeping up with changing personnel, which means that we need to repeat training for certain groups from time to time, as well as finding time for new initiatives to be taken and contemporary problems to be addressed.

Clearly the demand is such that we could spend a large proportion of our time training. However, important though it is, it is not as important as some of the other things we do. Our funding agencies expect us to devote most of our time to activities that can be seen to be immediately beneficial to them. This means that high on our list of priorities has to be the direct work we do with children who have been abused and their families, and also our making ourselves available for consultation to other professionals. Training has to take third place to these requirements. It is, nevertheless, as I hope this chapter will have shown, regarded by us with great seriousness and has, moreover, brought as many benefits to us as have been brought by us to others.

Undoubtedly we need to keep training at the forefront of our thinking if we are to continue to respond to the changing needs of our clientele. Current shortages in funding and ever increasing workloads, particularly within social services, makes it imperative that the training which we provide is affordable, accessible to all who need it, and relevant. Moreover, it must reflect the best that is available in research and practice so as to inform and inspire all those who work in the field of child abuse, including JACAT workers themselves.

Keeping the balance between all these activities and ensuring that colleagues do not become overloaded or overwhelmed is the task of the Co-ordinator. The compilation of a regular report, which includes a statistical breakdown of referrals, their outcomes and other activities such as the amount of training delivered, provides a way of giving feedback to us and to others about the allocation of time to our various activities.

Evidence-Based Practice

Just as JACAT uses its training programme as one of the ways of keeping in touch with its professional clientele, so it uses questionnaires and evaluation sheets to keep in touch with its other service users, cf. Alex McCahearty's research discused in Section Six. At the end of all conferences the audience is asked to fill in questionnaires on which we base any changes for the next conference. All groups for men and for women who care for children who have been sexually abused are also asked to complete evaluation forms. These are studied carefully, so that suggestions for improvement can be incorporated another time. A piece of research on adolescent groups was undertaken by a psychology student working with JACAT and a further study on the Follow Up Group is currently being undertaken by a university lecturer and a student (see Section Four on working with groups). These, together with the in-depth review of JACAT undertaken three years ago, which recommended expansion into other parts of Devon, a policy which JACAT is in the process of implementing, with its opening of a satellite branch in Newton Abbot to cover the Teignbridge area of Devon, all help JACAT to make its practice evidence based.

The creation of a cohesive whole from workers whose experience and training is dissimilar requires much effort.

Further reading

Iwaniec, D. and Pinkerton, J. (1998) *Making Research Work: Promoting Child Care Policy and Practice.* Chichester: Wiley and Sons.

Kiesler, D. (1971) Experimental Designs in Psychotherapy Research. In Bergin, A.E. and Garfield, S.L. (Eds.) *Handbook of Psychotherapy and Behaviour Change*. Chichester: Wiley and Sons.

Monck, E. (1997) Evaluating Therapeutic Intervention with Sexually Abused Children. *Child Abuse Review*. 6: 3, 163–77.

Parkinson, P. (1997) *Child Abuse and the Churches*. London: Hodder and Stoughton.

Roberts, V.Z. (1994) The Organisation of Work. In Obholzer, A. and Roberts, V.Z. (Eds.) *The Unconscious at Work*. London: Routledge.

Rogers, A. and Pilgrim, D. (1997) The Contribution of Lay Knowledge to the Understanding and Promotion of Mental Health. *Journal of Mental Health*. 6: 1, 23–35.

Section Two: **Consultations**

2.1 **Introduction to Consultations**

Ann Catchpole

Child abuse is not a unitary phenomenon. The causes and manifestations of child abuse are multiple and diverse. This is why service responses need to be varied and sensitive.

(Hardiker et al.,, 1996)

Introduction

JACAT was set up with the intention, as part of its brief, of providing an advisory service to professionals working in the area of child abuse. It had become clear already that even the lead professionals needed help in reaching sensible conclusions when working within this complex area. This remains the case even though it would be fair to say that there is now a much wider knowledge base than existed in JACAT's early days. However, hand in hand with increased awareness of the issues have come increased workloads, higher expectations from government and courts alike, and a clearer understanding of the harm done if mistakes are made.

Of all those professionals who use JACAT's expertise, it is social workers who are bearing the brunt of these ever-increasing demands. Until 2003 it was social workers who most used the consultation service offered at JACAT. Thus, during the year from April 1999 to March 2000, about 65 per cent of JACAT's consultations were instigated by social services, 30 per cent by health services and five per cent by others (including the police, the education service and voluntary bodies). Three years later, during the year from April 2002 to March 2003, there was change but not radical change: 61 per cent social services, 26 per cent health services, and 13 percent the others. (In most cases, often at JACAT's request, other involved agencies also attended the consultation.) However, the figures for the year from April 2004 to March 2005 show a marked change: a fall to 38.5 per cent for social service referrals, a rise to 49 per cent for health referrals, with the figure for other sources remaining steady at 12.5 per cent.

A full analysis of these figures has not yet been undertaken but it appears that school nurses and GPs are responsible for most of the increase. This seems to reflect the fact that social services are closing cases very quickly after the investigation is complete, and are leaving their health colleagues to do much of the monitoring that they used to do. This in turn means that it is schools, who have to refer through the school nurse, and health personnel who remain in contact with families where abuse has been a concern and who are, therefore, in a position to make a referral to JACAT when the time is appropriate.

JACAT offers an initial one-off consultation to any professional who requests its help, whether or not they come from health or social services, the two funding bodies. It does so in order to make sure that vulnerable children are not left without a service because of restrictions on its availability. If further work is required from JACAT, whatever its nature, then a referral has to be made through one of the funding agencies. This is seldom a problem, since the urgency of the case and the neediness of the child are established by the consultation, and ways for making a referral can be explored at the same time.

Telephone Service

JACAT offers a telephone consultation service to any professional with concerns about child abuse. Members of the team cover each day of the week on a rota basis, including weekends. This is not an emergency service and in no way replicates the services of the police, the NSPCC, or the social services. Those on telephone duty go about their regular work, collecting from the answer-phone or the secretary any messages to which they must respond. Sometimes attempts are made by the caller to by-pass the system or to avoid making a referral to the appropriate body when child protection is an issue. In these cases JACAT clearly states that such a referral must be made and that, if this is not done, then the referral will be made by JACAT itself. However, the majority of telephone consultations are genuine requests for help in interpreting data or in identifying the way forward. This may include a proper consideration of the appropriateness of referring a case for investigation. Calls come from professionals of all kinds: solicitors, social workers or court welfare officers wanting advice about the effect of contact for children with those who have abused them, teachers seeking clarity about the meaning of some observed play or a piece which a child has written, hospital workers wanting help in interpreting symptoms, or doctors asking for advice about how to help a patient whose family has been torn apart by the effects of child abuse. The list is long and infinitely varied.

During the year between April 2002 and March 2003 about 20 per cent of JACAT's consultations took place over the phone. This represents a rise of three per cent in three years. The figures for April 2004 to March 2005 tell a different story with roughly ten per cent of initial consultations taking place over the phone. However, some caution has to be expressed here as it may be that like is not being compared with like. There is some evidence to suggest that phone calls which were initially a consultation to see if therapeutic or other intervention were indicated, are possibly only recorded as consultations when a second and fuller consultation at JACAT does not follow the first.

In offering a face-to-face consultation JACAT tries to make the best possible use of its varied membership, according to the perceived needs of the case. Of course, the fuller the original referral the easier it is to achieve this. Wherever possible more than one person is used for each consultation: social workers are balanced with psychologists, men with women, and the inexperienced with the more experienced. This enables JACAT to offer a wide range of expertise and experience as well as creating the sense that the referrer is well understood. It has the additional benefit of enabling JACAT members to learn from each other and to pass on their knowledge to secondees and trainees without cost to the person seeking help.

When JACAT began, most of its work came through direct referrals: requests on paper or over the phone, usually by health visitors or social workers, and generally asking for direct work with a child. Naturally JACAT responded accordingly. However, over the years it has become apparent that not all children and young people who meet the simple criteria for referral (that is, having been victims of some kind of abuse), are wanting therapy, ready for therapy, and in a sufficiently secure situation to make therapy appropriate and safe. Moreover, there may be other ways of helping which would be much more advantageous. These are the sorts of issues that are explored at a consultation before work of any kind is agreed and set in motion.

Consultation or Referral?

Nowadays most JACAT referrals, therefore, unless they appear very clear-cut or involve children who are already known, are met with a request that the referrer come in for a consultation. Since families in which abuse has occurred are often receiving the attentions of a number of professionals the requested consultation may be widened by the inclusion of these others, so that the fullest possible picture of the situation may be obtained. Such requests are not always welcomed by the professionals concerned, since they are generally pressed for time and anxious that something should be done, preferably by someone other than themselves, and quickly. However, it would seem from the informal feedback which is received and from the more formal survey carried out (see Section Six) that the sense of careful consideration and planning is appreciated by most users. It is, after all, greatly to the distress of most workers that so little time is available for reflection on even the most complex cases. 'To work effectively, child protection workers need to have structured opportunities to reflect on practice, judgements, feelings and prejudices – opportunities that are generally not available when resources are scarce and case loads too high' (Cashmore, 1997). JACAT can provide just such an opportunity.

In many cases one referral may not be enough. It may be necessary to widen the net to include the carers of the child or children under consideration, to obtain their views about the child's readiness for therapy and their own needs, or to make a judgement about their ability to support the child during the therapeutic process. It is at this stage that the focus will often change from the child to the carer as it becomes obvious that that is where the need for assistance is greatest: either as a prelude to work with the child, to run in conjunction with the child's work, or to replace it altogether. There is sometimes a good deal of resistance from either professionals or carers or both to the idea that the child is not yet ready for therapy. In their view the child has been abused and needs help, therefore the child should have help. Similarly it is sometimes difficult for parents, other carers or professionals to realise that they may be the ones who are most in need of assistance, or who need to act to protect the child. Yet most, in the end, are willing to accept that it is better not to focus on the child as being the needy one if such a focus is not justified, and that many children will be best helped by those closest to them rather than by a professional therapist. Pauline Hardiker, from the School of Social Work in the University of Leicester, who spoke at JACAT's 1997 conference *Prevention in Practice*, said in her address on the social policy context of welfare that 'in a professional model of welfare, prevention is relevant at every level of intervention: the aim is to prevent the need whenever possible for a more intrusive intervention'. Such is, indeed, the aim of the JACAT consultation.

It is during the consultation process that consideration is given as to the likely effectiveness of therapy, whether family, individual or group, at this time. Many of the children needing therapy are, sadly, not in a position to receive it safely and effectively. There are a number of pointers to possible success or failure.

Most important of these is the child or young person's own desire to receive this type of help. It is not necessary for them to know precisely the type of help needed or to be able to express the reasons for seeking this help, but some sort of a request must be made. Next in importance is the willingness of the person who looks after the child, whether parent or professional carer, both to see the need for such help and to be ready to support the child right through the process, accepting the fact that this may not be easy and may even threaten an already fragile relationship. It is essential, too, that parents who have had some part to play in their child's distress, even if not as the child's abuser, are willing to acknowledge this part and to accept their need for help too. The existing relationship between the child's family and the caring services is often crucial in determining the outcome of treatment and may act as an indication of the likely nature of the relationship between parent and therapist. Where families are still caught up in their own private hell of addiction, promiscuity or mental illness, the outcome for the child, however good the treatment offered, is likely to be poor. The consultation process, if carefully carried out, should reveal most of these factors and enable JACAT members to make an accurate prognosis of the likely success or otherwise of therapy.

Sometimes JACAT requests a further consultation because the first consultation has left the best way forward still unclear. In this event the JACAT member or members will ask that they may take the matter to the team on the occasion of their next weekly meeting to try to resolve the difficulty. On rare occasions this will result in a further member of the team, whose expertise in a specific area may prove valuable, joining the next consultation.

Conclusion

The consultation process provides an excellent illustration of the merits and advantages of working together across the boundaries of agency or professional training:

- Clear and accurate information can be obtained at the outset, or sought out if it is not readily available.
- Practical considerations can be explored.
- The realities of what may be possible can be admitted.
- A way forward which is acceptable to all can be reached together.

The chances of misunderstanding, mis-reporting or forgetting to impart important information, which constitute the ingredients of poor communication between professionals, and which have been so often highlighted as the primary cause of the loss of a child's life, are much more easily avoided by this process. Cumbersome and slow as it must sometimes seem, it does appear to represent the surest and safest way of reaching a decision concerning the welfare of a child.

The remainder of this Section describes the process in greater detail, one using a particular example, the other describing the evolution of consultation at a personal and professional level.

2.2 A Consultation Service for Foster and Adoptive Parents

Susan Holt

Adoption Support

The Adoption and Children Act received Royal Assent in November 2002. Its intention is to speed up the adoption process, increase the number of children adopted, create a framework to safeguard the welfare of adopted children and provide support for adopted families. Its implementation has far reaching implications for the ways in which local authorities respond to the needs of adopted families, with the emphasis shifting away from finding and matching parents and children, towards offering an integrated 'service for life'.

The Act represents a culmination of the growing awareness that the nature of adoption has changed. Very few babies are now placed for adoption but there are increasing numbers of older children with histories of abuse and neglect being placed with new families. At JACAT this has been reflected in the steady increase in the numbers of adopted children and young people, and their families, being referred. Current JACAT members all report that more than half their workload is with adopted or fostered children and their carers. This chapter will describe the approach that we developed several years ago in response to what has become a growing need, and the way we have had to adapt our practice to the new demands.

All referrals to the JACAT team are funnelled through the Team Co-ordinator and are discussed at the weekly referral Team Meeting. In 1994 we noticed that we were receiving a small but steady flow of referrals of adopted children and their carers. It was clear that all the children referred had experienced abuse or neglect of some kind (in fact, usually multiple abuse) and would thus meet our criteria for referral. However, the personal and professional experiences of team members prompted us to think that we needed to offer a service that was specifically tailored to the needs of those involved in adoption, whilst at the same time recognising that we were not a post-adoption service *per se*.

As explained in the introductory chapter on *The Context*, all team members are part-time and hold posts in other agencies. My core training is as an educational psychologist, and when I first joined the team I was working as an educational psychologist covering a patch of rural schools. During one academic year I was consulted by two head teachers about sibling groups that had been placed for adoption from metropolitan areas. My involvement with these children, their teachers and prospective adoptive parents, made me aware of many issues, not all of which fall within the scope of this chapter. Most acutely, I became aware of how difficult it was for adoptive parents to gain access to help without feeling that they were failures. In fact one of the adoptive mothers told me that when she reported, after many months of struggle, that she felt things were improving at home she was told by a child psychiatrist that this was because she and her husband were getting used to being parents. This statement, although I am sure it was meant to be affirming, had the effect of demoralising the parents, who felt that the very real emotional and behavioural problems of their three children were of no consequence or, even worse, imagined by them.

Our discussions with professional colleagues wishing to refer adopted children for therapy also identified several issues that we felt were specific to adoptive families:

- The pain of loss for all involved in the process was frequently unacknowledged.
- It was very common for adoptive parents to have inadequate and incomplete information about their children, leading to feelings of dis-empowerment.
- Parents felt ambivalent about seeking help, on the one hand fearing that they would be labelled as inadequate but on the other hand wanting help. In the first instance this request for help was usually sought for the children as individuals.
- Parents had an on-going need for information and understanding about the effects of abuse and neglect on a child's development, especially the effects on the attachment and re-attachment process.

Most professionals recognised that the adoptive child's loss of their birth parents was traumatic even when they had not been in any way adequate as parents, but few gave sufficient weight to other losses such as pets, wider family, friends and their roots in the community of their birth and upbringing.

Even less acknowledged was that some adoptive parents were often trying to cope with welcoming a child into their home while still coming to terms with the realisation that they themselves were never going to have birth children of their own. In other cases a natural child might be struggling with the loss of their status as the only child in the family.

Howe (1998) writes that major shifts in child care policy and practice over the last two decades have led to changes in the character of adoption. The media interest referred to at the beginning of this chapter has helped the public to become aware that the vast majority of children currently placed for and needing adoption are not small babies: in 1998/99 the average age of looked after children who become adopted was four years and four months. By 2004 the average age had risen slightly to four years and five months, with 30 per cent being between five and nine years and 6 per cent between ten and sixteen years (BAAF, 2005).

However, how many prospective adopters embark on the adoption process with any real knowledge of what adoption may mean for the adoptee at a psychological level, or indeed what the impact of their past experiences have been and will be on their development? Consequently, 'it seems that the role of the modern adopter has become more important, more demanding and more difficult [and] the emotional balancing act that many adopters now have to perform requires parenting of a high order and people of rare motivation' (BAAF, 2005).

Facts and Figures

Government statistics for England show that a total of 2,200 children were adopted from care during 1999. This represents slightly more than half of all children adopted in England, most of the remainder being adopted by step-parents or relatives. It represents a small rise in numbers over the previous five years (thus, 2,000 children adopted from care in 1995). Of the 2,200 in 1999, only 200 were children aged less than one year at the time of adoption, with the majority of children (1,300) being adopted between the ages of one and four years. There were 55,300 children in care in England in 1999. BAAF figures show that 3,700 children were adopted from care in the year ending March 2004. Of these only 210 were under one year old. Despite the push for adoption, encouraged by the new legislation, and the earlier attempts of the 1989 Children Act to enable children to remain at home wherever possible, the numbers of children in care had risen to 61,100 by March 2004. See Surveying Adoption: A comprehensive analysis of local authority adoptions 1998–1999 (BAAF, England), 2000.

Information about the numbers of adoptions that fail each year is not easy to come by. The Department of Health (telephone conversation) quote a figure of fifty failed adoptions for the year ending March 1999, but adds a rider that they have little confidence in this figure because they do not believe that local authorities are keeping accurate records. However, 82 per cent of children placed with a view to adoption went on to be adopted in the year ending March 1999, and of the remainder 12 per cent were placed again with prospective adopters. Though official figures for failed adoptions may be unreliable JACAT is receiving an increasing number of requests for help from would-be adopters who, having fostered a child for some time, struggle to reach a point where they feel able to adopt the child. These cases are particularly time-consuming and usually involve work with both would-be-adoptive parents and the child. Two recent cases have involved such work over more than a year, reflecting the complexity and the difficulty of caring for such damaged children.

What we do understand, from talking to adoptive parents who have experienced it at first hand, as well as from professionals who placed a child, and from children whose adoption broke down, is that the pain and hurt surrounding a failed adoption is enormous and affects everyone involved in the process.

The Impact of Early History

What do we know about the long-term effects of abuse and neglect? Although there is a growing body of research on the effects of sexual abuse, domestic violence, and child maltreatment in general, we will never know enough. It is impossible to gain a true picture of what has occurred, or not occurred, when our informants are the child victims of maltreatment. My experience of providing psychological advice in child care legal work has taught me how little is actually 'known', and also how hard it is for professionals (including myself) to see, hear and act upon what is known. Thus with any one child who has been taken into care and placed for adoption it is likely that any documented material will only represent the tip of the iceberg in terms of what they have experienced.

Lyons-Ruth and Jacobvitz (1999) state that the literature on child abuse and neglect has established that there are many negative developmental outcomes associated with maltreatment, and they list the following:

- Poor peer relationships, with increased levels of withdrawal and avoidance of peers.
- The display of an increased level of aggression towards peers (especially physically abused children).
- Unusual or aggressive behaviours in response to the distress of peers.
- Increased levels of depressive symptoms.

- Compromised school functioning in comparison to peers.
- More negative and less coherent representational models of the self and others.
- A high level of maltreated children displaying disorganized patterns of attachment to caregivers.

Danya Glaser (2000) summarises the research evidence on the effects of neglect and abuse on brain development and functioning. She pays attention to the physiological responses to stress and the long-term effects of the stress response. She links the resultant dysfunctional response to frightening experiences and feelings of passive fear to the behaviours associated with disorganised or controlling attachment patterns. She also cites research that indicates that security of attachment with the primary caregiver acts as a buffer to stress situations.

Central to current thinking about adoption is the effect of maltreatment on attachment, and of course it is a *sine qua non* that an adoptee will need to attach to their new parents, and the adoptive parents will need to bond with their adopted child. Howe (quoted earlier) interviewed over 100 parents of adopted children, whose children had reached late adolescence, and who between them had adopted over 300 children from babies through to older children. His aim was to find out how things had turned out. Of particular relevance here is the impact of pre-placement environments on post-placement social development.

Howe categorised the children by attachment type, from secure through to non-attached, and identified six patterns of adoption which emerged from discussion with adopters:

- secure/stable
- anxious/compliant
- short-term testing
- angry
- detached
- and casual.

Howe observed that while the adoptive parents had encountered very disturbed behaviour patterns, only a few of the adoptions had broken down irretrievably. These were in those cases where the children were described as angry or detached.

Of significance for us at JACAT is that his research showed that very few of the adopters had found the input of professionals (educational psychologists, child psychiatrists, psychotherapists) to be useful or effective. Parents felt that such professionals demonstrated little understanding of adoption, the child's psychology or the parents' distress. Howe also found that the more parents could make sense of their children the more they seemed able to stay with them.

Daniel Hughes (1998) also speaks of the slowness with which professionals have come to terms with the impact of abuse, particularly where it is emotional abuse or neglect. He writes: 'The devastating effect of pervasive emotional neglect is only slowly entering into court hearings and influencing the subsequent decisions that are being made regarding the lives of these children. Reactive attachment disorder is one of the most severe consequences of profound neglect, and its damaging effects on the development of children is increasingly being recognised. When a child is unable to trust even the best parents, the damage that has been done to his self and his capacity to experience nurturance and a reciprocal relationship is immeasurable. Such a child, without significant, successful interventions, will not assume a secure place in our society.'

Making Sense and Staying with it – our Consultative Approach

Every JACAT member holds an active therapeutic caseload, and we believe that this is vital in order to keep us 'up to scratch' in terms of our practice and theoretical knowledge. It is also the aspect of our work from which we derive most satisfaction. However, we accept that individual and family therapies, be they long- or medium-term, are expensive ways of bringing about change, and we have used a consultative approach with fellow professionals since our inception. We see this as a cost-effective way of assisting colleagues to assist clients, and one in which workers in the difficult area of child abuse can feel supported and valued, rather than de-skilled by the 'experts'.

It was this same sense of empowerment and affirmation that we wanted to bring to the work we had been doing with adoptive families and colleagues working in this area. We believed that if we were to treat adopters as if they were clients or patients, this would be experienced by them as a failure on our part to recognise their different status. Whilst we recognise that adoptive parents are not professionals in mental health work, and should not be treated as such, we feel that they should be given access to professional help as a matter of right. This help should be offered before situations become too entrenched or unmanageable and before adoptive parents feel that they are failing.

We decided that the most appropriate way to offer help would be via our consultation system. In this way adopters could have access to members of the team with particular interests or experience in adoption, initially with a face-to-face consultation. Access to the service at the appropriate level could then be negotiated. In essence we wished to make the process as easy and non-bureaucratic as possible.

The aims of our service are to help adopters make sense of their children, and, just as importantly, to understand their reactions and feelings towards them. In addressing these key issues we hope to increase the likelihood of adoptive parents 'sticking with it'. We are not a dedicated post-adoption service but have seen a need to bring our understanding of the effects of abuse on child development into the adoption arena.

Our consultation approach is essentially a non-hierarchical one where the parents remain in control and in charge, being at liberty to act upon or reject any advice given. Huffington (1996) describes the range of activities that can be described as consultation, ranging from a non-directive, almost counselling, approach to problem solving, through to providing expert opinion. She proposes that anyone acting as a consultant needs to be able to slide up and down the scale from uninvolved (client as expert) through to planning intervention (professional as expert) according to the demands of the situation. The key in consultation is that the locus of responsibility rests with the client. Whilst Huffington's work relates to providing consultation to institutions and organisations, we have found that it is precisely this ability to slide up and down the consultation scale that makes this approach particularly suitable for adopters. We are able to use our expert knowledge about child abuse whilst at the same time learning from each individual family about what adoption means for them.

Adoption and the Re-attachment Process

Without doubt our understanding of the complexity of the attachment process and the ramifications of disturbed and distorted attachment experiences on a child's development is growing all the time. However, whilst this body of knowledge continues to accumulate it seems that providing accurate and up-to-date information about a child's background and its likely effects on them is a task that is too frequently covered inadequately by those involved in the adoption process. This leaves both child and adoptive parents with an 'experience vacuum'. In Parker's book (1999) research is cited stating that only 50 per cent of adopters felt that the information received on their children was sufficient or up-to-date, and in some cases adopters felt that some facts had been deliberately withheld or distorted. One third of families in this study were not allowed to see the agency's file on their child. We are often involved in trying to help adoptive parents extract information from social services.

Adoption is about hope and new beginnings, but it is also about loss, separation and pain. If newly constructed families are to bond, grow and develop together, then each family member needs their life experiences, good and bad, to be recognised, respected and held in mind. In attempting to assist adoptive families in this process of development and attachment we have developed a fairly simple model which attempts to analyse how families deal with this process. In adoption, the development of 'family-ness' is an ongoing process, and thus the model looks at adoptive parents and adopted children in parallel.

Using this model in consultation with adopters it is possible for us to make a decision about how far along the continuum (from parents as experts to professionals as experts) we need to pitch our work. It also helps us to determine if at any stage we need to offer any other interventions – either from within our own team or by calling on other resources.

Tables to illustrate this model can be found on pages 33–4.

Case Study – Using a consultation approach to engage with a family

Sarah and Michael were a childless couple who were in the process of adopting a sibling group of three children, aged nine, eight and eighteen months. They were referred to us by the adoption agency who had taken on the support and social work role with this family on behalf of the children's local authority.

Sarah had extensive experience of working with children but was planning to continue a full-time job while her husband was going to give up work to become the main carer. Sarah and Michael had sought a consultation with JACAT because Tim, aged nine, had been found playing 'sexy games' with his younger sister and little brother.

A colleague and I undertook a series of consultations with Sarah and Michael, during which we explored many issues apart from, but including, the 'sexy play'. It became clear early on that this couple would never have sought help from the Child and Adolescent Mental Health Service as they felt that this would stigmatise them as failing parents. However they found it acceptable to consult with us about how to deal with problems with the children. During the consultations we learned that the family had good support networks of family and church but at this stage in the process (the children had been placed for four months) they did not feel able to voice their worries and anxieties to others.

We were able to talk about strategies for helping the other children in the family to keep safe, and also to demonstrate to the parents that Tim's sexualised play came to the fore when he felt anxious or had been in trouble. Both parents found Tim the least attractive and most demanding of the three children, but Michael agreed to make special time to spend with Tim and to do activities with him that would boost his esteem.

In the course of our meetings we found Sarah very resistant to any suggestion that the children might be experiencing feelings of loss and sadness relating to their birth family or previous foster carers. She could find no evidence of this and felt that they had 'taken over' the family home very quickly and were relieved to be in a permanent home. Whilst we felt that this was certainly likely to be true in part we also felt that there was evidence that the two older children were displaying distress, albeit through destructive and challenging behaviour. We became clearer about why Sarah found it hard to hold in mind the children's living past when her husband told us that she too was adopted and had always been very secure in the love of her adopted parents. This issue became important as we began to realise that Sarah had been adopted as an infant and was drawing erroneous parallels between her experiences as someone who had been adopted as a baby and those of her three children adopted at a later age. Having understood this we also hypothesised that this couple had not really grieved for the loss of their own unborn children and that this was hindering them in truly connecting with the two older children. They were far more able to see what the toddler needed.

Our next step was to refer the whole family to one of the family therapists in our team in order to emphasise their 'family-ness' and to avoid the trap of labelling Tim as the troublesome family member. The parents agreed to this but would never agree to wait in the waiting room with other 'problem families'!

Comment

How children are prepared for the move into a new family, and how this is managed can have a significant impact on the placement. Our work in the consultation service has taught us that there appears to be no acknowledged good way of doing this, and that very often pragmatics dictate how introductions are handled, rather than the needs of all those involved.

Case Study – The impact of inadequate preparation

Rowena and Mark were a childless couple in their thirties. Mark was a teacher and Rowena worked from home. Milly and Bobby were children of mixed race aged seven and four and had experienced severe neglect before being taken into care. Rowena and Mark sought advice from our service about Milly whom Rowena was finding it very hard to like. Mark was very forthright about the shoddy service he felt they had received from the children's Social Services department, and also made it clear that he sought help from us because a team member had impressed him as knowing 'what she was talking about' at a talk to prospective *adopters*.

Rowena's ethnicity reflected that of the children, and she explained that she had immediately taken to Milly when she had read about her because she had had to look after and protect Bobby – just like Rowena had done with her own younger brother. The reality had, however, proved very different once the children had moved in. Rowena found that Milly often ignored her and appeared to make a deliberate play for Mark, that she played Rowena and Mark off against each other, and that she appeared to be always acting a part and never showing any spontaneous pleasure or enjoyment. Bobby on the other hand was disobedient and challenging but was showing signs of making a meaningful attachment to both Rowena and Mark.

We learned that the children had only met Mark and Rowena once before they moved 200 miles away from their home town and foster carers to live with them. The rationale for this had been to tie in with Mark's long summer vacation but of course this had left the children feeling that they had been uprooted from everything they knew to live with virtual strangers.

Over the course of the consultations the split between Rowena and Mark over the children became very marked. Rowena could find nothing kind or positive to say about Milly, and Mark felt she was being too judgmental and hasty in her reactions. Mark also located the problem firmly in Rowena's court and was angry that she appeared to be jeopardising their only chance of being parents.

Over several sessions we worked hard at trying to help both parents understand why Milly was showing such detached and rejecting behaviour. Mark found it easier to be patient and to allow Milly space and time, but Rowena found this impossible. After much heart searching the couple decided not to proceed with the adoption, and although both would have wanted to keep Bobby they felt the children needed each other.

In this instance the consultation service provided a safe space for this couple to explore some very painful issues, not only about the children but also about their relationship. Rowena was able to see how she had invested a part of herself in Milly, and how angry she had been when she found that her attempts at befriending and helping Milly were rejected. Rowena had seen herself as a child in Milly and had wanted to give the child Rowena all the benefit of what the adult Rowena had learnt.

Mark had desperately wanted to recreate a family – his own parents had died when he was a young boy and he felt robbed of his childhood. Again he wanted to nurture his own inner child through these two children, the whole business being so much more painful for both of them as Rowena could not have children.

While it is impossible to be certain that the hasty introduction intensified the parents' reactions and the children's stress levels, it is our view that the way in which this was handled increased the risk of a disrupted placement. The agency involved in the assessment of Rowena and Mark had recognised that things were not going right early on in the placement (hence the referral to JACAT) but failed to take into account the psychological impact of what they had learned about the couple's motivation and issues regarding loss. As part of our ongoing support of this couple Rowena continued to see one of our workers individually and the couple were referred for couple counselling.

In this instance it seems that the combined determination of everyone involved to bring about a fairy tale happy ending contributed to the breakdown in placement. It is a tribute to Mark and Rowena that they worked hard at helping the children move on.

Comment

All the adopted children that have been referred to JACAT have suffered abuse and neglect in some form. Within this sample of children and young people very few seem to have any detailed knowledge or history of their background, and whilst this can be understood at one level as a response to trauma on the part of the child, we also find that adoptive parents are similarly hazy or uncertain about background history. On occasion it has seemed that professionals have shown a callous disregard for the needs and rights of adopted children to know about their history.

Case Study – Denial of the adopted child's right to their history

Janet, whose adopted parent first consulted us when she was four, still had no Life Story Book at eight, despite repeated efforts by her adoptive mother before and after the adoption to get Janet's social worker to do this work. She has no contact with her mother or her sister, who still lives at home with her birth mother, despite an agreement that contact should take place twice a year.

Michael was fourteen and had been adopted for twelve years. His parents sought help regarding stealing, poor hygiene and poor peer relationships. After an initial consultation it seemed important to meet with Michael to find out what he felt. Michael desperately wanted to see his younger sister, with whom he used to meet up each year, but whom he had not seen for five years. He did not understand why this contact had stopped. He felt ashamed at being adopted but did not know why. He tried to deal with his birth mum and dad by pretending they did not exist, and he did not have a way of describing them or thinking about them.

Michaela was referred because of sexualised behaviour at school. She was six years old and had been excluded from school. She had been taken into care aged two with her older brother Peter, and initially they had been fostered together. However, Peter had been found simulating intercourse with Michaela, and she had been moved to another foster home. Michaela herself had no idea where she might have learned to be sexy with other children, and she was confused about why she never saw her older brother. She thought that she behaved as she did because she was bad, and thus could hardly bear to talk about what she had done. She also believed that she was so unlovable that acknowledging what had happened at school would be the last straw, leading to her adoptive parents rejecting her.

Comment

Sometimes adoptive parents find the anger and fury that their children provoke in them frightening and debilitating. In these circumstances we have found it helpful to talk from an expert position about the processes of transference, counter-transference and projection, as a way of helping parents make sense of their reactions. A knowledge of the child's history helps us to do this more effectively.

Case Study – Feelings aroused in carers

Sharon was a lone parent with two teenage children. She had cared for Tina as a foster carer since she was eighteen months old, and was now planning to adopt her. Sharon desperately wanted to make up for the deprivation and rejection that Tina had experienced, and was a calm and creative parent.

Tina was a very challenging little girl who would set out to provoke Sharon and her children with taunts, non-compliance and general disruption of the family. Sharon fought extremely hard at keeping her own rising feelings of fury and hurt at bay whilst Tina seemed unaffected by her outbursts and could switch them off and turn them on at will.

Exploration with Sharon about Tina's background revealed that her birth mother had been unable to deal with what could be seen as developmentally appropriate behaviour, temper tantrums or exploratory behaviours and had responded by becoming ill and, it is suspected, even giving Tina medication to sedate her.

Sharon could see that Tina would feel far too frightened to experience the full force of her anger towards her birth mother or indeed feel able to express any negative feelings about or to her. Consequently Sharon was the receptacle of Tina's unbearable angry feelings – both those she could not feel herself (projection) and also those that belonged to her birth mother (transference). Sharon, because of her own personality and experience, in turn found it hard to say just how angry she felt with Tina and indeed with her birth mother, and consequently was becoming physically ill under the strain. Sharon's two older children took a stand about what they would tolerate from Tina, thus enabling Sharon to be firmer and clearer with Tina.

Conclusion

The JACAT consultation service for adoptive parents offers a flexible intervention for adoptive families where there is a history of abuse and neglect. Adoptive parents of abused children take on some of the most disturbed and challenging children in the care system, and in our experience are often left to cope alone or with very limited help. We have found that a consultation approach can offer access to expertise and experience in the sphere of child abuse and neglect without de-skilling or 'pathologising' parents.

Entering our service via consultation can also mean that parents are more willing to accept therapeutic help for themselves or their children at a later stage, and in this respect consultation has been an important tool in engaging with clients.

Table 1: Becoming an Adoptive Family – Parents

Stages	Attitudes	Issues
Making the commitment to adopt	Recognition that the adopted child will not be a replacement for longed-for or lost children.	Commitment, if a couple, of both partners to deal with the complexities of being an adoptive family. Infertility and the need to create/recreate.
	Acceptance that the child will have a living past.	Capacity to contemplate and bear pain, the parent's own and that of the child.
Thinking through adoption	Ability to acknowledge hopes and fears	How the couple deal with feelings: their level of emotional literacy
	Acceptance of the need for everyone to adjust to new roles.	Views and attitudes on contact with birth family
The adoptive family	Attitudes to its own needs and those of the child.	Resolving conflict between the needs of an adult couple and the needs of the child, and recognising their own needs.
	Capacity to deal with challenge.	Working through feelings of anger, hurt and guilt. An ability to set boundaries.
	Acceptance of the reality of the past.	Capacity to help the child deal with feelings of loss and split loyalty without becoming depressed or overwhelmed. Dealing with contact with the birth family, and feelings about this. Need for a supportive network of professionals, family and friends to share problems without feeling bad.
	Becoming a unique and special family.	Establishing 'this family' culture – establishment of a bank of shared memories and experiences.

Table 2: Becoming an Adoptive Family – The Child

Stages	Attitudes	Issues
Making the commitment to adoption	Wanting a 'keeping family'	The child's conceptual understanding of family as well as of birth family experiences
	Understanding that the past will not be obliterated by adoption	Quality of preparation work done with the child The child's ways of coping with any trauma/abuse
	Belief that birth family has given for adoption	The child's knowledge of his/her own history and internal representation of this Psychological freedom to move on.
Thinking through adoption	The ability to acknowledge hopes and fears	The child's ability to express feelings and wishes
	Acceptance of the need for everyone to adjust to new roles	Views and attitudes on contact with birth family
Becoming a family	The capacity or potential to trust	The need to feel safe, and strategies for achieving this
	The capacity to deal with challenge	Working through feelings of anger hurt and guilt. Ability to accept boundaries
	Acceptance of the reality of the past	Recognising that a traumatic past may be interfering with the capacity to make new attachments Dealing with contact with birth family, and feelings about this Balancing the need to revisit issues in past against not being allowed to get on with the here and now
	Becoming a unique and special family	Sharing in 'this family' culture: the establishment of a bank of shared memories and experiences

Note: The above has to be considered in relation to child's age and developmental level.

2.3 A Consultation Service for Professionals and Others

Ann Catchpole

The Nature of Consultation

Over the years the patterns of consultations at JACAT have changed radically. In the beginning consultations were reserved for professionals only. Professionals still come, and in considerable numbers, but others come too, notably foster carers and adoptive carers and natural parents. The number of consultation slots has had to be trebled and it is seldom possible for more than two team members to be present for any one consultation. Consultation has become much more than a single initial meeting to determine the nature of the work required. It is now one of the major tools for doing the work itself, as JACAT members and those consulting them meet on a regular basis to try and find solutions to testing cases. It is one of the prime examples of co-operative working.

In allocating cases for consultation to team members every care is taken to try to match the needs of the case to the skills and background of those offering consultation and to make sure that more complex cases have more than one worker. However, the complexity of the case is not always apparent from the referral and occasionally, like other team members, I find myself offering consultation on my own which can still be daunting. However, *all* my colleagues find it daunting at times and are not afraid to say so. If we find ourselves out of our depth and in need of advice from colleagues with a different background and expertise it is always possible to say so and to offer a further consultation when such expertise will be at hand.

The consultation process as a lifeline

Where cases are unusually complex, and when therefore they demand of workers almost more emotional energy and staying power than it is possible to offer, the consultation process may itself provide a lifeline. Working with child abuse is almost as lonely for the worker, at times, as it is for those families who have experienced it. It can cause despair, breakdown, burnout, job abandonment, and even suicide for workers who are not properly supported. JACAT has observed most of these phenomena across the various professions: the police, teachers, social workers, health visitors, family centre workers, and those who work for voluntary agencies, all of whom come for consultation.

Case Study – Providing a lifeline

One day a social worker arrived for a consultation in such a distressed state that he was clearly almost at breaking point. He suspected that he had uncovered a network of sexual abuse which encompassed many families but it was impossible to prove because of the unreliable nature of the evidence provided by the children concerned, most of whom were disabled or had learning difficulties. His frustration and helplessness at his failure to protect these children were the major cause of his distress. He felt unsupported by his managers and was considering leaving his job.

The plight of this social worker alerted us to the growing need to look after the workers themselves as well as those they were trying to help, and we soon found ourselves offering support to others caught up in the same situation. As a social worker myself, with the responsibility for a caseload made up entirely of children and families in which abuse had occurred, I am well placed to be able to empathise with the feelings of a professional under that sort of stress and to recognise that there are always likely to be many more workers out there struggling with their own distress.

In many cases, too, workers are liable to reflect the bewilderment of the families whom they are trying to help. Child abuse of whatever kind has at its centre a child, but its effects do not stop there. The ripples spread ever outwards, affecting all with whom that child or their family come in contact: school, youth club, work place, all may feel its influence. Small wonder, then, that families, and those who work with them, feel overwhelmed and do not know where to start to try to alleviate the distress.

Complex cases

Often JACAT is best able to help by acknowledging the complexity of the case and the demands it places upon the workers, and by offering to see the worker or workers who face the issues first hand on a regular basis so that they can share the burden. Of course, without the close emotional involvement that work of this nature often brings with it for the worker, JACAT is, to change the metaphor, in a better place to separate the wood from the trees and to offer some hope of a way forward. Such consultations may go on for many months or years and may involve one professional or many, one JACAT worker or several. They may occur as frequently as weekly or as infrequently as three times a year. There is no set pattern: each is set up to meet the particular needs of the case. Where large investigations are concerned or complex family issues involving a number of professionals from a variety of fields, JACAT may offer support or advice to all who take part. Such an exercise can take its toll in turn on the JACAT worker or workers concerned, as many of the painful effects of the case are transferred to them. During a recent complex police investigation every single member of the team was involved with one aspect or another of the enquiry. For some of us, myself included, matters were made more complicated by the fact that we were involved through the other half of our work and, therefore, unavailable as a worker to JACAT.

Consultation with Non-professionals

Sometimes JACAT offers a consultation to people who are not professionals but who are struggling with some issue concerning the abuse of children. However, the non-professional, often a non-abusing parent of the young person concerned, would normally be accompanied by a professional. This ensures that there is someone there who accepts responsibility for the case and can put in practice whatever is needed following the consultation. JACAT is not a front-line agency. It requires others to look after families in their entirety. More often, the first consultation will be with the professional alone, and the other person will join the process for further consultation or consultations. Much can be achieved on these occasions to strengthen the confidence of the client in the primary worker as they see the worker consulting on their behalf and being supported in the process of determining, with him or her, what is best for the child or young person. Such consultations can be empowering for all concerned.

Case Study – The non-professional

One such consultation involved a young mother whose daughter had been sexually abused by her erstwhile partner, the father of her children. Her social worker had been asked to make a report for the court concerning the contact between the woman's other child and his father, such contact having been to that point not just unsupervised but also having involved over night stays with him. The social worker had asked for a joint consultation for herself and the child's mother.

When they came, both felt that the situation was not right but were unclear as to precisely why, or what could be done about it. As a result of exploring the impact of the current situation upon each of the two children involved, the extraordinary mixed messages which they would be receiving as a result of it, and the options for doing something different, much was achieved: the woman decided to stop contact for the son, thereby paying attention to his request that he should not be made to see his father, the social worker determined to support her in this move via his court report, the son began to tell both mother and social worker about further abuse he had experienced while staying with his father, and the little girl's distress at her brother's continued contact with him began to ease when this contact stopped. In addition the relationship between son and mother, and between one sibling and another, greatly improved. And all that from one consultation! Moreover, the social worker declared afterwards that his eyes had been opened concerning many of the issues.

This case highlights one of the issues with which JACAT often finds itself wrestling: contact between children and an abusive parent. Since the 1989 Children Act there seems to have been a growing presumption that children should remain in contact with their fathers following divorce or separation, whether or not the fathers have been violent towards their partners, or even to their children. Or, at the very least, the courts make a ruling that denies the father contact to one child, whom he is known to have abused, while maintaining it with another. Recent research indicates that in many cases this exposes the child in contact with the father to further risk of abuse of many kinds. 'There was a clear overlap between the existence of domestic violence and the abuse of children during contact, whether physical, sexual or emotional' (Hester and Pearson, 1998). The JACAT consultation process offers a forum in which careful judgements can be made on such difficult matters, and workers and clients can be empowered to put decisions into practice.

The consequences of not protecting a child from domestic violence are graphically spelt out in this excerpt from a poem by Selina Nicholas (1995) entitled Ongoing Violence:

> So het up, I sensed your violence –
> you laid your force right into me.
> I tried to run, I tried to hide,
> Frightened of such energy.
> No one saw what was happening,
> not many saw the real you.
> Behind closed doors my life was different,
> yet on my face were vital clues.
> A troubled kid was how I started
> when mother went so far away,
> always fighting with those around
> with common rules to disobey.
> Unfair denial, rotten future,
> stolen innocence because of you,
> myself withdrawing, holding emotions,
> growing up as anger grew.
> Daytime turned to distant darktime
> nightime didn't come at all,
> as the violence became more frequent
> I disliked myself a little more.
> One step forwards, two steps back
> though struggling on I've not got far,
> the inward death, you killed my spirit
> on-going misery, unseen scar.

Professionals' Meetings

Part of the on-going consultation process is the type of meeting that could loosely be called a 'professionals' meeting'. These take place on a regular basis over a period of time. They offer a forum for shared information, encouragement to the various workers involved, and a way of making sure that all the participants in the case are keeping pace with each other and acting together. Often, in complex cases which involve children who are perceived to be at continued risk, or who offer particularly difficult challenges, JACAT will chair such meetings as well as offering other professional input to them. In many cases, in order to accommodate other professionals, JACAT will meet outside Exeter. Often JACAT may have more than one worker involved in the case, working variously with the child, or with the carers, or advising the professionals – sometimes, indeed, doing all three. Such situations stretch our resources to the limits but are worthwhile if they serve to maintain children at home in safety and to preserve placements which are at risk of breakdown whilst enabling workers to recognise, through pooled information, when it is imperative to move a child from an unsafe situation. It is to be hoped that such regular and detailed sharing of information has helped to prevent further tragedies like those in which investigations have identified lack of communication among professionals as leading to the death of a child.

It would be wrong to suggest that JACAT's involvement in a case is always welcomed. Sometimes it is necessary to draw the attention of other professionals to what JACAT regards as dangerous shortcomings in practice or provision which make the undertaking of the desired therapy impossible or leaves the child in danger. Often JACAT holds on to cases like a terrier, refusing to be diverted from our purpose until such time as changes for the better occur. Though senior management may find this tenacity worrying, it is often welcomed by the workers in the field who have seen their potential for intervention reduced more and more over the years. Hopefully, the presence among JACAT members of representatives of those services which consult it means that its interventions come from a position of understanding the strains under which others work. Similarly, the representatives from the management of social services, health, education, probation and the police, who make up our advisory body, give JACAT a forum for on-going discussions about tendencies in service provision which cause it concern.

Advice or On-going Work?

Some consultations held at JACAT are not about a request for work but are specifically requests for advice only. Often such meetings will themselves stem from an initial phone call that indicates that the matter would benefit from more time for consideration than a phone call allows. Sometimes the professional seeking advice may wish for help in interpreting the behaviour of a child or young person who appears to be exhibiting sexualised behaviour: teachers may ask for help in dealing with this kind of behaviour in a school setting; senior churchmen may want to discuss matters relating to the alleged abuse of a child by a member of the clergy; play-group leaders may wish to discuss the ramifications of an enquiry into abuse within their system; schools and colleges may seek advice about ways of supporting colleagues when a number of pupils have been caught up in a ring of abuse.

Some of these consultations occur on a one-off basis and do not lead to further work. However, it is frequently the case that consultations do lead to further work, whether it be a number of further consultations, the provision of individual therapy for a child or young person, group work, or support for carers. Tony Morrison, in his excellent article in *Child Abuse and Neglect*, highlights the difficulties experienced not only by clients but also by professionals when advice is first sought. 'Anxiety runs like a vein throughout the child protection process. It is present in the anxious or unrewarding attachment that forms the family context in which abuse may occur. It is present in the highly charged atmosphere of the parents' first encounter with professionals concerned about their child. It is present too within the child professional system, as child abuse represents a crisis not only for the family but also for the professional network' (Morrison, 1996). It seems that the process of involving professionals in detailed consultation greatly increases their confidence that JACAT can offer a worthwhile service. This advantage is heightened by the involvement, where possible, of the would-be client or carer of that client, at the consultation stage, so that, again, confidence is established. Not surprisingly there is more hope of successful engagement when clients are not asked to venture into the unknown and terrifying deeps of therapy without having an opportunity to test the waters. The ordeal of this first meeting for some clients is amply illustrated by the shaking of their limbs and the difficulty they experience in speaking at all. This is where the presence of a supportive professional accompanying them can be so helpful. Fortunately, once the ice is broken, the session usually brings a relief in tension, often expressed in tears.

Consultations are sometimes set up in an attempt to decide where work for a child should best take place or what the nature of this work should be. There is some overlap between the services offered by Child and Adolescent Mental Health Services (CAMHS) and by JACAT. Sometimes indeed referrals are made to both services. It is not always clear which service should pick up the case. CAMHS has the services of psychiatrists who can provide medication and a psychiatric assessment, something which JACAT does not offer. However, because of the demand for its services, and the wide area of problems that it covers, its criteria for offering a service are high and children or young people have to be in considerable distress before they can be accessed. JACAT has a much narrower remit, dealing, as it does, only with children who have been abused, and families which have been affected by abuse. This sometimes means that JACAT can offer a service when CAMHS cannot. Occasionally both JACAT and CAMHS may be involved with the same family, offering different services, and there may be some disagreement about which form of treatment should be offered. In these cases a meeting is arranged so that the matter can be thrashed out and agreement reached or, at the very least, the professional with responsibility for the case, generally the social worker, enabled to hear the pros and cons of each position and reach an informed decision. On the whole, fortunately, each service is happy to consult with the other for the benefit of the client.

At its best, the consultation process is also therapeutic in itself, offering relief to a beleaguered worker who can share, perhaps for the first time, what it feels like to be working with such a case, or some consolation to a victim who learns for the first time that they or their family are not alone in experiencing the devastation of abuse. Sometimes both professionals and clients arrive for consultation angry at the way in which the system has let them down, and doubtful about the possibility of achieving anything this time round. If the consultation is conducted thoroughly, sympathetically, and respectfully, some of this anger and despair can be dissipated. Abuse thrives on secrecy, control and division. It is banished by openness, empowerment and working together. The JACAT consultation process tries to put these three things into practice. To quote from a poem entitled Getting On, again written by Selina Nicholas (1995: 35), herself a survivor of child sexual abuse, who attended a JACAT group for mothers of children who have been sexually abused, the first consultation with JACAT may be the first step in:

> Coming to terms with my past
> redirecting the blame,
> Re-adjusting my life-style,
> letting go of the pain.
> Stamping out darkest misfortune,
> facing all life I have left.
> Taking another step forwards,
> being ahead of the rest.

2.4 Consultations: Conclusions

Ann Catchpole

The previous two chapters will, I hope, have demonstrated that the consultation process, as used by JACAT, is a flexible and useful tool. First and foremost, it offers a way of gathering information which far surpasses even the most thorough referral, since it allows supplementary questions to be asked and the views of all those present to be heard. Matters which may not have seemed important to the referrer may assume much greater importance when viewed as part of the wider picture, or interpreted by experienced practitioners. The consultation process also offers an opportunity to assess the potential for change among the would-be clients, especially but not exclusively if they are present, and to make a judgement about who would be best suited to carry out a given piece of work. Sometimes, when considering a referral beforehand, JACAT members have identified someone whom they believe could well undertake the necessary work with the client only to find, in the consultation, that the nature of the work needed is not what was anticipated and requires, therefore, a different worker. The consultation is often, most crucially, about reaching agreement on the type of work needed, whether the time is ripe for such work to be undertaken, whether someone is available to do this work, either from among JACAT members or beyond, and whether adequate support is available for those who will be looking after the child or young person while the work is undertaken. So many decisions! No wonder more than a single consultation of three-quarters of an hour is sometimes needed in order to reach agreement about the best way forward. The process may be slow and painstaking but, because all have participated in the decision-making, there is a good chance that all will stand by the decisions and act upon them. JACAT has no power to compel others to accept its decisions: that power lies with the care manager, and it can only rely upon its ability to persuade and the openness of its methods.

I hope Section Two will also have shown how JACAT has refined the way in which it has used consultations and increased the scope of those it engages in the process. As consultations have become more complex we have become increasingly aware of the need to record the decisions reached, or the advice given, since the discussion is often far-reaching, with many possibilities explored, before a common mind is reached. Accordingly one of the JACAT members will always take notes. These notes form the basis for the report which is made back to the team on the following Monday, and are also the basis for the letter which now follows a consultation. This letter is a relatively new innovation, but we hope it will lead to greater efficiency and do away with those occasions, fortunately few in number, when there is some dispute afterwards about just what was said!

The consultation process has grown to reflect JACAT's multi-disciplinary make-up and its preference for working with other agencies whenever possible. It also reflects its belief that child abuse will only be successfully combated by a holistic approach. Many dangers threaten if agencies do not work together but instead adopt a secretive and possessive approach. Abusive families will be able to divide one professional from another, sympathetic workers may find themselves inadvertently colluding with parents to the detriment of the children, and information which is not shared by all can be crucially misunderstood or ignored, and lead to an incomplete picture and the failure to take action. On a less serious level, but still with potentially detrimental effects on the abused child, families may be given conflicting advice because professionals are not working together; conversely, they may be left without crucial advice because each worker believes it to have been given by another. At the beginning of an investigation families may be asked to allow policemen or women, social workers, family support workers and health visitors into their home. All will come asking questions, some will come offering advice. Once the investigation is over many, if not all of these professionals, will vanish like snow in summer, leaving the family to pick up its own pieces and put itself together again, an attempt as likely to succeed as that of 'all the king's horses and all the king's men' who tried to 'put Humpty together again'. It is often at this stage that JACAT will receive a phone-call from the lone professional who is still in touch with the family, be it health visitor, teacher, doctor or social worker, asking for a consultation. Such a consultation should go some way towards the child or children concerned avoiding the twin misfortunes of 'falling between the gaps' or 'over-servicing' (Cashmore, 1997). As she says, collaboration may not be a panacea but it is undoubtedly a good deal more effective than lack of collaboration. Indeed it may be one of the best ways of preventing the further abuse of children by the very systems which have been put in place to protect them.

Section Three: **Working with Individuals**

3.1 Introduction to Working with Individuals

Paul O'Reilly

Introduction

As trained professional therapists able to work with adults and adolescents as well as individual children, it is our stated preference only to work with individual children in exceptional circumstances. The adults who refer children to us, and the parents or carers of those children, usually expect us to concentrate our efforts on 'sorting them out'. However, this can all too easily have the effect of scapegoating the children and of increasing the already present tendency for all parties, including the children themselves, to regard the children as 'the problem'. Our interventions of choice are as follows:

- Support and consultation with other workers.
- Support and consultation with the families and carers of young people who have been abused.
- Group work with young people who have been abused.
- Group work with the parents (especially mothers) of young people who have been abused.
- As a last resort, individual work with young people.

This section deals with the last of these and describes instances of individual work with young people and clarifies why it might be that such work is needed by certain young people given their exceptional circumstances. Research in other areas of distress, such as young people diagnosed with anorexia nervosa, shows clearly that the intervention of preference is family therapy until the young person reaches an age of somewhere between 14 and 18 years. By this age there is a move from family therapy to individual work with the young person for themselves.

Though family work is still required (Dare et al., 1995), in the field of child sexual abuse it is clear that individual therapy and group therapy with young people are both efficacious, given the right circumstances (Trowell, 1999). A clear balance is to be achieved between the work that might be offered to a young person within the context in which they live and behave, and therapeutic work which is particular to the young person.

In the case of the areas of work illustrated in this section, one of the recurring themes is that support and maintenance of carers is necessary. This is the case even though care has to be exercised to preserve the young person's privacy within the bounds of the direct work. There is no doubt at all that the more individual work with the young person takes place the more input is needed to help the carers of that young person support them and maintain the therapeutic endeavour.

It is clear from all the illustrations in this section that engagement of the young person in the work, and the prevention of sabotage of the work, which may occur at any point in time, is difficult but essential. Obviously a young person has to be both available to make use of the therapeutic space offered, and also inclined to do so. By 'available' we mean able and motivated to experience again their painful and damaging personal history; by 'inclined' we mean that the young person can robustly maintain a relationship with the therapist and resist any possible sabotage or ambivalence that might reside in carers whether informal (familial) or professional. Many of the common processes that occur in clinical work with adults also occur with greater intensity with respect to children and young people. Just like adult clients, children find it difficult to believe that they could be worthwhile, that they might be treated respectfully by another person, especially an adult, and that an adult might hold them in mind over an extended period of time. Moreover, they find it hard to understand that privacy will be maintained, that trust will not be broken, and that the relationship with another adult will in itself be used as an aid to personal development. In the therapeutic process there is a particular poignancy for young people who wish to remain loyal to their family of origin, including the abuser, at the same time as wishing to make use of the developing relationship with the therapist.

The development and maintenance of a therapeutic alliance with a young person can take a long time. Young people can make use of 'acting out' to both test the limits of the therapy arrangement and to see whether the badness which they feel in themselves makes them without worth in the eyes of the therapist. As demonstrated in the following chapters there are particular difficulties in maintaining privacy, pacing the work, and coping with the transference relationship that is formed. On top of this is the painful experience of the limitations imposed on the therapist by the real world, demonstrated in the issues of inter-agency planning (especially around young people who are both victims and victimisers) and in the challenge to obtain the provision of resources over an extended period of 18 months or between two and three years.

Joint Agency Offers Variety

In a joint-agency multi-professional system such as JACAT it is possible to use a variety of methods of work, and provide a variety of media with which to do the work. In all such work the consistent containment of the child is essential whichever the method or medium of work chosen. The chapters in this section illustrate some of these working practices.

Amongst these methods of intervention, cognitive behavioural therapy may be useful as a technique in working with abused children, though not every child will be able to respond to this method. Ross and O'Carroll (2004) have reviewed the outcome of a number of studies where a post-traumatic conceptualisation was used to plan treatment and intervention. It appears that individual differences in response to abuse are related to three intermediating variables: the severity of the abuse, the availability of social support, and attributional styles regarding the causes of negative life events. Another highly significant factor appears to be the child's developmental stage at the time of abuse. In JACAT we have found not only that the effectiveness of working with children is likely to be strongly influenced by the family context but also that both children and carers can benefit from the use of techniques such as cognitive therapy.

Despite our reluctance to intervene directly with children, it is clearly a necessity that individual therapeutic intervention occurs for particular young people because of their unique life story. The people who care for them informally or formally may not be in a position to offer the neutral acceptance that a therapist might, and in fact carers of young people have a much more important task to perform than those who offer therapy or therapeutic input. They have to give the young person a message of being worthwhile in the setting of their everyday living. In order to carry out this demanding task they may need help themselves.

The chapters in this section contain examples of the kind of individual work that might be necessary in a therapeutic service system such as JACAT. There are interventions with young people who have been abused, with young people who are greatly at risk anyway through their disabilities and who have been abused, and with young people who are extremely challenging because they victimise others and are highly likely to have been victimised themselves.

3.2 Working with Young Children

Carole Town

The builder men have made all the houses finished. It was all messy and muddy before. Don't they look nice?

Introduction

The work we do at JACAT is aimed at addressing the therapeutic needs of children and families where abuse has occurred. Although the majority of our referrals are of children who have suffered sexual abuse, when we begin to work with these children and their families it is usually more important to address the fact of having been abused than decide upon the particular form of maltreatment experienced. The emotional and psychological harm experienced by abused children is a common thread linking all forms of abuse. In Lizzie's story a number of the issues common to working with all such children are illustrated.

Case Study – Lizzie

Lizzie and I were gazing out of the therapy room window. The window overlooked a small development of new houses. We had begun our work together 18 months previously, at which time the site was little more than a muddy area with one winding tarmac entrance road. From time to time during our weekly meetings we would stand at the window and note the progress on the building site. In the early stages Lizzie had voiced concern when the mechanical diggers had created deep trenches for the foundations and the pipe work. Later she had become anxious and somewhat fearful at the sound of the noisy machinery and men's shouting voices. Once the walls of the houses began to grow taller she voiced approval and she was especially pleased when the roofs were completed. Lizzie's comment on the finished state of the houses was made on the second to last session of our work together.

Throughout our work I had commented on the parallel between the building of the houses and the repair and rebuilding going on in the playroom as Lizzie struggled via her play and our conversations to rebuild her life.

In reply to Lizzie's original comment, I said, 'I am wondering if you're pleased that some of the messiness you used to feel is more sorted now?' Lizzie gave me one of her startlingly bright smiles and then turned back into the room to begin her play for the session.

The Referral

We had received the referral for Lizzie from her social worker. As is our usual practice at JACAT we had offered an initial consultation for the social worker and the foster carer, Laura. In this first meeting with myself and another team member we were given the information that follows.

Background and History

Lizzie was five years old and had been in her current foster placement for eight months. She and her older half-brother Tom, then aged seven years, had been removed from their mother's care approximately twelve months prior to this. Lizzie's mother, Kay, was known to be working as a prostitute, and there had been concerns for some time about her care of Lizzie and Tom. Both children's names were on the local authority Child Protection Register in the categories of neglect and likely sexual abuse.

The local authority had been attempting to offer support to Kay for the previous two years. Their concerns had been triggered by information provided by an acquaintance of Kay's. It appeared that Kay would frequently leave Lizzie and Tom in the care of a variety of adults, some of whom were known to be regular drug-users. In addition, the teachers at Tom's school had expressed concern about things Tom had said which suggested that both children were witnessing violence towards their mother, perpetrated by male visitors to the home. There were also concerns about Tom's sexualised behaviour towards female members of staff and towards girls in his class.

The local authority applied for and was granted interim care orders, and then full care orders, on both children after Kay left the children with a female friend and did not return to collect them. Although Kay had made telephone contact with Lizzie's social worker she had not seen or directly contacted Lizzie or Tom since.

Lizzie and Tom had experienced three changes of temporary foster care placements before being placed together in a short-term foster placement. This foster carer had reported a close and caring relationship between the children, but on a number of occasions she had had to stop Tom from engaging in sexual behaviour with Lizzie.

In seeking to make permanent plans for the children the local authority made contact with Lizzie's father, Steve. Steve and Kay had never lived together, and so Lizzie had never known her father. He had recently re-established a connection with his previous partner, Laura, who was the mother of his two other children, Johnnie aged nine years and Sarah aged seven years. Although Steve and Laura were not living together at this time, Laura came forward and made a very strong bid to take on the care of Lizzie. Following a careful vetting and assessment process it was decided that Lizzie should be placed with Laura, and Lizzie's two half-siblings, Johnnie and Sarah.

Tom had been placed separately. By this time Tom had begun to disclose a history of frequent exposure to the sexual activities of his mother and her clients. During these disclosures it was clear that Lizzie, to a lesser extent, had been required to be present during the activities. Lizzie had never spoken about this. Tom also said he had been made to be sexual with Lizzie. Tom had been offered and was undertaking therapeutic work in a specialist unit for children who had been extensively exposed to sexually abusive experiences. Arrangements were made for Tom and Lizzie to have indirect contact, initially with cards, letters and phone calls, with the possibility of direct supervised contact to be arranged in the future.

Current Situation and Concerns

Laura described Lizzie as a lively, articulate and bright little girl. She was beginning to settle into her new family and school but continued to struggle with the clear rules and boundaries Laura placed around her behaviour. Laura showed considerable insight into Lizzie's difficulties, and it was clear that she was very committed to her care.

The concerns Laura mentioned were:

- Lizzie had shown some sexualised behaviour with Johnnie, Sarah and some friends' children. Laura had addressed this directly with Lizzie, and had told Johnnie and Sarah that they must let her know if they had any further concerns about this.
- Lizzie had periods when she seemed 'switched off' and in a world of her own. In addition, Lizzie had frequent outbursts of very angry and non-compliant behaviours.
- Lizzie was having difficulties getting on with other children at school and often came home saying that no one liked her.
- Lizzie was able to talk about her brother Tom, asking if he was all right and saying she wanted to see him, but she was not willing to talk with Laura about Kay.

Laura also expressed concern about Lizzie in the future and was very keen to secure help now for her, in order to prevent difficulties later in her life. Laura and the social worker were requesting individual work for Lizzie.

Comment

One of the decisions to be made in an initial consultation meeting is regarding the most effective way for help to be offered. Particularly with very young children, or with those who have had a recent change of carer, we consider whether joint work with the child and main carer (usually mother or foster-mother) is advised, or even whether indirect work through time offered to the mother or carer alone is more appropriate.

In considering Lizzie's needs we took into account the duration and nature of her abusive experiences, her presentation and the behaviours of concern, and the resources available for her support. We also drew upon our knowledge of child development, including the development of attachments, and on our knowledge of the dynamics of abuse.

The history we had been given suggested that Lizzie had experienced long-term, unreliable and inconsistent care from her mother, culminating in total abandonment. In addition, Lizzie had witnessed her mother being physically hurt by other adults, and she herself had been exposed to and involved in adult sexuality. All these things had occurred before Lizzie was three years of age.

Lizzie's current behaviour was causing concern at home with Laura, and at home and school with her peers. Lizzie was also demonstrating considerable anger and a sense of not feeling liked.

Our knowledge of child development tells us that during the first years of life the young child is engaged in the process of building assumptions about themselves, about others, and about the nature of the world. These assumptions arise from the way the child experiences being cared for and the actions they observe in others. Assumptions of self-worth, self-efficacy and predictability in the world, are engendered by the experience of reliable, nurturing and age-appropriate care-taking.

Our knowledge of the impact of abuse in childhood, especially during these early formative years, tells us that children can develop a range of strategies with which to cope with the pain, trauma and confusion experienced when their needs are not met:

- If a totally dependent younger child is to resolve the dilemma of being hurt or harmed by the very person responsible for their well-being, the child may come to the conclusion that they themselves are to blame, i.e. 'If something bad is happening to me then it has to be because I deserve it: I am bad'. If the child subsequently experiences being left or abandoned by their parent this is likely to confirm this belief in their own badness. Children can let us know about this belief through behaving badly.
- If a young child experiences her or his need for physical and emotional care being disregarded, then that child is likely to conclude that such needs are not important and that they are not worthy of being cared for. Children can let us know this by their lack of self-care or by rejection of good care from others.
- If a young child observes and experiences frequent situations of fear and alarm they are likely to conclude that the world is a dangerous place. Children can let us know this through hyper-vigilance, unsettled behaviour and fearful reactions in certain situations.
- If a young child has not experienced close and nurturing relationships with adults they are likely to conclude that it is not safe to invest too much in relationships. Children can let us know about this by engaging in indiscriminate or superficial relationships, or by having difficulty in developing and sustaining relationships.
- If a young child has been required to gratify the sexual needs of adults they may conclude that this is the way they are expected to behave in order to be accepted or to please others. Children can let us know about this by sexualised behaviour towards adults, other children or in their play.

Laura's description of Lizzie suggested that she was functioning at an age-appropriate level both physically and intellectually. The areas of concern mentioned by Laura suggested that Lizzie was struggling to sort out confusion in her emotional world, particularly in relation to her sense of herself as acceptable, and with respect to appropriate expression of her feelings. She also needed help to deal with her confusion about sexual behaviour, although Laura had already provided very clear information for Lizzie and also taken account of Johnnie's and Sarah's needs.

Laura was also keen to make herself available for any work that might be advised for herself in addition to the specific work requested for Lizzie. Lizzie was, therefore, in a permanent placement with good support and a carer who was prepared and able to work alongside any direct work offered to Lizzie, and she thus fulfilled several of the major criteria for successful intervention.

It was decided that I would see Lizzie weekly, for four weeks initially, in order to see if she could respond to a non-directive play therapy approach. If Lizzie seemed able to make use of this way of working I would continue to see her on a weekly basis for a long-term period. In fact, Lizzie responded well to these initial four meetings, and so I continued with what developed into an 18-month piece of work.

Laura was offered time by another team member with meetings every six to eight weeks during this period of work.

Planning for the Work

At that time we had two possible venues for seeing children at JACAT. I decided to use the venue away from the main hospital site. This venue comprises an ordinary dwelling house that we have been able to equip with two playrooms, a group room with easy chairs and a second sitting room suitable for meeting with parents. There is also a kitchen, a bathroom and a small office and equipment store room.

I decided to meet with Lizzie in the general playroom that is equipped with play material suitable for younger children. This includes a playhouse with kitchen materials, soft toys and puppets, a beanbag and easy chair, a child-sized table and chairs, dolls and doll play equipment including a doll's pram, drawing materials with paper, and playdoh.

In discussion with Laura it was agreed that I would see Lizzie immediately after school. Laura was able to bring her and collect her regularly. These practical arrangements need to be clarified at the outset of a piece of work, and for some children it is necessary to have other agency support for transporting the child to and from therapy sessions, along with a familiar adult.

Laura and I also agreed that I would be updated about any significant issues in Lizzie's life by my team colleague who was offering time to meet with Laura. This arrangement took account of the need to keep my weekly time focused on Lizzie herself rather than needing to develop any lengthy conversations with Laura on these occasions.

Comment

A long-term piece of work involving weekly sessions with a child can become intense and demanding. I therefore arranged regular consultation sessions with a colleague from the psychology department. This was an important part of the planning since it provided me with a regular time to process the material arising in the therapy sessions.

Themes in the Work

Over the 18-month period of weekly meetings there was clearly a great deal of material to process. However a number of main themes emerged out of this work.

The key theme which emerged very early on in our meetings, and which was present in some way in most sessions, was that Lizzie's exploration of her sense of herself was made in relation to significant people in her life, and primarily in relation to her mother. This main theme had two separate but closely linked strands. The first of these strands seemed to be Lizzie's need to re-experience the earliest stages of her life when, as a baby, she had been totally dependent on her mother. The second strand was Lizzie's need to test out this 'mother figure' in order to see if she, Lizzie, would be rejected because of the badness she felt was within her. In addition to these key themes I became aware of Lizzie's fearfulness and sense of potential threat or danger, as indicated by her reaction to other people's presence in the house on some occasions during our sessions.

In pursuing these key themes Lizzie spent a period of time in each session during the first twelve months of our meetings, squeezed into the doll's pram as a 'baby' who would then require soothing, pushing around, feeding (from a baby feeding bottle) and generally being cared for.

Lizzie also developed ways of trying to help me understand how she had been cared for previously. Some of these ways seemed to be attempts at making me into a controlling, denying and punitive 'mother' who would not give Lizzie enough. For example, we began our meetings with a drink and biscuit: Lizzie would regularly challenge me as to how many biscuits she could have, or tell me I had brought the wrong biscuits as she did not like the ones on offer.

In our play with the kitchen equipment Lizzie would frequently prepare food for me to eat which she would then ask me to pretend was too hot or nasty-tasting, or she would 'trick' me by giving me an empty plate. During this play Lizzie could change her voice from a soft gentle tone to a high-pitched shrieking tone, issuing harsh criticism, and then refusing to allow me to eat or to play.

On other occasions Lizzie refused to comply with the rules within the playroom, limited as they were and mainly aimed at ensuring safety or preventing damage – for example, she would climb on to the table close to the window, or threaten to tear the books. She would then become very anxious, seeking reassurance that I still liked her, or that I was not cross with her.

During the middle part of our period of work together Lizzie moved on to exploring the relationships between the important people in her life. I had heard from Laura via her meetings with my colleague that Lizzie had begun to join Johnnie and Sarah in their visits to see their father, Steve. In our sessions Lizzie began using drawing to depict members of her family and on one occasion struggled to decide where to position Tom in a drawing that also included Laura, Steve, Johnnie, Sarah and herself. Lizzie was obviously struggling with the two separate parts of her family – the family she had experienced for the first three years of her life, which had included Tom, and the family she was now with, which did not include Tom.

On a later occasion she drew a wedding picture with Laura as bride, a male figure that changed from being Steve, as bridegroom, to 'not Steve' and back again, and herself as a bridesmaid. In this same session Lizzie was able to talk directly about Kay as she differentiated between Kay who was her mother and Laura who was her stepmother.

I heard later, via Laura's meeting with my colleague, that following this session Lizzie had become very upset when she fell at home and hurt her leg. Laura sensed that Lizzie's distress was more than could be accounted for by the physical hurt to her leg, and when she gently prompted Lizzie, Lizzie was able to say that she was feeling very sad about Kay. Laura took this opportunity to re-explain to Lizzie that the reason she was no longer with her mother was because Kay had not been able to look after her properly. Lizzie was able to say to Laura that she had thought that Kay did not like her.

Although on many occasions Lizzie and I would be the only users of the building at the time of her sessions, there were times when other workers would be present, using other rooms. On these occasions Lizzie would be obviously anxious when she heard people pass the door of our playroom or go up and down the stairs. In addition, Lizzie noticed the hatch-way at the top of the stairs, into the loft area. She needed reassurance that there was no one in the loft. These anxieties seemed to link into another recurrent theme in Lizzie's play which involved shutting herself into the playhouse, with the windows carefully covered with curtains, in order to prevent 'the strangers' entering. On one occasion Lizzie was able to talk about this fear of 'the strangers' as she said once she had seen 'a stranger hurt mummy in the bathroom'. We were able to talk about how frightening this must have been for a little girl, and how children needed to know that adults can protect children from danger.

I learned from Laura's meeting with my colleague that during the week before the above session, the mother of another child in Lizzie's class at school had been the victim of a violent assault at home. It was therefore possible to return to the issue of dangerous people in the following session with Lizzie. Lizzie said she had told Laura that when she grew up she was not going to get married 'because men could beat up ladies'.

A regular part of the routine of our meetings, in the early stages, was that Lizzie would run ahead into the playroom and hide. I would then have to find her – under the table, behind the chair, etc. – before she would go on to choose other activities. Another routine which developed beyond these hiding games was that of 'statues'. Lizzie was amazingly adept at suddenly freezing in mid-action, often when dancing, which she loved to do.

I could make some sense of these hiding and statue games in terms of her uncertainty in allowing me to 'see' what was going on for her, or her need in the past to have 'frozen' as a survival strategy in times of threat or danger. However, there were other parts of her play that remained a chaotic puzzle to me. I wondered on these occasions whether this is what Lizzie needed me to experience – the sense of muddle and confusion she felt in her own life.

During Lizzie's play, when incidents appeared to have significance in relation to these themes of therapy, I would comment on the possible meanings. As time went on Lizzie became able to let me know how she felt about these comments. Sometimes she would silently concur, with a look that suggested she could hear and accept what I had to say, at other times she would respond verbally by developing a conversation, and on other occasions it was clear that she had difficulty with what I had said. I felt, at times, that her difficulty was because of her wish not to have to acknowledge, accept or deal with, the painful feelings involved, but at other times I felt my comments were unhelpful or unnecessary as Lizzie was using the non-verbal play experience as the most appropriate way of processing her own experiences.

As our work together progressed Lizzie began to leave behind some of the early baby play. She used the dolls more as babies, rather than as herself, and took on the role of parent, demonstrating appropriate care and feeding behaviours towards them. Her puppet play also showed fewer traumatic accidents happening to the baby hedgehog and rabbit puppets. The reports I was hearing, via my colleague who was working with Laura, suggested that Lizzie was being more successful in her peer-group relationships and her behaviour at home was generally calmer.

Bringing the Work to a Close

Some fifteen months into the work we agreed a finishing date, which we worked towards over a period of about three months. Once we had agreed a finishing date Lizzie went through a period when the early baby play returned, including Lizzie's attempting to squeeze back into the doll's pram! We were able to use this physical evidence of her growth to talk about her emotional growth and she was then able to move on to seeking reassurance in ways more appropriate to her chronological age.

Our work ended at a time when there were no other major changes due in Lizzie's life and she was experiencing some very positive feedback about her achievements in school in particular.

Two years after our work ended we received a message from Laura asking for an appointment. I saw Laura alone and heard that Lizzie's behaviour was again causing concern, with renewed angry outbursts at home. It appeared that Laura had recently ended a relationship with a man she had been seeing for approximately one year. Lizzie had begun to develop a very positive relationship with this man and had been upset to learn that he was no longer going to be around. I offered one further appointment to meet with Laura and Lizzie together. In this session Lizzie continued to say to Laura that she was worried that Laura might also send her away. Laura was therefore able to offer Lizzie the reassurance she needed that this would not happen. In contacting Laura some weeks later she reported that Lizzie was settling again and their close relationship had resumed.

Some Considerations for Work with Younger Children

In thinking about the needs of younger children aged 8 years and under, two characteristics of this age group are particularly important for us to take into account when planning an effective response. The first is the high level of dependency on adults of these young children, and the second is the role of play in the development of young children.

Young children's high level of dependency on adults is a central factor mediating the harmful impact of abusive treatment by adults. This is true for all types of abuse, physical abuse, emotional abuse, sexual abuse and neglect.

Younger children's lack of physical strength and skill, relative to an adult, puts them in the position of not being able to defend themselves or to escape from physical attack. Such experiences can add an enduring sense of helplessness and powerlessness to the pain suffered from the physical hurt or harm.

Emotionally and psychologically the child's dependency on adults places them in a position from which it is difficult, if not impossible, to challenge or question the adult's actions. Children are told that it is 'naughty' to disobey adults and they must do as adults say. Additionally, whilst children are still cognitively at the stage of making sense of the world from their own perspective rather than others' perspectives, the conclusions they reach when faced with 'bad' things happening to them is that they themselves must be 'bad'. When an adult punishes a child this punishment is therefore seen by the child as deserved. Children frequently retain and elaborate on this message of their own badness, incorporating it into their view of themselves. Their lack of experience of alternative ways of being treated may also mean that children believe their own harsh treatment is normal.

Sexual abuse of the young child puts that child in the position of being made use of by an adult for the adult's own sexual and other needs. This leads to the child's experiencing a betrayal of trust in the adult who should be there to take account of the child's needs. The trauma of developmentally inappropriate exposure to adult sexuality, the betrayal of trust by an adult and the frequently given message that the child is responsible for the abuse, combine to produce the lasting effects seen in children who have been abused in this way.

Younger children's dependency on adults is therefore an essential factor to be considered in reaching an understanding of the impact on children of ill treatment at the hands of adults. It is also important to keep this dependency in mind when decisions need to be made about the best way to offer help to the young child who has been abused.

In order to benefit from any direct individual work that will address the consequences of abuse, children need to be in a safe and supportive living situation. The messages they receive in therapy about the importance of their needs should be congruent with the care they are receiving in their day-to-day life. Young children will also be dependent on the support of their parents or carers for managing any increase in troubled or troubling behaviours during the process of therapy. Children who feel they are still at risk of further abuse, or who have had a recent change of carer, will probably not be in a position to undertake such work.

A second characteristic of young children which must be taken into consideration when planning therapeutic work is the central role of play in their lives. It is important to bear this in mind in any assessment process, or the planning of any work with parents or carers, but it is most important of all when direct individual work with a young child is being considered. Play as a natural means of communication and processing for young children can help adults to understand about the child's world and offer a way of working with children.

As part of an assessment process it is important to ask about the ways in which the child uses play. This can tell us about issues with which the child is struggling as well as the child's need, and ability, to make use of the medium of play in therapeutic work. Parents or carers can be helped to use their observations of their child's play, both with play materials and with playmates, as a way of gaining a greater understanding of any problems the child may have. Children may convey their distress, confusion or anger through play rather than through direct verbal communication. Adults who are able to understand these indirect communications are in a position to offer support to the child rather than feeling confused, and possibly tempted to respond critically or even punitively, when faced with behaviours that may create alarm in the adult. It is helpful for parents and other carers, and for children, to hear that the behaviours of concern can be seen as understandable responses to the situations the children have experienced rather than as indicators of something being wrong with the child.

In planning for direct individual work it is necessary to take account of the child's current stage of development as well as their age and stage of development at the time of the abuse. In offering a play environment for exploring and working through the confusions and traumas arising from the abuse it is important to remember that children may need to engage in play typical of a range of stages of development. The play materials provided and the understanding of the therapist will foster such exploration.

A child who has been denied play opportunities, as a consequence of neglect or abuse during the pre-school years, may, for example, benefit from permission in the therapy sessions to engage in play which is typical of a two, three or four-year-old, even though the child is chronologically older than this. Such play may not be as acceptable or possible in the child's day-to-day life.

Children may also make use of the message of acceptance, offered by the therapist, to play out themes of anger, punishment, control and destruction. The relationship with the therapist, and the boundaries and rules of the therapy sessions, can provide the safety necessary for the exploration of the negative feelings, associated with these themes, which are common in children who have been abused.

For some children it may be possible to build explicit links between the play themes developed in therapy and the child's actual abusive experiences; other children may benefit just from the opportunity to find ways of expressing very strong but confusing feelings via their play. It is particularly important with young children to take account of these non-verbal clues. Whilst children can be helped by being given verbal labels to make sense of some of the muddling emotional experiences with which they struggle, it is also necessary to take account of the purely physical and sensory quality of many early childhood experiences which can be recaptured and worked through in play.

The therapist will need to have the experience and skill to judge the most helpful level of intervention and comment for each child.

The therapist will also need to be able to guide the pace at which the child progresses through such work, including the point at which any piece of work needs to end. It is frequently the case that a child will make use of direct work for a period of time and then at a later stage in their development may need or wish to return for further work. Such a further request for therapeutic work can occur for a variety of reasons including both normative and unexpected life events. Events which may give rise to the need for further work could include a change of school, e.g. from primary to secondary, the introduction of new people into the child's life, e.g. a new child in the family or a new partner for the child's parent or carer, or unexpected traumatic events, such as illness, accidents or bereavements. It is also important to keep in mind the possibility of further abuse, given the increased vulnerability to future abuse of children who have been abused in their early years. The re-occurrence of distressed or troubling behaviours, in children who have previously experienced abuse, needs to be carefully assessed when considering the need for further direct work.

Conclusion

It is important for the ending process to include positive messages about the progress made during the work as well as allowing for the expression of the more negative feelings of anger and sadness which a child may have as the relationship with the therapist draws to an end. A carefully managed ending will increase the likelihood of the child's making good use of any further therapeutic help at a later stage in their development, if this is needed. Parents and carers will also benefit from understanding, and therefore being able to predict, the sorts of situations in the future that may provoke a return to some troubling behaviours in the child.

As was the case with Lizzie, we at JACAT often find that children need to return for further work when they reach another milestone in their development. This is particularly likely to happen when the initial work has taken place when the child is very young. It is important that this possibility is made clear to both parent and child, so that a need to return is not perceived as a failure.

3.3 Working with Adolescents

Anna Flanigan

And it's just a phase I'm going through. Just my hormones kicking in. It happens when you reach a Certain Age. I know because my Dad told me.

(Rebecca Ray, *A Certain Age*)

Introduction

When Harry Enfield's comic character Kevin reaches his 13th birthday, his father exclaims, 'He's losing the power of rational thought . . . he's become a teenager!' Both parents hold on to each other looking dismayed and bewildered. The father desperately tries to commiserate by saying to his wife, 'Don't worry, darling, it's only a phase, it only lasts for four or five years'. (Enfield, 1994)

The anticipated dread of the teenage years will be familiar to a lot of parents – 'the dread that your "tiny miracle" has turned into a raging bundle of aggression; the charming toddler has transformed into the "Incredible Sulk". And you are left wondering what went wrong!' (Dainow, 1994) This is the dread of feeling helpless, unloved, out of control and de-skilled as an adult, in the thrall of an energetic and potent adolescent; the confusion of dealing with rapid and violent changes of mood, feelings, behaviour and thoughts in someone who is no longer a child but not yet an adult. And all this when you are coping with your own personal and professional mid-life changes. It represents a heady cocktail of challenges to parents.

According to a recent government survey, most teenagers get on well with their parents. The survey found that out of the 2,500 teenagers interviewed nearly 75 per cent said that their parents were there for them when they needed them and 40 per cent said that they got on well with their parents. Nevertheless, the period of adolescence is a challenging time for parents and young people as they try to cope with the myriad changes in both family and individual life.

The prospect of working with this age group fills many therapists with similar feelings of dread. However, many adolescents require and seek individual counselling or psychotherapy. It will be necessary for therapists working with them to 'bear the essential paradoxes that are at the heart of the adolescent process' (Frankel, 1998). He cites a quote from Anna Freud as summing up these paradoxes.

Adolescents are excessively egoistic, regarding themselves as the centre of the universe and the sole object of interest, and yet at no time in later life are they capable of so much self-sacrifice and devotion. They form the most passionate love relations, only to break them off as abruptly as they began them. On the one hand, they throw themselves enthusiastically into the life of the community and, on the other, they have an overpowering need for solitude. They oscillate between blind submission to some self-chosen leader and defiant rebellion

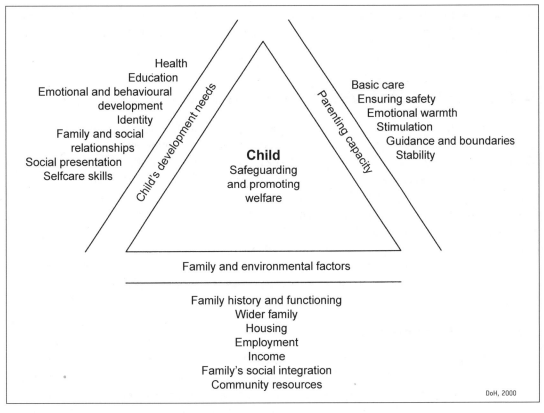

Health
Education
Emotional and behavioural development
Identity
Family and social relationships
Social presentation
Selfcare skills

Child's development needs

Parenting capacity

Basic care
Ensuring safety
Emotional warmth
Stimulation
Guidance and boundaries
Stability

Child
Safeguarding and promoting welfare

Family and environmental factors

Family history and functioning
Wider family
Housing
Employment
Income
Family's social integration
Community resources

DoH, 2000

Figure 1: Assessment framework

against any and every authority. They are selfish and materially minded and at the same time full of lofty idealism.

(Freud, 1966)

When working with this age group therapists can expect to have their personal and professional selves challenged in a way that is different from working with adults. They may need to be active and directive at times; they will be seen as, and respond as, a parental figure at times; they will certainly feel de-skilled, attacked and helpless at times. But they will also see the amazing capacity for thought, change, insight, tolerance, empathy and forgiveness that is present in many adolescents.

In his various audio tapes for parents (available from the Trust for the Study of Adolescence) John Coleman encourages and reassures parents by urging them not to mourn the child they fear they have lost but to celebrate and relish the adolescent they have now, who may become an unexpected good friend. Equally, the therapist can treasure those privileged moments of insight and connection with a young person as they share their feelings of pain, joy, loss, anger, despair, enthusiasm, optimism, and idealism.

This chapter will consider the particular demands on therapists working with teenagers who have experienced abuse. The term 'abuse' refers here to neglect, physical abuse, emotional abuse, and sexual abuse. However, particular emphasis will be placed on the two latter categories as they represent the highest number of referrals to JACAT. The clinical material predominantly refers to adolescent girls of sixteen years and under, as this reflects the author's past and present caseload.

A Framework for Working with Teenagers

In his article on working with adolescents in an in-patient unit, Singh suggests that workers should develop a 'therapeutic bearing ... which comprises human ordinariness, emotional openness and intellectual curiosity' (Singh, 1987). This means that workers should understand and appreciate adolescence as a stage of human development, should adopt a 'consistent therapeutic attitude' (Singh, 1987), and understand the principles of the therapeutic alliance and process. When working with young people who have been abused, workers should also have knowledge of the cause and effect of child abuse and be familiar with any relevant child protection procedures and legal requirements (see Figure 1).

I have found that holding in mind these issues enables me to work closely and effectively with teenagers whilst maintaining my separateness and integrity as a therapist and adult.

Theoretical orientation

It is important to have a theoretical orientation for this work. It is the foundation on which the practical application of therapy is based. It is where you can look for guidance and inspiration for the right intervention, or for explanation when seeking a way forward with a client. A young person is part of a social system usually dominated by the family unit, and for many of the young people referred to JACAT there are the additional complexities of the care system. The individual therapeutic relationship with a young person is only one part of an extremely complex set of relationships involved in child protection and child abuse work. It is necessary to consider the context in which therapy is carried out and to make sense of the family and professional interactions and relationships with which the young person will already be involved. An appreciation of systemic concepts is invaluable.

My basic training as an occupational therapist was informed by client-centred concepts:

- That everyone has a right to a healthy psychological as well as a physical life.
- That everyone is unique, with a personal dignity and worth.
- That everyone has potential, with a capacity for choice and change.
- That everyone can be an active agent in their own recovery.

However, if a young person is going to move towards recovery and make the necessary changes to achieve this, the systems around them must be able to shift enough to allow them to do so. At JACAT each member of the team is expected to have at least an intuitive sense, if not a theoretical knowledge, of systemic concepts. To work successfully with young people, particularly those in the care system or the child protection system, 'therapists need to take their place in the circle of people holding the safety net' (Hunter, 2001). This means clear, respectful, and open lines of communication with the other adults involved. It is necessary to form a therapeutic alliance with the individual young person but to see them in relation to their system as a whole and to find a way of working with that system and the client's relationship to it (McLeod, 1993).

Case Study – Kim

Kim, aged 14 years, is referred by her female social worker. A few months earlier Kim had disclosed sexual abuse by her paternal grandfather when she was aged eight years. Her parents are divorced following alleged domestic violence by Kim's father. Her parents still have a hostile relationship. She lives with her mother and younger brother. Her father does not accept the allegations, and family relations are strained. She is estranged from her father as a result but wishes to re-establish contact.

The Crown Prosecution Service had taken up the case, but they decided not to proceed to court because of the excessive distress caused to Kim by the prospect of being cross-examined. The police have interviewed her grandfather, and Kim feels believed by the adults within the professional system with whom she has been involved. Her social worker has been with Kim from the beginning and dealt with the initial interview. At the time of referral she continues to offer family support including some individual time for Kim. The request is for individual therapy for Kim, joint sessions with her mother, and sessions for her mother alone. We offer an initial consultation session and agree that I and another colleague will undertake the work.

Comment

Kim and her mother had a good initial experience of the professional system. The social worker has developed a working partnership with them by using the important concepts of family support, namely, acceptance of their circumstances and being a source of important information for them (cf. the chapter on Approaches to Family Work). She has extended that partnership with the referral to JACAT while keeping the family informed of the ongoing process. As a result they approach JACAT already feeling empowered and informed. Via consultation, my colleague and I can carry on this process and begin the development of a therapeutic alliance. Gradually, the individual work with Kim will move into a more dominant position in the system. It is likely that this will be successful with this initial liaison and networking. It may even be possible to involve Kim's father as appropriate.

Sequelae of abuse

The correlation between an abuse history and the adverse effect on physical, psychological and interpersonal functioning, both in the short and long-term, is well known and well documented. The sequelae of abuse include anxiety, depression, self-harm, poor interpersonal relationships, sexual problems, low self-esteem, mistrust of others and symptoms of post-traumatic stress disorder (PTSD) such as disassociation and sleep disturbance. It is known that adults who have experienced abuse are more likely than the general population to be admitted to a psychiatric hospital, to have addiction problems, and to show a higher incidence of heart disease, cancer and respiratory problems. It is also known that many children and adults never report their abuse, and the statistics available are only compiled from known cases, so the full scale of the problem remains unknown.

Adolescence as a stage of development

It is common for young people to present or re-present at JACAT in adolescence. This is the stage of development when young people are beginning the long process of change from dependence to independence and separation from family. They are trying to develop their own identity; their focus on relationships is transferring to peer friendships and intimate relationships, and they are becoming more aware of their own bodies.

At personal and immediate levels, sexuality brings with it the struggle for bodily integrity in the face of unyielding impulses and feelings that are evoked at puberty. There are terrible fears and insecurities about whether one's body can work well, in a co-ordinated way, such that one can feel competent and integrated while exploring sexuality with another. There is the terrifying possibility of things falling apart, not working, and not being in tune. The self is on the line as one submits to these feelings in the context of letting go of control with another person. The expression of physical love touches at the root of one's identity as the merging of intimacy, closeness and trust transforms the developing personality. (Frankel, 1998).

The process of adolescent development can be severely disrupted by abuse or the memory of abuse. It is no wonder that problems may emerge or re-emerge at this time.

Case Study – Sarah 1

Sarah was 11 years old. A family friend had sexually abused her before the age of two. He had also abused other children in the neighbourhood but there had been no prosecution. Sarah's family had moved to Exeter when she was about four. Her parents separated when she was six and her mother remarried about one year later. Sarah was a beautiful and vivacious girl. She loved drama and hoped to be an actress. She had recently started her periods and this presage of emerging womanhood and sexuality had thrown her into psychological turmoil. She had become withdrawn and anxious at times, and had become verbally and sometimes physically aggressive towards peers at school, especially boys. During the first six months of our work the account of a well-known MP's accidentally killing himself through auto-erotic strangulation appeared in all the papers. Sarah became extremely disturbed by this. She asked her parents to explain what it meant, but they got embarrassed, and angry, and accused her of being 'dirty'. She asked me to explain, which I did. She immediately looked relieved but still puzzled. After a few minutes she said, 'So, it's OK for me to have the fur rug in front of the fire and a bottle of wine?' It was my turn to be puzzled. I did not understand. She went on to talk about her fears that as someone who had been sexually abused she did not deserve anything other than kinky sex. The romantic ideal of candlelit sex in front of a blazing fire with someone she loved and who loved her was impossible. Every time she felt sexually aroused these thoughts had plagued her. Her body felt damaged and ruined and merely a receptacle for hurt and further abuse. She deliberately avoided and resisted any possibility of intimacy and closeness through relationships because it only served to remind her of the paradox of her need to be close and her own repulsiveness. It was a theme to which we returned many times.

How is therapy helpful?

Young people who have been abused can 'gain enormous relief from the opportunity to talk about and be heard unconditionally and uncritically, particularly when expressing feelings which might not be thought acceptable, such as positive feelings and a sense of loss and concern about the abuser' (Glaser, 1992). Carl Roger's ideas of empathy, unconditional positive regard and genuineness are an essential part of the therapeutic relationship. The young person can begin to feel valued and accepted; can begin to feel confirmed in their own identity; can begin to feel less isolated, less abnormal and strange; can begin to learn to trust another adult; and can begin to restructure on a cognitive level their chaotic and abusive past experiences and regain a sense of control and mastery. The therapist offers a predictable and reliable environment in which the young person can experiment with ways of feeling and being. Not only is this essential to the therapeutic relationship, but also to the developmental process which has been interrupted and delayed. 'Trust, the capacity to rely on an internal experience of love and protection, is shattered by trauma, and slowly reclaimed in therapeutic work' (Briggs, 1998).

The Therapeutic Encounter

The themes of therapy – betrayal, abandonment, trust, fear, envy, rage, rivalry, doubt – and the ways they are thought about, place the therapeutic encounter at the heart of our examination of human subjective experience.

(Orbach, 2000)

The beginning of a therapeutic relationship provokes anxiety all round. Client, family and therapist will have hopes, fears and expectations of what will happen or not happen. There will be ambiguities about what is known or not known, and by whom, about the abuse. By the time the young person is referred to JACAT, they can have undergone a number of intrusive procedures involved in the investigation, such as physical examination and a CAMAT interview (usually a joint interview conducted by the Child Protection Police and Social Services to listen to the child's evidence). Understandably, they and their family or carers can be wary of what they interpret as further exposure and intrusion into their lives. However, some information is essential for the therapist to assess suitability for therapy. 'There is always a need to consider a complex history of disturbing and difficult relationships affecting the young person. Treating the consequences of abuse means both trying to understand the impact of the trauma on the young person, and also understanding the qualities of the experiences the individual has known throughout life and the way these have been taken in, or internalised, to become the relationships which hold significance in the internal world' (Briggs, 1998).

Young people can have many prejudices about therapists or counsellors. In Rebecca Ray's novel, A Certain Age, the central character's friend, Holly, has to go for counselling. She muses about what the counsellor will be like: '.one of two categories. Either a fifty-year-old guy with half-moon spectacles and a frown that's too big for his face, or a woman of the same age with unshaved legs, shin-length skirts and too many smiles. I couldn't see Holly talking to any one like that.' (Ray, 1998)

It is unlikely that many of the young people who arrive at JACAT will have been referred independently. Usually, they have been sent by another professional, a parent or carer, or both.

The adult they encounter at JACAT may seem like an extension of their parents, another symbol of authority or another adult with the potential to abuse them. If the therapist they meet is male, the latter feelings may be compounded for it is still the case that the majority of child abusers are male, particularly in sexual abuse. There is some evidence that adolescent girls can have difficulty in talking about sexual abuse to a male therapist, although it is also known that many young women bond well with male workers (Moon et al., 2000). The clinical consideration should be one of caution when assigning male workers to young women who have been abused, with special reference to sexual abuse. Of course, the same caution should apply to young men and the gender of their therapist, although it is difficult to back this up from the research. It is the practice at JACAT always to consult the young people themselves and to attempt to respect their wishes with regard to the gender of their therapist.

Confidentiality and privacy

The therapeutic encounter is intrinsically private and personal. The world behind the doors of the therapy room is enclosed and closeted. These boundaries are necessary as they help to create an atmosphere of confidentiality and containment. From the inside this can feel safe and holding, from the outside it can appear excluding and secretive, particularly to parents, carers or other professionals. Abuse thrives in a culture of secrecy and fragmentation. It is vital to explain and demonstrate the difference between secrecy and privacy to both the young person and their family or carers. The other people involved with the young person have to understand and appreciate the need for privacy in order not to sabotage the therapeutic relationship. There are ways of including them, without their being in the same room as the teenager and the therapist. For example, there can be regular reviews with parents present, or parallel family work can be arranged. However, confidentiality must remain paramount. This is an important issue for adolescents, particularly for those who have experienced abuse.

One of the developmental tasks of adolescence is to achieve emotional and physical separation from parents. The act of abuse involves the inappropriate crossing of adult boundaries. In order to take account of this paradox, and to model appropriate adult behaviour, it is crucial to respect, hold and maintain boundaries within the therapeutic encounter. If there is to be any sharing of information, it is beneficial to agree with the teenager first what is possible to share. Young people do not always know the rules of therapy. They will need to understand from the therapist what is expected of them in individual or family work, as well as the role of their therapist in both settings.

One of the constant tensions for therapists is to maintain the balance between creating a safe and containing environment, so that therapeutic change can be facilitated, and the continued protection of clients from further abuse. Issues of child protection have changed the concept and old assumptions of confidentiality. Therapists working with children and young people have a different duty of care than they have when working with adults. Although, at JACAT, it is the case that the abuse is known and recognised, it is possible that further disclosures will be made about past or present abuse during therapy. All members of the team are bound by the local child protection procedures and adhere to the guidelines regarding the sharing of information. For the young person this means that the usual confidentiality of the therapy room can be limited and may have to be breached. This can be a precarious and difficult time for both client and therapist.

The idea of conditional confidentiality can be confusing, and the young person may not be sure what they are able to discuss safely. It is preferable to be open about the ramifications of child protection and to talk about the possible need for involving other professionals. It is helpful to talk about confidentiality in general in the initial session. Of course this is no guarantee that the young person will remember what has been said if it becomes necessary to breach confidentiality. My experience is that most young people disclose because they want the abuse to stop, or they need to share more information and they think you will help them, even though they do not always fully understand what happens next. However, it cannot be assumed that any young person who shares risky information is automatically asking for you to act to protect them. They may simply want to understand and have insight into what is happening to them and what they are feeling, and to use the process of counselling or therapy they are being offered. A breach of confidentiality may precipitate an immediate withdrawal from the work. The hope is that the client's trust and the therapeutic alliance can be maintained alongside the development of a partnership with colleagues within the child protection system.

The understanding, tolerance and appreciation of differing professional roles are vital in order to establish a working relationship and the rules regarding the flow of information between the therapist and other professionals. The aims of investigation are inevitably different from those of therapy. What is deemed successful in terms of protection, and maybe prosecution, will not necessarily be deemed therapeutic. Social workers will need to know how therapists think and work, and vice versa. For me, as a therapist in a joint agency team it has been an invaluable experience to have fellow team members who are also field social workers. This has given me the opportunity to gain insight into both individual social work practice and agency procedures and politics, and, in return, the opportunity to explain and unveil the process of the therapeutic encounter. As a team, this mix of professions and agencies enables us continually to ponder and wrestle with the complexities of the working partnerships that must be entered into if the needs of the client are to remain paramount. For me, the benefits of this ongoing process have generalised to my relationships with other colleagues in the wider child protection system.

Disclosures

The issue of disclosure is especially complicated in the period before court cases in which a client is giving evidence. It is important that children and young people are heard, believed and taken seriously. This can be validated, both within families and in society at large, by the judicial system.

It has been a prevailing myth that young people cannot receive therapy before court cases are concluded. This could mean a wait of months, sometimes even years, for therapy, and resulted in much unnecessary distress for clients and families. The Crown Prosecution Service now issues guidelines that state that the therapeutic needs of the child must be paramount. The prosecution of the abuser is not necessarily seen as everything. The differing needs and emphases of the systems involved must be met within the spirit of the Children Act while keeping the needs of the child as the most important consideration. In this context, individual work is advised, although group work is still frowned upon because of the risk of cross-contamination between young peoples' stories.

Disclosures can occur at any stage of the therapeutic encounter. They 'can affect the therapist's openness to the communications of the young person, and they are vulnerable to being pulled or nudged, either towards denying the abuse, its seriousness and its implication, or, at the other end of the spectrum, to becoming over actively involved in discovering, and rooting out the truth' (Briggs, 1998).

Case Study – Mary

I worked with Mary for over two years. She had a long care history with a number of foster placements and one failed adoption. At the time I met her she was 13 years old and living with foster parents following the breakdown of her adoptive placement. She had an early history of emotional abuse and neglect with some unconfirmed suspicions of sexual abuse by her birth parents or her former carers. The concerns were about her poor personal hygiene and self-care in general, her sexualised behaviour particularly around male teachers at school, and her difficulty with peer relationships. She looked and dressed like a boy. This was a legacy from her adoptive home where any sign of femininity or sexuality was severely suppressed. About 18 months into the work she disclosed to a member of staff at school that her male foster carer was sexually abusing her. She was removed from the foster home and placed in a residential school.

Mary had always been very active in the therapy work. She used symbolic play a great deal and would create elaborate scenarios in which we would both have to take an active part. The play for some weeks had indicated that a disclosure of some kind was imminent which was likely to be of a sexual nature. My supervisor at the time was a very experienced male therapist. Both of us thought the evidence from the play indicated that the disclosure was about past events. On hearing about her disclosure I immediately felt shocked, and then guilty and upset, that I had not seen the 'here and now' quality of her play. I felt disconsolate, de-skilled as a therapist and bewildered at how I could not have interpreted her communications accurately. How could the combination of two experienced therapists have missed what was going on? There were no such recriminations from Mary. She said that working through the issues in the play had helped her to say something, but not to me. She said she had been trying to tell me but when I did not 'get it' she told someone else.

In my supervision I agonised about what had happened. I realised that there were a number of events that had contributed to my 'blindness'. The suspicion was that Mary had been sexually abused in the past. My wish to uncover the truth about that past had allowed me to miss Mary's more subtle communications about her present danger. Her foster carers were known to be experienced and thought to be able. Mary was considered to have improved a lot in their care with increased confidence and less reported difficulties with peers. She was assumed to be safe by the professionals involved, including myself. We had always worked at a symbolic level and this had led to some ambiguity on my part about how to talk to her on a more concrete and factual level. I think I wanted the abuse to be in the past because unconsciously I could not tolerate the thought of Mary's being abused again. I wanted to hang on to the idea of life getting better for her, and I now think she did not want to disappoint me and ruin my hopes for her. So she protected me and my 'vision' of her. As I write, those old feelings of 'How could I have missed it?' are rekindled. It illustrates for me the powerful forces at work that prevent children and young people from disclosing abuse, and others from recognising its existence. All the more amazing that so many can take the risk and speak out about their pain.

Young people who have experienced abuse will have developed ways of coping with the ongoing pain, distress, and fear and will have evolved a number of tactics to help them feel in control. Admitting to any feelings may seem like a letting go of this control, and will be unfamiliar and scary. It is as if the control is going back to an adult (in the person of the therapist) who could harm and further abuse them. The trust in oneself and others is so fundamentally damaged by abuse that it can take a long time to develop it and establish it again within the therapeutic encounter. We are fortunate at JACAT to have no imposed time constraints on our work. This opens up the possibility of working at the clients' pace.

Children and young people who have been abused present with a wide range of personal and interpersonal relationship problems. The healing process can take many months or years. In an agency where post-abuse services are the core business and main focus it is possible to take account of the specific therapeutic needs of such children and young people, and their families. It is our experience that the work may be done in phases that coincide with maturation and developmental stages, so a child may return more than once to continue the work.

All members of the team can develop their expertise in direct work with clients, whether it is individual, group or family. No team member is full-time at JACAT, but the experience they bring from their other areas of work acts as both a foil, and an enhancer, to the specialist work of the team.

Interventions

In any therapeutic encounter the therapist feels the constant tension between when, and when not to make an intervention. There are inevitable periods of silence. The use of silence is important to the therapeutic process. Silence offers time for reflection, and for more to be said but it can also be construed as hostile and obstructive. When working with teenagers, it is not helpful to allow long periods of silence, even if they are initiated by the adolescent themselves. They can interpret these as threatening and overwhelming and a disincentive to talk further. Equally, the therapist can fill the silent space with endless talk as a reflection of their own anxiety, which is also unhelpful. A young person's persistent silence is one of the most anxiety-provoking forms of communication for the therapist, who can be left feeling hopeless, helpless, de-skilled and angry. Looking for the underlying meaning of the silence as a communication is constructive and productive, but it may be that the silence becomes so intractable that the work will need to be terminated. There can be a number of reasons for this: the timing of the work may have been wrong, or the young person may not be as ready to talk as originally thought. Often the young person will drop out themselves.

Case Study – Nicky

Nicky had agreed to attend for an initial six sessions when aged 14 years. She had been sexually abused by her stepfather involving mutual masturbation and digital penetration. She became increasingly silent as the sessions progressed, and finally dropped out of therapy after three sessions, with no explanation. She rang me up two years later asking to come back and talk. She explained that she had stopped talking to me before because she could not tell me that her stepfather had raped her. She had worried that if she had stayed in therapy I would have guessed because I 'could see inside her head' or I would have wheedled it out of her. She was now ready to talk so she had come back.

This fear of an omnipotent therapist who has the magical ability to read minds is a common one. The victims of abuse feel contaminated and damaged by their experience. This leads to a belief that either others can see this badness or that the badness is so well hidden that if anyone did see it, that person would immediately become contaminated as well, leading to immediate rejection.

Case Study – Sarah 2

After a week's break in her therapy due to my illness, the behaviour of Sarah (see Case study Sarah 1 above) in the next session fluctuated between being verbally hostile and maintaining long periods of silence. She appeared very angry with me. I assumed this was due to the break and her fury at me for abandoning her and so fuelling her feelings of worthlessness. But I sensed that I was missing something. My supervisor suggested that maybe Sarah had worries that she was so unbearable that she had made me ill. In the next session I suggested this to her. She cried and said that she had thought that her 'badness' had leaked out of herself and into me, making me ill. Her hostility the week before had been an attempt to drive me away before I got too ill and had to abandon her anyway. I was able to explain that it was the flu' virus that had made me ill, and to reiterate a commitment to her and the relationship between us.

Mood swings

It is not surprising that teenagers can be resistant to help from adults. Adolescence involves a long period of experimentation, evolving various strategies for breaking parental ties which can result in an oscillating pattern between wanting to be cared for as a child and wanting to be treated as an adult. The swing between the two can be rapid and unpredictable.

This behaviour is mirrored in the therapeutic encounter, with the adolescent demanding closeness and caring one minute, and fending off all offers of help the next. The difference in mood between sessions can also be startling. In one session the young person can appear devoid of all hope and full of despair, and the next they bounce in having got a new boyfriend, a new job, new clothes and feeling that the world is a fantastic place in which to live. The therapist can feel they are on a rollercoaster of emotions. It can be difficult to make careful and well-considered clinical judgements. The therapist can, on the one hand, feel relieved that the young person's mood has lifted but, on the other, feel foolish and angry with their client for 'deceiving' them.

There is a danger that therapists will become hostile and rigid in return, prompted by feeling de-skilled and out of control. It is important to remember that the behaviour of adolescents is a reflection of their inner world and an indication of their level of both joy and distress. They can behave in an outrageous and provocative way without meaning to do so. A wise therapist looks for the underlying meaning of the behaviour in order to formulate a response. Given the possible rapid fluctuation in mood in each session the therapist has to develop the ability to extemporise and remain flexible in order to respond to the unexpected, to be tolerant and to remain holding and containing. All this contributes to an atmosphere in which the young person can be accepted and heard in an uncritical way, and can allow them to begin to explore their deeper anxieties.

However, a therapist can be thrown off track by a sudden and unexpected personal question such as 'Have you ever been abused?', or a hostile remark such as 'What do you fucking know or care, you've never been abused?' Sometimes these questions are genuinely as innocent as they appear but they are telling and efficient challenges to boundaries and can leave the therapist disoriented and feeling intimidated and rattled. If the remarks are said in an aggressive way the therapist can also feel genuinely frightened. The usual response to fear and threat is to become defensive. A defensive response is not conducive to insight and understanding. Therapists need to remain flexible and imaginative in their responses: to know when to ignore remarks; to know when to respond with an answer; to know when to talk about underlying meaning; to know when to use humour; to know when to share their own feelings; to know how not to get side-tracked into dead-end confrontations at the expense of more important issues; to know how to react to their own fear and remain contained and containing.

A young person may have learnt to shut out painful feelings by averting any discussion about them. A common way of doing this is shorthand verbal responses that are designed to block any response from another person, such as 'Dunno', 'Don't care', or 'It's boring' (Jezzard, 1994). It is important to respect this method of communication. It can give the young person space to think and reinforce their sense of separateness from you.

Case Study – Ruth

Ruth was 16 years old. She had been sexually abused at ten years by a known paedophile. She had been interviewed by the police at the time, along with other suspected victims, but had denied anything had happened to her. The professionals involved always believed that she had been abused but could not prove it. Her shorthand block to painful emotions in our sessions was the word 'whatever'. She said it when I got too close to her deeper feelings and if she wanted to provoke and annoy me – a manoeuvre to put me off the track. I learnt not to take the response at face value and how to stay alert for the underlying meaning. This was not easy. Ruth had not been used to talking about her feelings or to using the words to describe them accurately. She wanted to tell me the details of the abuse because there were things she had never told anyone. After about 15 months of work she was able to say that the man had raped her. She continued to use 'whatever' but her insight into the meaning of why she said it gave its use more of a conscious, deliberate and playful quality.

Being the adult

No matter what theoretical orientation the therapist chooses they will have been an adolescent themselves. This brings a peculiar resonance to the work. However, adolescents rarely want to hear a therapist's personal reminiscences of their own adolescence. There are times when an attempt at self-disclosure can provide helpful insight, but it needs to be used sparingly and with caution. Inexperienced therapists can believe it is a way of joining with their client, an indication of what Singh meant by human ordinariness (Singh, 1987).

Adolescents need you to be an adult. Winnicott suggests that 'the big challenge from the adolescent is to the bit of ourselves that has not had its adolescence' (Winnicott, 1965). This can lead to resentment and intolerance of adolescent behaviour. He believed that we should accept, relish and celebrate adolescent immaturity and not try to emulate it, disregard it, or understand it. Adolescents cannot be aware of their own immaturity but the very fact of it does offer challenges to adults, such as the reminder of their own waning potency, unfulfilled expectations or potential, as well as the painful or pleasurable memories of their own adolescence. It is important to meet those challenges as an adult. 'Adults are needed if adolescents are to have life and liveliness' (Winnicott, 1986). This means adults must stand up to the challenges in a safe, contained and non-retaliatory way, secure in their own identity and point of view. It is that difference that enables the adolescent to explore and experiment with their own identity.

Therapists, as adults, are on show and on trial for both their ability as practitioners and their robustness as grown-ups. Young people do not want therapists to be like them, but they do need you to understand them, and listen to their experiences and point of view. Finding a language that is mutually understood is helpful. The language of therapy can be esoteric and make the young person feel stupid and small. Jezzard (1994) suggests that rather than make some complicated, smart interpretation it is better to offer views and comments as choices that can either be accepted or disregarded as the young person chooses. Each young person will have their own family words, slang words and street language with which the therapist will need to be familiar. For example, I found myself some years ago in an awkward situation with a young women who was telling me how many boys she had 'got off with' one night at a party. At that time, I thought 'got off with' meant 'having sex with'. What I learnt from her was that it meant kissing, which gave the ensuing conversation a whole different meaning!

Conclusion

I find it deeply moving, at times, to be allowed to share the inner world of the young people I see at JACAT. They have experienced the most extraordinary traumas at the hands of other adults and I continue to be amazed at their capacity for trust, love, forgiveness, joy and insight as well as rage, intolerance, and grief. It is satisfying and rewarding to witness change and personal growth and development in another human being. It is a privilege to watch a young person move from victim to survivor status and recognise and realise that 'having been abused' is not the only way of describing themselves in the world: to paraphrase Singh (1987), to know they can acquire adolescent 'ordinariness'.

3.4 Working with Children and Young People with Disabilities

Jo Bromley

Introduction

The experience in JACAT of working with young people who have disabilities is limited. Given the known vulnerability of such young people to abuse, the question immediately arises as to why so few are referred for help to the service. The answer partly lies in the fact that JACAT is a post-investigation child abuse team, which implies that the fact of abuse is acknowledged. There are, however, other more complex considerations to be held in mind. 'In most jurisdictions today, children of all ages can be deemed competent witnesses, but their credibility is often doubted; they have even been equated with intoxicated and mentally ill adults.' (Lamb et al., 1994) It is also well known that relatively few cases of disclosed child abuse reach the judicial system. Since the successful presentation of evidence in criminal cases so often depends upon the linguistic and presentational skills of the witness it is not surprising that even fewer cases of child abuse reach the court when the victim is a child or young person with a disability. It appears to us in JACAT that this has an effect on the civil decisions that are made about whether or not to begin an investigation into a possible case of child abuse, when the putative victim is a child who is disabled. Prosecution guidelines in our judicial system still tend to be biased against the child witness despite attempts at reform in recent years. When this bias is brought to bear, as well as the well-practised and calculated strategies employed by abusers to maintain the abuse as secret, the vulnerability of children and young people, and the means by which they might be protected, become issues of citizenship, shared responsibility and service delivery.

Both inside and outside the therapeutic domain there are complex matters to be considered. The nature of the disability itself may cause problems. There may simply (sic) be a belief among the carers of, or workers with, young people that no one could possibly abuse a disabled young person. Sometimes the challenge of maintaining an open, if slow and complicated, communication with a young disabled victim may be too much. A young disabled victim may feel that their degree of dependency makes disclosure too great a risk because of the loss of support involved. It is salutary to reflect that 'in this country we do not know how many disabled children have been abused, nor do we know what happens to them – what they receive in terms of service or interventions, and whether or how many of their abusers are identified and prosecuted', and that the Department of Health does not require Social Service Departments to record 'disability' (Cooke and Standen, 2002).

Some Definitions

There have also been recent changes in the terminology used by the statutory systems. The World Health Organisation (1996) offered a way of thinking about disability that proposed three levels: impairment, disability and handicap. Take the case of my colleague and co-author, Paul O'Reilly. Paul has an impairment, in that he is short-sighted. Fortunately he can compensate by wearing glasses. However, when he is in the swimming pool without his glasses he is disabled. If he were not able to see at all he would be handicapped in one particular way. Moreover, the situation is made more complex by his feeling of vulnerability and doubt about his resilience when he is without glasses. There are also social and cultural norms that affect the way in which people who are different are perceived. It is clear, too, that the issue of availability of specialist tools, resources and service provision will influence the degree of handicap experienced.

The most recent change in terminology has been the use of the term 'special needs'. This is a term which was used primarily in the sphere of education but which has more recently been embraced by social services and the health service with much wider connotations than that of educational needs. The 1989 Children Act brought disabled children into the mainstream of legislation by defining them as 'children in need' and by placing upon the police, local authorities, health and education authorities the responsibility for their protection. However, 'recent research suggests that disabled children living away from home are not being afforded the full protection of the Children Act'. Coupled with the Department of Health's recognition that 'disabled children are more likely to live away from home, to be accommodated on a short or long-term basis and be in state-funded residential education', this must give rise to concern (Paul and Cawson, 2002).

In the current climate 'disability' provision exists as part of a continuum spanning a wide range of special needs. Wherever possible the young person with disabilities will be located in mainstream service provision. For the purposes of this chapter, the term 'disability' refers to one or more of physical, neurological, sensory and learning impairment. The fact of disability has usually been taken into account at the point of referral. Westcott (1993) suggests that the risk of abuse to children with disabilities may be as much as 50 per cent higher than that of the non-disabled population. According to Marchant and Page (1992), the four factors contributing to this higher risk are:

- societal values
- the child's experiences
- the child's difficulties in telling about abuse
- the denial by professionals

This may help us to understand the complexity of abuse disclosures by children and young people with disabilities. Abuse is often systematic and victims are more likely to be abused by someone known to them and in a position of trust than by unknown people. This makes the telling of the fact a difficulty. Coherent disclosures are required by service providers in order to achieve the best potential for protection. Coherent communication is likely to be reduced in the context of limited communicative ability. Marchant and Page (1992) refer to the lack in skills interface in the separate fields of child protection and abuse, calling for the 'bridging of the gap' between the two areas by either dual specialism or joint working. Without one or other of these the potential for denial by professionals about the fact of child abuse within the disabled community is increased, and in turn, so is the risk of harm and increased vulnerability to the children and young people (see Westcott, 1993).

Core Issues

Westcott and Jones (1999) as quoted in Oosterhoorn and Kendrick (2001) isolate three core issues which affect the vulnerability of disabled children, namely dependency, institutional care and communication. Children and young people with disabilities are more likely to rely on the assistance and support of a significant number of carers and other involved adults than their mainstream contemporaries. In many cases this includes the on-going, and often lifelong, provision of intimate care: washing, bathing, dressing and toileting. In the context of vulnerability to potential abuse a significant part of the child's life is exposed to the breach of power and trust in relationships. Given what Oosterhoorn and Kendrick (2001) describe as the 'legitimacy' of the child-carer boundary as the usual unit of personal care it is increasingly likely that the pair will construct and maintain a position of unquestioned validity in the child's eyes, a position which excludes others from that pair. Therefore, when the abuse of power and trust does occur within the child-carer context, familiarity will make it less likely that the child or young person will have a concept of harm and it will be highly unlikely that the nature of the unit of care will be questioned with regard to appropriateness of touch and interaction. Whilst in general one may hold the concept of goodwill and intent in the child-carer unit, in the specific area of child abuse there is an inherent dilemma in addressing the issue of dependency and the appropriateness of the care context.

Abuse Awareness

Oosterhoorn and Kendrick (2001) highlight the use of residential care and special facilities for children and young people with disabilities as places for increased likelihood of abuse. It is therefore unsurprising though no less shocking to hear that perpetrators of physical, sexual and emotional abuse are attracted to work in social care settings and, furthermore, that children and young people of vulnerable populations may be at increased risk. Recent press stories about internet child pornography and the involvement of numerous men in professions which give ready access to children emphasise this matter.

A balance of pro-active strategies may help to reduce risk in specialist care and support settings. Policies supporting the rights of individuals with disabilities are a basic requirement of specialist settings. Clarity of disciplinary routes when policy and practice guidelines are breached, and a style of management that makes clear its accountability and responsibility across all levels of the organisation, are essential. Careful recruitment of staff is another way of attempting to reduce the potential for harm within specialist facilities. Screening for criminal convictions, making use of employment references, well thought out interviews for appointments, and clarification of the commitment and motivation of the organisation to promote and protect the well-being of service users may deter some perpetrators. Such strategies also offer an implicit message to new staff concerning the standards of the setting and practice in which they will be working. The new Criminal Records Unit will be of great assistance once it is satisfactorily staffed.

Abuse awareness training for staff within specialist facilities for children and young people with disabilities provides a further layer of preventative and pro-active involvement. As part of an induction package it orientates staff members towards an ethos which believes in the rights of people with disabilities, and models good practice in terms of the expectations of the organisation and the shared task of care for service users. Specialist input by services that are able to offer a meta-position to practice may help facilitate insight and energy for review and progression. Two kinds of specialist are required here: specialists about abuse and specialists about disability. Maximal skills in consultation and facilitation are essential.

(Note: Here meta-position means being able to consider practice issues from a perspective which includes consideration of the many contexts within which the practice takes place – at the individual level, the client-worker relationship, the context of the client, the agency context of the worker, and other relevant contexts or systems that might impinge (education system, legal system, neighbourhood network are some examples).)

Communication Difficulties

Oosterhoorn and Kendrick (2001) report on the communication difficulties that children with disabilities have about the issue of abuse. They highlight the difficulties of using communication systems. Often the system itself is a reflection of the child's ability to manage only a limited number of concepts about their life and world. For instance, 'Makaton . . . the most widely used communication system [has only just developed] signs covering general personal growth and development, emotions, feelings and relationships, and with supplementary vocabulary specific to abuse and bullying for sexuality and abuse'. There are languages with appropriate signs in these areas but these were found not to be widely used in institutions, home to some of the most vulnerable disabled children. Furthermore, the person who controls choice over the extension of language on communicator systems is likely to be the carer or educator. It is also usual for children to make use of symbols on their communicator simply because they are there. However, the over-use of a symbol is not a sufficient reason for withholding it from a communication system when its presence may prevent or draw attention to harm to the child. It is also important to be able to recognise the child's level of understanding about general life concepts, the specific concept of abuse and whether the child is able to recognise the fact of their own abuse experiences.

In my experience of child abuse disclosure, investigation and healing, it is not unusual to hear the abusive experiences described as a game or way of caring. The former suggests a mutual interaction for which the victim can therefore be deemed 'partly accountable' and feel as if so, whilst the latter implies normal caring behaviour on the part of the perpetrator for which the victim should feel 'grateful' or guilty if not so. Both carry a heavy overlay of emotional abuse that is internalised by the child or young person as part of the emotional burden which forms and maintains a sense of the need for secrecy. In the case of children or young people who have a disability it may be more difficult to unravel these grooming processes. For example, as in Case Study – Communication difficulties, a perpetrator's code name for the abuse may not be recognisable beyond the perpetrator/victim dyad, and communication difficulties may make disclosure impossible.

Case Study – Communication difficulties

When Michelle, aged 15, with spina bifida and speech difficulties, told respite care staff of the game 'window-time' that her father played at night-time, the staff became concerned. Following the passing on of limited information, a social worker visited the family home and asked permission of the parents to speak with the children of the household, separately. Michelle reiterated her telling of the 'game'. Her brother, Philip, aged six and able-bodied, substantiated the main points of the game. It involved heavy physical manipulation and twisting of Michelle's body and limbs, which were painful and stiff at the best of times, and inappropriate touching around her knees and inside her thighs. Philip described the same style of twisting done to him by his father as being like playing 'Chinese burns'. The parents were warned about the father's behaviour by the social worker. Michelle's mother did not believe that her husband would behave in such a way, and reminded social workers and care staff that she had been trying to get help with the burden of caring for Michelle and for the challenging behaviour that she had been posing for several months. Michelle did not speak of 'window time' again. Communication between parents and respite staff deteriorated until it consisted simply of basic hand-over information. The case was closed by social services. Eighteen months later Michelle moved to a residential placement.

Joint Working

Our position at JACAT is to work cases jointly where abuse has occurred against children and young people with disabilities. At the point of referral all cases are discussed within the multi-disciplinary Team Meeting. Where a complex issue arises it is usual to invite the referrer to join us for a discussion of the case. When part of the complexity is the fact that the young person is disabled the team invites a member of staff from that specialism to join the consultation process. For example, where a learning difficulty is identified then a member of the new Joint Agencies Team (a multi-disciplinary team established to care for the requirements of 'special needs' children) with that specialism would be invited. Sometimes it is unclear whether or not the difficulties arise primarily from disability or from the effects of abuse. Indeed, in many ways the experience of abuse itself, and its well-documented immediate and long-term effects, may be a disabling experience for many survivors. Furthermore, only detailed history-taking and tracking of the events that led up to the abuse make it possible to see what made that child more vulnerable than others, and what their special needs may be.

Through the consultation process it is possible to prioritise the more pressing need and to determine who is better placed to do the work, a JACAT member, or a member of the joint working agency. Sometimes the abuse is clearly identified as the primary focus for intervention but at other times the impact of disability and its complexities in the child's life cycle are considered the priority. Where the former is the case and a JACAT worker holds the responsibility for the therapeutic work, specialist resources and consultation will be sought to bolster the input. There are several good packages available to support work with children with disabilities, offering creative options and styles of intervention as a vehicle for communication, the engagement process, and clarity about what might be possible in a given situation.

Children who continue to suffer abuse after investigations have taken place experience the external world – and this includes therapy – as limited in its capacity to hear about abuse, limited in its ability to stop abuse, and limited in its potential to be helpful. When a child feels like this the potential for therapy to heal is stunted. The child's need for security and stability must, therefore, be addressed before therapy can be undertaken. Since in disclosure and investigation work so much of the process depends upon the child's ability to use a voice that can be heard, children and young people with disabilities are more likely to end up in a 'no change' position after disclosure than are their non-disabled peers in similar situations because of that very problem of finding a voice that can truly be heard.

Choosing a setting

The therapeutic setting is also of relevance in this specialist area of joint working. Disabled access is of the utmost importance. The accessibility of a building, including disabled parking spaces, ramps, wide and easy open-and-hold doors, visibility at reception, and lift access, all give good messages about the ways in which people with disability are held in mind by the organisation.

Case Study – Access

I met with a woman whose son, Conrad, aged nine, has cerebral palsy and is reliant on the use of a wheel-chair on a full-time basis. Following a request for help with his challenging behaviour, the GP made a referral to the local Child Guidance Clinic. The mother reported on the initial appointment during our conversation. They had arrived to learn that the car park was at the back of the building and the main entrance not visible from where they had parked. As was customary she took the wheelchair from the car and settled her son in it. On reaching the front of the building they discovered a short, steep set of steps. Realising that it would be difficult to gain entry to the building that way the woman returned to the car park, put the wheel-chair away and carried her son into the building through the rear entrance. Upon entering the building the woman had to carry her son up three flights of steps in order to locate the therapy room. It was agreed by child, mother and therapist not to return downstairs for the wheelchair but to prop the boy up with cushions in an armchair. I asked the mother how she felt the session had been for them. She replied: 'Oh, it was OK. To be honest, I can't remember much about what was said, but we'll go back again. I'll go a bit earlier next time, and I've asked whether it would be possible to meet in a downstairs room so that I can go back for the wheel-chair.'

The comments of this parent in Case Study – Access highlight the importance of accommodating the most basic of disability requirements, in this case, access to the building and the use of an appropriate room. JACAT, which shares the building and its parking area with Child Health and Psychology, has a disabled parking space right outside the front door, wheel-chair access, good visibility at reception and downstairs rooms. One would assume, therefore, that all would be well for disabled clients. However, there is one major snag: the disabled parking space, though kept free, cannot be reached by any car because of the cars which are persistently parked outside the parking bays, blocking the way in. The availability of specialist help is not enough: the co-operation of the work force is also essential!

It is important to consider the issues of familiarity for children with disability when deciding where a piece of work should take place. As a joint worker it is likely that there will be a choice of venues available. For instance, a family may be used to visiting the disability teams' offices to meet with a community nurse or occupational therapist, and this might prove a better venue than asking the family to attend appointments at a place with which they are not familiar. This will have to be weighed up against the potential benefit of separating the therapeutic work from other previous or on-going matters. The boundaries of the therapeutic endeavour can offer a useful parallel to the importance of respecting boundaries of privacy and individuality in the abused child or young person. This in turn should be echoed by the adults to whom the focus of care and containment for the healing process falls. With this in mind, the joint working position can be used to full advantage. In post-abuse work with carers also it is possible to adapt models to include the presence of a known worker to facilitate ease of communication and to reduce the risk of carers' getting caught up in explanations of their child or young person's disability, rather than their healing. Striking a balance of communication with the children, young people and their carers requires a concentration on the current relationship with the therapist, holding in mind the thread of engagement which runs throughout the sessions, and maintaining a live focus on seeking to provide a service that is valued by its users.

Sustaining communication

One of the tasks of the professionals in joint-working is to sustain the collaboration through a willingness to remain engaged in difficult issues, using and tuning in to both verbal and non-verbal forms of communication. This may be particularly pertinent to working with disability issues and abuse, where the subtlety of communication may be above and beyond spoken language.

Case Study – Sustaining communication is an extract from a solution-focused supervision session and highlights how professionals get caught up in their own fears about communication difficulties. The style of input is based upon the work of our colleagues at the Brief Therapy Practice in London. Solution-focused consultation is often used to help move beyond a problem-based difficulty and to focus thought on positives and strengths.

Case Study – Sustaining communication

A community nurse sought support in talking with her client, Susie, about her experiences of abuse. Susie was aged 13 years and had been on the community nurse's caseload for about a year. She had cerebral palsy, resulting in some mobility and speech difficulties, both of which show deterioration when she is tired or stressed. She has an able-bodied eight-year-old sister, and they both live in the family home with their birth parents. Both girls are currently on the Child Protection Register under the category of 'likely physical abuse' and 'actual emotional abuse'. The Child Protection investigation had found insufficient evidence to establish actual physical harm but had clearly established that the father had threatened to use violence and had used harsh punishment in the past. The younger sister had also been interviewed as part of the investigation, following Susie's disclosures of physical harm, managing to say that she was fearful of her father, but unable to add further to this at the time.

The community nurse was worried about how best to proceed. She felt alarmed that matters had escalated and she might feel 'out of her depth'. It was important that she left the consultation feeling empowered and able to proceed with clarity.

A conversation between the nurse and the supervisor took place as follows:

Supervisor: 'What is your best hope for this consultation?'

Community Nurse: 'I'm hoping to clarify my thoughts in preparing to visit a young person who was abused by her father.'

Supervisor: 'What will you notice about yourself which will tell you that your hopes have been met?'

Community Nurse: 'Er . I'll be clear about my role and feel confident to talk with my client.'

Supervisor: 'What do you notice about yourself when you are clear and confident in your work?'

Community Nurse: 'That I'm not worrying about the way I ask her about how things are, and being sure that she's able to respond.'

Supervisor: 'So if you weren't worrying about the way you talk with her, what would you be doing instead?'

Community Nurse: 'I'd just be getting on with it.'

Supervisor: 'And if you were "just getting on with it" what would your client notice about you that would be different?'

Community Nurse: 'My thoughts and feelings would go together, and I'd flow in my conversation with her. So I guess she'd notice that our conversation was going well.'

Supervisor: 'What would she notice about you that would tell her that the conversation was going well?'

Community Nurse: 'I'd be making eye-contact, smiling, prompted and prompting in our chat.'

Supervisor: 'What else?'

Community Nurse: 'Warmth, I feel, and genuine regard for her, Susie, that is.'

Supervisor: 'What would you see in Susie that would make you think that she noticed these things?'

Community Nurse: 'She'd be more connected, make eye contact, smile too, you know.'

Supervisor: 'What else?'

Community Nurse: 'Oh, I don't know. um . Oh, I do. She'd use her head to regulate the distance between us when the conversation gets tough, facing me fully when its OK and turning profile and her head slightly bowed when she's sad. She's great at that.'

Supervisor: 'What do you notice about the way Susie uses body movements that tells you about how the session is going?'

Community Nurse: 'Angle, tilt, tiredness, avoidance, etc.'

Partnership and Vulnerability

Parents and carers tend to speak of professionals as available to discuss the issues associated with becoming the parent of a disabled child, initially welcoming the place that such professionals hold in the family's life. This is despite wishing it were not so. Over time the family system shifts and a process of adaptation ensues. The notion of being a family that encompasses members with disability takes priority over the fact of disability itself. Many family members whose lives are affected by the physical impact and emotions and practicalities of disablement refer to the impact as a fading phenomenon, often resulting in the disability's becoming 'invisible' within the family setting. The family may become more focused and clear about ways in which they feel professional systems can best be of assistance. Often this is in relationship to equipment, financial aid and, for some families, respite supportive care. Such conversations, often based on 'loss or lack' of resources and facilities, may reflect the position of the child with disability, in that, whilst children with disabilities may internalise messages of not being 'normal' or 'good enough', deficit models of disability prevail.

The issues concerning a young person's interactions with others are complex. Opportunities to practise social encounters and achieve intimacy, both physical and emotional, are greatly reduced outside the relationship between parent-carer and child. For the child or young person with disablement needs, the degree to which they experience their thoughts, perspectives and opinions being valued and respected may largely depend upon the interpretations made by significant carers and professional helpers. However well-intended these interpretations may be, it is likely that there will not always be – and maybe should not be – a meeting of like minds about key issues. During the communication process a shift in emphasis, motivation, understanding and effect may occur which is the result of one person acting on behalf of another. Any attempt to communicate information that is considered undesirable at any level may result in a negative reaction. For most people with disabilities such a response will heighten feelings of isolation and vulnerability and may effectively result in silencing the voice of the disabled person.

Partnership with parents and carers is a central notion of disability service provision. Professionals look to parents and carers to further initial lines of enquiry about the needs of their children. Yet often such communication embraces minimal dialogue with the person for whom the provision is intended, and professionals often experience tension in balancing the relationships and needs within the family. Rarely does it seem possible to secure private and individual time with the child or young person to discuss their wishes and beliefs. Concern that any disruption to the way of going about business may impact negatively upon the alliance between the adults, and as a result have a negative effect upon the child, tends to dominate the process. In fact such behaviour perpetuates the silencing of the voices of people with disabilities.

With practice, communication improves, and by retaining a position of inclusion the professional gains confidence in managing the fears and tensions which lead to misunderstanding. Once the focus of the problem shifts then it is possible to believe that communication can take place with the professionals' being able to seek solutions with the child or young person. This whole process enables a child with communication difficulties to extend their ability. The slower the pace, the more space offered, and the greater the time taken to be clear about information, the more the child will be imbued with confidence about the positive intent of those involved. The process of listening with respectful regard and good intent is in itself enabling and confirming. It is also likely that the quality and reliability of information gained in this way will be much improved. One of the tasks of the professionals is to contain the interaction through a willingness to remain engaged in non-verbal forms of communication, if need be, and in doing so to allow themselves to tune into the subtlety of human communication that is above and beyond spoken language.

Focusing on the positives and strengths in one's own communication contributes a large proportion of the energy required in communicating with children and young people who have disabilities. It is important to remember that the child or young person with 'no communication' does not exist, with the exception of those children whose central nervous system no longer functions. Central to communication is the nature and quality of the relationship.

The Abuse of Power and Trust in Relationships

We have already considered the ways in which children and young people with disabilities experience increased dependency on their parents or carers. We have also noted that children and young people are more likely to be abused by people with whom they have a trusting and often valued relationship. Thus children who are abused are at increased risk of being physically, sexually, emotionally and psychologically abused by people who are known to them, trusted by them, and seen to be reliable in acting on their behalf. For children with disabilities this may include speaking for them, making decisions on their behalf, giving physical and often intimate care and administrating medication. These 'people of trust' are the very people who determine how the outside world views the child's competence and understanding. In our child protection system there is a variety of possibilities for improvement which would enable children and young people with disabilities to speak out about their abuse. In part this would entail heightening the awareness of all professionals involved in the child protection process about communication strategies and needs of people with disabilities.

Extremes of distress are often negatively re-framed where children and young people with disabilities are concerned, with acting-out behaviour seen as, at best, 'deviant and attention-seeking' and at worst, framed as 'mental deficiency or illness'. Children who use a variety of behaviour such as head banging, rocking, screeching and biting may be demonstrating acute distress. We know that psychosis is closely associated with childhood trauma, but it is rare for such a possibility to be considered where a primary disability exists. The concept of 'locked in' trauma is not new and is sometimes considered in metaphoric terms as a 'Pandora's box'. To open the box, and release the trauma and internalised anxiety, is a huge task for any survivor of abuse. The increased complexity of living with trauma alongside disablement is likely to exacerbate symptomatology and impinge on the survivor's perceptions of safety in the external world once he or she has disclosed.

Taking a position of zero tolerance about the abuse of power and trust in human relationships is vital, with a belief that all people have a right to physical, sexual, emotional and psychological care. Educating mainstream and disabled communities in issues of appreciation and disability awareness is important in valuing children and young people with disabilities. This helps to dispel myths associated with the behaviour and motivation of people with disabilities, and also helps to promote the experience of confidence, independence and autonomy in the disabled community. Furthermore, it becomes increasingly possible to hold in mind the extent of the increased vulnerability of children and young people with disabilities as part of, yet separate from, the context of their potential for development. This may in turn propel people to act on signs and symptoms, disclosures and instincts when situations feel inimical to the rights of individuals.

Physical ease of arrival, entry to the building, and the reaching of a specific location where the police interview, or CAMAT interview, will take place sends highly positive messages about the dignity and respect with which children and young people with disabilities, and their message they bring, are held. In Exeter, for instance, there is no disabled access to the CAMAT suite. The implied message is clear: this is not a place where children and young people with disabilities are expected to be. Ease of access should be a priority before the bringing of disclosure and the airing of allegations. The process of lifting and handling may also be unhelpful to the children and young people. They may feel actual pain during transfers and experience increased vulnerability through the process, which in turn may affect their confidence and self-perception during interview.

For some time now there has been a focus on the limitations of the Crown Prosecution Service's system in hearing child abuse cases, and its ability or willingness to hear prosecution evidence in a child-friendly way. This concern has, in the main, been driven by the wish to prevent the oft-mentioned abuse by systems that youngsters who have appeared in court talk about. In fact, consequential to the impact of the abuse in childhood, prosecution witnesses are often subject to further abuse and trauma as past events are re-examined in the prosecution process.

New advice and guidance through *Speaking up for Justice* (DoH, 2002) may begin to make a difference. Disabled children and young people could not be thought of as other than vulnerable, and likely to be intimidated. When investigative and court processes change to take account of such young people change may become possible throughout the civil systems, especially social services, health and education services.

Clearly each individual has the right to a fair trial, but it is a commonly held view that the prosecution process in child abuse cases is heavily weighted in favour of the perpetrator, and it is certainly true that relatively few cases come to court. This perpetuates an uphill struggle to protect children and young people in general and specifically those with disabilities. Those children who find it so hard to be heard are also far more likely to be denied protective intervention through the court system on the basis that they are unlikely to provide 'good quality evidence' and are seen, by virtue of their disability, as 'unreliable witnesses'.

The following case study provides an example of how it is possible to give young people with disabilities a chance to speak for themselves. Initially Tom's abuse had been acknowledged in the child protection process through the voice of another child. This had ensured that Tom was recognised as a child who had been abused but did not provide him with the cathartic experience of speaking for himself. The therapist, using all the help available from those who knew Tom, together with her own skills and patience, helped Tom find his voice.

Case Study – Finding a voice

Tom attended the local School for the Deaf from 'out of county', and an extra-contractual referral was made from the local authority who were responsible for his care. This involved a great deal of communication and paperwork across the areas in which he lived and the area where he attended school, and waiting for permission to go ahead due to funding issues, which delayed the onset of therapy by almost a year.

Tom was ten years old when he began individual counselling. He had 'hearing difficulties' and used a radio-aid for schoolwork, lip-reading of moderate ability, and Sign Supported English (SSE) with peers and teachers. He had been placed at the residential school a term before his ninth birthday, following investigations in his birth family of childhood sexual abuse, triggered by his older sister's allegations against their maternal grandfather. His sister had disclosed her own sexual abuse and alleged that Tom had also been abused by their grandfather. Tom had never disclosed abuse, and had not been interviewed, but had been placed on the Child Protection Register under the category of 'actual sexual abuse' and 'actual emotional abuse'. These categories were accepted as true and named at the Child Protection Meeting despite the lack of disclosure by Tom in order to make it possible for professionals to act on his behalf. Tom's grandfather pleaded guilty to a charge of indecent assault on a female under 16 years of age, and served a two-year prison sentence for that offence. Tom's mother later disclosed childhood sexual abuse by her father. The standard of care at home had been considered poor, and it was felt that Tom's special needs would be better catered for at a residential school for the deaf.

The therapist began the work by establishing dialogue with the School for the Deaf. The school staff felt that Tom was able to communicate on a one-to-one basis with the therapist, without the use of an interpreter. In fact, he had learned to use sign language since he joined the school. Most pupils at the school tended to use Sign Supported English due to the curriculum requirements of English language studies and reading. Sign Supported English is a sign structure that follows the grammatical construction of English language and translates word-for-word. British sign language is a visuo-gestural sign system that has a different grammatical construction to English language and cannot be directly translated in many forms without some loss of intent or meaning.

The therapist received information about Tom's cognitive ability, shortness of attention span and emotional affect. In the light of this helpful information the therapist offered weekly counselling sessions, with each session lasting 45 minutes rather than the standard hour-long sessions. The therapist also heard about Tom's behaviour during the school week and his difficulties in adjusting to routines following weekends at home.

With this in mind another JACAT team member had joined the consultation process, offering advice and consultation to the school about behaviour management and supporting the staff in understanding the abuse issues. Of particular relevance were 'containment' issues, given that Tom had a tendency to run away from adults when boundaries were defined. Behavioural strategies included positive reinforcement of good behaviour, ignoring negatives, and facilitating an atmosphere of positive regard. Tom's behaviour was reframed from 'attention-seeking' to 'attention-needing', and rich conversations ensued with the school staff about Tom's needs against a backdrop of neglect and abusive experiences. The staff actively sought opportunities to make Tom feel included and valued, i.e. asking him to help with small tasks and activities concerning projects that the school was involved with. These opportunities appeared to give Tom a sense of value and purpose. As a result he actively sought things to do, and showed appreciation of his belongings and environment.

The therapist met Tom with his key worker initially to find out from Tom whether he would have preferred an interpreter to be present. Tom had been clear that he would not. The therapist had explained during the first meeting that she had limited sign skills, but that she was confident that they would find ways to understand each other over time. It was agreed at that point that if either of them felt it necessary, a proficient signer would be invited to join them. In fact this was not required throughout the course of counselling.

Over a period of time Tom and his therapist developed a narrative about their work together. The theme was of 'learning': Tom learned to communicate about his feelings, and the therapist learned to communicate about deaf issues and sign use. This offered a reciprocal style where both giving and receiving were valued. In the therapeutic relationship both held positions of knowledge and experience to 'give' and curiosity in the receiving of many stories. Thus it was possible to deconstruct and explore issues associated with both deafness and abuse separately, and to reconstruct an alternative narrative that took account of both in Tom's life.

A variety of therapeutic media were used to express emotional effect, including drawing and painting, plasticine modelling, puppet play and role play. The therapist also used a card game called 'Capture a Feeling' that offered opportunities to anticipate and reflect upon emotional expression in a variety of scenarios. Tom became very attached to the idea of the game and rewrote the rules and adapted the scenarios many times over, to practice current situations and reflect on past events. He also used the game to tell of difficulties he had at school, using the game itself as a 'confession' time and then moving into puppet play to re-enact scenarios and explore alternative behaviours and consequences.

It was through the process of puppet and role play that Tom underwent a form of catharsis that had been considered by the referrers to be highly unlikely. He had never mentioned his grandfather in relation to any abusive experiences. He had been able to speak of and draw his grandfather in relation to his absence but drew pictures of a 'man behind bars' on several occasions. The therapist observed a blankness of emotional expression when Tom drew these pictures. It had been suggested by the school staff that Tom would not have an 'emotional template' for his experiences, due to early gaps in cognitive and affective representation. However, the 'Capture a Feeling' game had offered a different perspective on emotional availability, and Tom's anger and distress at school had not suggested any lack of emotion. In the counselling sessions the therapist had experienced more of a dissociative response when Tom spoke about or drew his grandfather.

Over a period of weeks the puppets in the therapy room became an increasing feature of Tom's work. He set up scenarios and invented scripts to be used in the meetings, often with themes of 'disappearance' or 'surprise'. Having developed a relatively sophisticated ensemble of characters he began a process of restructuring the therapy room, by moving furniture, setting up 'secret' areas and making a bed in one corner of the room. He recreated and adapted this arrangement over a further four weeks of activity. He had then introduced a repetitive role play of 'burglars' where he allocated roles and scripts to himself and his therapist.

The 'burglars' scenario had then been re-enacted by Tom with his therapist during the following two sessions, with the therapist offering no interpretation of events, but curiosity about the process. Tom had then proceeded to repeat the procedure with himself as the burglar. The usual distractions had occurred on two repetitions, followed by the 'disappearance' of the burglar and the bedtime routine. On the last occasion Tom had changed his behaviour, so that when the distractions were complete, the therapist turned to find Tom already lying under the bed cover in anticipation of the therapist enacting the bedtime routine.

The therapist had made an appropriate response within the boundary of the enactment. She had begun to walk across the room, stopped, raised her head and spoke of feeling uncomfortable about seeing the 'burglar' in bed. She had clearly named the fact that it was not OK for an adult to get into bed with a child, and within the enactment took herself off to a chair in the other corner of the room and sat down. Tom had lain still under the blanket for a little while before declaring the role play complete. He had continued with the usual clearing up arrangements before sitting opposite the therapist, making full eye contact for a protracted period in silence and had then nodded, commenting that the therapist had done a good thing. The two had then deconstructed parts of the role play with regard to safety issues and eventually the therapist had been able to comment on the content, querying whether it connected with Tom's experiences of abuse by his grandfather. Tom had nodded and when the therapist had asked him to clarify his response, he had spoken a clear 'yes'.

From that time it appeared that Tom had completed his business in therapy and spent several weeks engaged in play with board games that had previously been used as 'cooling off' activities during the last ten minutes or so of sessions. He had shown no further interest in role play or the puppets, and when asked whether he wished to do so had replied that he had 'done it', giving the therapist a puzzled stare, which she later described as a 'withering look'.

The sessions ended at the natural break for the summer holidays, with the school staff reporting some improvement in Tom's behaviour at school, and definite improvement in his behaviour on return from weekends at home. There continued to be concern about Tom's level of functioning at school, which was attended to through their educational psychology provision. Despite knowing that he could return to counselling if he wanted to, and its actually being suggested to him on two separate occasions to our knowledge, Tom did not return to JACAT for any further counselling.

Conclusion

Life will continue to be difficult for disabled children and adolescents and their carers. The advances in the ways in which systems and agencies are striving to include challenged and challenging young people will, hopefully, be fundamentally empowering. However, many more will be abused and many will continue to be abused. The user/carer movement and the attempts by social services and health services to involve users and carers in both constructing particular care packages and the general planning of services should make some positive difference. Nonetheless disabled children and young people are at greater risk than those who have no disability, for the reasons stated earlier in this chapter.

Reluctance and resistance about the fact of abuse will remain throughout society and its systems. Vigilance is required by all adults who are involved in the care of disabled young people. Careful and empowering listening should be the minimum we all will accept. Perhaps more 'witnessing' of accounts by disabled adult survivors of abuse will mean that more will become possible with respect to safety and recovery.

3.5 Working with Young Male Sexual Offenders

Brian Johnson

Introduction

There is a group of boys and young men who give rise to concern because of their sexual behaviour. For a significant number their sexual behaviour is considered to constitute an abuse of other young people.

Working with this group of young people is not easy. Sometimes they are known to be victims of abuse themselves but even when the details are not known or there has been no disclosure the assumption is usually made that this is so. This presents a conundrum for those who care for them. As abusers they may well present a threat to other children within their family home, at school or at large in the community. As victims they need the support of all who come in contact with them. Many of the parents who attend groups at JACAT, or seek support and advice in other ways, struggle with this dilemma.

One of the functions of leaders of groups and of those who conduct family consultations is to try to help natural or adoptive parents understand how it is that their son, or occasionally daughter, has sexually abused other children. In terms of our experience of working with such young people the possible reasons seem numerous but all require a thorough knowledge of the young person's history if some possible explanation is to be given. In his chapter entitled 'Causal Explanations' Kevin Epps gives a detailed account of the available literature on this subject and summarises what the literature demonstrates. He points out that learning is the one theme which dominates the literature and the theoretical models that it describes: all practitioners are seeking to instruct their clients in new ways of behaving which decrease the chance that they will re-offend.

We have a commitment at JACAT to working with these young people who can be thought of as both victim and victimiser. This is the story of my work with one such young person.

The Referral

Andrew and Ben were two teenagers who had been adopted at an early age. Andrew was the older boy, but at referral he was not causing as many problems as his younger brother. Accordingly it was Ben who was first referred to JACAT. The initial referral was the result of an approach by the adoptive parents, David and Elizabeth, via the post-adoption support worker. David and Elizabeth thought that past abuse might be having an adverse effect on Ben, and considered that he was getting to the stage when he might be able to share issues and worries regarding his pre-adoptive past. As is our practice, a consultation was arranged involving the adoptive parents, the support social worker and two JACAT team members, of whom I was one.

The consultation

During the consultation David and Elizabeth told us as much of the boys' history as they knew. The boys' early life had been one of inconsistency and uncertainty. There was evidence that they had witnessed domestic violence. They were neglected, and there was a strong suspicion that they might have been subject to sexual abuse. The early years' information was patchy, and although the social worker tried to fill in the gaps she was unable to offer much more, as the boys had come from out of the area and a full early history had not been forthcoming.

From David and Elizabeth we were given a picture of the boys as presenting with mild learning difficulties, with Ben being the more intellectually able. He was starting to demonstrate anger and distress, which the adoptive parents considered had a causal link with issues in his early life. Ben had been told about the meeting and he had indicated a willingness to be involved in seeing someone from JACAT, if it was considered appropriate.

The JACAT workers involved in the consultation thought that it would be useful to offer a limited number of individual sessions to Ben. We hoped that he would start to engage in working on the issues which might emerge during those sessions. Again, as is our practice within JACAT, this was discussed with colleagues at the next Team Meeting before a formal offer of sessions was made.

The Initial Work with Ben

The offer to Ben and his family was for individual therapeutic work for Ben with a female clinical psychologist from the JACAT team. At the time it was felt that a woman would be less alarming to him. He himself had not expressed a preference either way. The following is my account of what I heard at our regular meetings about the work.

On the first of the planned sessions Ben spent time exploring the room, looking in every cupboard, drawer and toy box. He talked freely, and a theme that soon emerged was that he considered himself 'little' in comparison with his brother (who is taller) and his peers at school. He expressed a wish to be bigger, and didn't like being the smallest in the family.

At the start of the second session, he rushed into the room as if on a mission. After a quick look around he went over to a white board fixed to the wall and wrote the word 'SEX' on it, and then asked if it was all right to talk about sex. He started talking about males lying on top of females and the other way around. He then went on to explain that there are two ways of having sex. The first was practising sex when younger and you don't take all your clothes off. The second was when the boy unzipped and took his willy out and the girl pulled her dress up. He was asked if his parents or school had told him about these things. Ben said that they talked about it in maths. He then lay on the floor to illustrate the correct position. He then asked the therapist if she wanted to have sex with him. The therapist explained that she didn't have sex with children, and that it was not necessary for him to offer to have sex with her in order for her to work with him. Ben went on to say that 'my brother practises sex with me and I don't like it'. The therapist clarified the word 'practised'.

It was explained to Ben that his Mum and Dad needed to know about this so that they could help him, and he agreed that they should be told. On leaving the room and rejoining his parents, Ben told them, 'Andrew wants to have sex with me.' This was felt to be a very useful and positive event. The immediacy was remarkable. As Ben stepped out of the therapy room into the waiting area he made his disclosure to his parents. Andrew was present at the time, and he did not deny anything that was being said. In fact, he was nodding and appeared to be confirming his involvement. The parents themselves did not appear unduly dismayed at the time, but later they explained that they were shaken and so shocked that they actually felt out of their depth. However, they had confidence in us. Since they did not want to be punitive to either of the boys they maintained the appearance of relative calm.

As it happened, David and Elizabeth had travelled separately to the appointment in their cars. It was decided therefore that the boys should travel home separately. It was considered that Ben trusted his parents and that armed with this new (if very worrying) information they would be able to keep the boys safe.

At this stage the professionals clearly had some thinking to do. The situation was unusual, given that it appeared to be the younger boy who was taking the initiative. Moreover, his brother did not seem to be taking the routes of denial or minimisation which are usually adopted by alleged perpetrators. In addition, neither boy seemed to be inhibited in any way about discussing his sexual activities.

JACAT was then involved in a number of meetings concerning the child protection process. The outcome of this was that no formal police or criminal process was to be pursued. The boys' names would not be placed on the Child Protection Register as, although it was acknowledged that both boys were involved in sexually abusive behaviour, no advantage could be seen in their being registered. It was felt to be possibly too heavy-handed and might also be experienced negatively by the parents. There was nonetheless a plan. JACAT was requested to remain involved, both therapeutically and in thinking with the adults in this family about the safety of the boys and possibly others.

Comment

In the late 1990s, when these events took place, it was common practice for social services to try to avoid placing children on the child protection register when their parents were deemed to be both co-operative with the authorities and able, with assistance, to protect their children and to protect other children from them. It was also uncommon to register children who were abusing other children but who had no known history of abuse themselves, as was the case with Ben. Nowadays, the situation remains patchy in Devon with some parts automatically calling a child protection meeting on behalf of the abuser as well as the abused while others do not. JACAT believes that all children who abuse other children should be the subject of a child protection meeting in order to elicit the facts, obtain help for the offender so that he may cease offending, and form a plan which will protect other children from harm.

It was at this point we considered it appropriate to introduce a further intervention for this family. We are fortunate in JACAT to have the flexibility and range of skills that make possible a multiplicity of engagements. Possible combinations of work were considered in a JACAT team meeting, and it was decided to try the following approach. First, the clinical psychologist who started to work with Ben would support and work with the parents. As she is well-versed in systemic thinking she would also act in overseeing and holding all the work in mind. Second, a male clinical psychologist would try to engage and work with Ben. Third, I would try to work with Andrew, as I have been involved in working with boys and young men whose sexual behaviour is problematic.

As I have already mentioned, Andrew, though he had a recognisable learning difficulty, appeared to have a reasonable understanding of language. It was thought that he probably possessed a degree of comprehension that would enable him to engage successfully in the cognitive behavioural approach that I have employed when working with young boys whose sexual behaviour is a problem. This approach is constructed around a structured cognitive method which is the amalgamation of several other existing programmes, designed for use with groups and modified in this case for working with individuals. The programme begins by establishing the expectations of client and carer, setting ground rules, determining the readiness of the young person for work, and gathering information from all possible sources. It then takes the young person through an assessment of the degree of acknowledgement of what he has done, and of his intellectual and then emotional awareness of the impact on his victim. I hope to obtain from the client a description of his activities, and to bring him to a point where he has developed empathy towards the victim and a willingness to co-operate with the support networks which will be essential for the management of risk. In Andrew's case these were his parents, his teachers and JACAT.

The Work with Andrew

At the time of working with Andrew, JACAT had a number of premises, one of which was a three-bedroom house in a residential area separate from our main base on the hospital campus. The arrangement of this house included three play and therapy rooms and a wet room where painting, the use of clay and other messy work could be undertaken. I used this house as often as I could when working with young people who might pose a risk to other children, as I could book the whole house and thereby avoid contact with other vulnerable clients. I decided to use one of the play and therapy rooms for the work with Andrew, and this also meant that whoever brought Andrew could have a room in which to wait.

The therapy room itself was furnished with a small table, two chairs, beanbags and a wide range of toys. The room also contained a wooden structure that stood in a corner creating a roofless playhouse with a door, curtained windows and a feeling of a safe and contained space.

The work with Andrew soon took on a regular pattern. He would arrive in a state of excitement, 'all in a rush', usually with his school shirt hanging out and his tie pulled to one side, looking as if he had been running, not just sitting in a car for half an hour. We would then spend five or ten minutes catching up on what had happened since our last meeting, twenty minutes working on whatever task I had set, and twenty or thirty minutes of his playing freely with the toys and the play house.

It became apparent from the first session that the model I had used in the past was not going to be applicable with Andrew. I have found that even when working with very young and unsophisticated boys whose sexual behaviour is of concern, the first step ('why am I here?') is usually a difficult one. The difficulty springs from my challenging their attempts at minimisation and denial. I will not accept 'they told me to' or even 'I've been in trouble' but only an acknowledgement (within the capability and understanding of the young person concerned) of the behaviours of concern. It usually takes a lot of work to get to this point. Andrew, however, exhibited no sign of denial or minimisation: when asked 'Why are you here?' he replied, 'Because I do sex with my brother'. I then asked: 'Where do you do sex with your brother?' He replied, 'In the bedroom'. 'Does he want you to do it with him?' 'No,' he answered. 'Do you ask him to keep it a secret?' 'Yes.' When I enquired as to why it had to be kept a secret, he told me that it was naughty. I then asked him if he had sex with anyone else. 'Yes, with Robin [his teddy] and my pillow.' At this point I was a little taken aback as it often takes many weeks to get a young person to a place where they can start to talk openly about what they do. Andrew was clearly operating on a very different level. I think he had very little comprehension of the magnitude of what he was saying. As far as he was concerned, it was the adults around him who had a problem, not he or his brother, who, in his eyes, were fine.

Comment

Most children and young people have an instinctive wariness about talking about sexual matters in front of adults, understanding that this is frowned upon.

A JACAT colleague reminded me of an experience she had had with a young boy whom she had to talk to at school. In her role as field social worker she had been asked to see what the boy had to say following a disclosure of abuse which his older brother had made. The boy had been relaxed and happy enough to chatter to her until he sensed that the topic of sexual abuse was being approached. At this point he clammed up completely and refused to say anything more.

This is a pattern that is often repeated on occasions when children are interviewed by the police and makes it very difficult to proceed with the case against the perpetrator.

Clearly Andrew was not following this much more usual pattern.

A Different Way of Working

What then did this openness on the part of Andrew signify? It seemed possible that it could be attributable to his early history, about which we knew very little detail, or to his innate learning difficulties, or both. Becker (1991) and O'Brien (1992) researched case material and produced a model which indicated that when looking at a juvenile sex offender one would expect to find certain pre-disposing factors: sexual abuse, or unclear sexual boundaries or deviant sexual mores which left the young person unaware of the normal consequences of his actions. Here we were hampered by the paucity of our knowledge of his early life so I needed to find a way of understanding how Andrew perceived things. I wanted to work towards his feeling safer and being less of a danger to himself and others.

I was used to working with boys and young men who from a very early age had developed complex, and sophisticated but skewed thinking as a way of maintaining their behaviour. Andrew on the other hand presented a very different way of operating. He seemed to have the ability to converse using quite sophisticated and complex language. However, his internal emotional understanding of the world was anything but sophisticated. He was very simplistic and concrete in his thinking.

I started on the long task of trying to understand how Andrew perceived what was happening in his life. On one occasion Andrew and I were talking about the future. He had given me a well-practised and stereotypical picture: school, exams, college, work and marriage, although he clearly had little understanding of what it all meant. I offered him a 'magic wand' and said I could grant him three wishes regarding his future. I asked him to consider that he was grown up, say 25, and to formulate the three wishes to decide what his life would be like. He immediately said he wished (1) that he would have lots of money; (2) that he would be a famous footballer; and (3) that he would have a lovely girl friend.

We then talked about those wishes, and I reflected on related things such as good health to enjoy the money, and that maybe if he were a famous footballer he would have lots of money anyway and so need not waste a wish. Andrew then did what he does so well and was soon running with the fantasy, telling me that not only would he probably be well-off as a famous footballer but also that he would be able to get a girl friend without using magic. I then offered to take back one wish and give him another. I told him to think about it as it was a 'one wish one time' offer. He thought for some time, then said: 'OK, you can take the money wish back', and when asked what his final wish would be he replied: 'A big car'.

The way in which he covered up a profound lack of real understanding with a verbal veneer of sophistication meant that I had to be constantly aware that what Andrew was really like in thought and feeling did not synchronise with what he might say. On another occasion, when working on 'good touch, bad touch' – we had a very interesting time over good and bad – we started talking about appropriate clothing. When asked: 'Would it be alright for you to be dressed just in your shorts on a beach?' Andrew replied, 'Yes'. I went further and enquired if it would be alright if a girl of his age were to wear just her shorts on the beach. At first he said, 'Yes', but then after a quick rethink he changed to 'No'. I enquired why it was all right for him to just wear shorts on the beach and not for a girl. He replied, 'Cos she has tits'. After saying 'tits' he became animated and was clearly becoming aroused. He went on to say that 'girls have blue tits'. I was not clear at that moment what associations he was making, so I asked what he meant. He clearly believed that some girls had blue breasts. That thought was highly erotic as his arousal clearly indicated.

Later when thinking about the case with other team members we discussed what might have informed Andrew's 'blue tits' belief. This, and a lot more time with Andrew, led me to the following conclusion. In eroticising and objectifying girl's breasts, he had put them in a category with other things he considered to be 'naughty' sexual things and labelled them 'blue' as in 'blue' films. The abstract nature of the word 'blue' in this context was lost because he was so concrete in his thinking.

The more I worked with Andrew the more it became apparent that the difference between his presentation and his actual understanding was the key to working on the risk he presented to himself and others.

A Change in Direction

My work practice now became far more directive. I started offering fewer alternative scenarios as a means of helping him develop an understanding. Instead I gave him simple rules:

- You must not go into your brother's bedroom.
- When you feel the need to do sexual things, you must talk to your parents.
- You must not take other peoples things (such as Mum's underwear) and then use them for masturbation.

Through the other JACAT team members involved with this family, we started getting Andrew's parents to set very clear and unambiguous boundaries. In keeping with this style of clear directional work I started looking at ways of changing his use of sexual arousal as a means of minimising or denying feelings of sadness and fear. I wanted to help him find alternative ways to deal with these distressing emotions. This involved challenging him on every occasion that he appeared to be becoming eroticised. This happened mostly on the occasions when he was trying to remember something uncomfortable or was having to concentrate on the task we were working on. He would start to become agitated and flushed, his breathing would become heavy, and he was often visibly erect. Whenever this happened, I would stop whatever we were engaged on to describe what was happening. I would tell him simply and firmly that he was becoming sexually aroused and that it was not appropriate. I explained that if he felt uncomfortable, fed up or bored he should let me know. I could then help him deal with his discomfort without the need for him to escape into sexual arousal.

I went on to talk with him about what other things he could do when he started to feel the need to be sexy. This was a difficult question for him. I wanted him to learn that sometimes he was using sexy feelings to avoid pain but that sometimes it was for sex. Quite a challenge for all males! We considered such strategies as asking to leave the room, or thinking of something he likes (other than sex) such as holidays, computer games and favourite foods.

As the work with me and at home progressed — that is to say, setting and consistently reinforcing boundaries, coupled with the provision of safe activities — Andrew started to be seen as posing far less of a risk to himself and others. He also started to present in a more relaxed and confident way within our sessions. I was getting reports from home that he was far less inclined to want to 'sneak off' with his brother, and, in fact, was going to the other end of the spectrum and was sticking closely to his parents.

It appeared that he was beginning to take some responsibility for his own actions which has to be the main preoccupation of all therapeutic work with such young offenders.

Comment

Adam Jenkins, in his book *Invitations to Responsibility* was an early influence on my way of working with young people and he, together with Finklehor and Wyre, also informed the kind of treatment programme I followed with my clients.

At this point in our work I was just beginning to think that perhaps we had found a method of moving Andrew towards a safer way of being when we started to get hints that there was more to come. He began to be able to recall and describe in far more detail what happened when he was with his brother Ben. On one occasion he was explaining how they were both playing outside the school on a parents' evening. He told of his feelings of discomfort when he realised that his parents were no longer in sight. At first I thought that the feelings of discomfort and fear were the result of his feeling unsupervised and at risk of instigating sexual activity. However on reflection I began to suspect that he might not have been afraid of being the instigator but rather of being the recipient of inappropriate sexual advances. In subsequent sessions it became evident that despite Andrew's willingness and active participation, his younger brother Ben was far more powerful and in control of the sexual activity than had previously been thought. As Andrew became more able to talk about what was happening and thereby keep himself and others safe, Ben became overtly sexual and aggressive within his therapy sessions. Ben started to blame his therapist and JACAT for interfering in his life by stopping him from having sex. But that, as they say, is another story.

The work with Andrew finished soon after this turn of events, with Andrew's parents continuing to reinforce his boundaries and to keep open communication with him, the understanding with JACAT being that we would continue to offer support at any stage if it were needed. The work with Ben, however, was just beginning.

Conclusion

Though many professionals come into contact with children who are known to be both victims and abusers they are seldom confronted with first hand evidence of their sexualised behaviour. When they are, as is frequently the case with parents, natural, foster and adoptive, most are horrified, many disgusted, some to the point of requesting that the young person concerned be re-housed elsewhere, and all profoundly in need of help. Much of the content of this chapter has been toned down so as not to give unnecessary offence but some graphic descriptions remain in order to help professionals and others see and understand more clearly the impact of sexual abuse on outlook and behaviour and how it affects those who care for children who act in this way and how it is possible for the therapist to cope with this behaviour in safety and with integrity.

The case of Ben and Andrew is a good example of the complexities of trying to work with young people about their sexualised behaviour. Situations are often not as they first appear. There has to be a willingness then to widen one's thinking and sometimes to subject it to the more objective view of colleagues. As adoption and fostering often throw together children who have been sexually abused, sometimes without any knowledge of this abuse by those with whom they are placed, it is only too easy to make assumptions about who is the abuser and who is the abused. These may later turn out to be wrong. Seniority of itself does not necessarily bring power; other matters such as size, intellectual, emotional and psychological development may have a bearing on where the power lies between two children, as will most assuredly their individual life history.

Andrew's case also illustrates the necessity of being able to work with young people in a variety of ways. His verbal ability, in part the product of having been brought up by adoptive parents who were highly articulate, meant that he flattered to deceive. The cognitive approach often used with other young men did not work in this case, and an alternative had to be found.

The importance of working with the whole family was obviously crucial here, as was the willing co-operation of JACAT colleagues to give of their time to make this possible. Had the parents not been enabled to set boundaries for the boys which made Andrew feel safer at home it is unlikely that he would have been able to speak out. Without the offer of therapy for Ben too, the task would have been incomplete, and an unsafe situation become more unsafe as the boys grew older and perhaps able to extend their operation more easily beyond the home.

3.6 Working with Adults Sexually Abused as Children

Nick Booth

Introduction

Nick Booth was asked to write this chapter in order to give the perspective of a worker in the adult sphere of mental health. Nick has worked as a clinical psychologist and family therapist in Devon for over thirty years. He is currently Head of Psychotherapy Services, part of the Primary Care Trust in Plymouth. Conversations with him had indicated that during the course of his work he had met many adults whose mental health problems appeared to be largely the result of sexual abuse suffered in childhood. We wondered whether these problems might have been avoided, or at least lessened, by proper help and treatment before adulthood. We felt that Nick might be able to throw some light on the subject from his experiences as an adult worker. (Editor)

The Context

It is only relatively recently that we have become aware of the magnitude of suffering that has been caused by the sexual abuse of children in our society. This chapter, which focuses on adults who have been involved with adult mental health services, looks at the consequences of neglecting sexual abuse in childhood, and illustrates the difficulty that adult survivors find in accessing services that meet their needs. As a clinical psychologist and psychotherapist working in the field of adult mental health, much of my work has been with those who are trying to come to terms with their childhood experience of sexual abuse and its consequences. This chapter uses the fictional case (based upon a number of individual cases) of Mary and also of Sarah to illustrate the problems that these clients face.

Estimates of the prevalence of child sexual abuse (CSA) suggest that up to 51 per cent of females and 16 per cent of males in the adult population have suffered from this form of abuse (Hagar et al., 1998). The majority of abusers are male.

Not all victims of CSA suffer from long term consequences (Baker and Duncan, 1986; Herman et al., 1986; Kendall-Tackett et al., 1993). The nature, duration and severity of the abuse, the personality characteristics of the victim, their relationship with the abuser, family characteristics, peer relationships and positive or compensatory life events, will all determine an individual's long-term response to trauma. Whilst little is known as yet about the protective factors which may be specific to CSA, the concept of resilience is helpful in understanding how some individuals have a lower risk of developing subsequent disorder following childhood disadvantage (Rutter, 1999). Nevertheless, there is now substantial evidence of the pervasive and enduring impact of CSA on the lives of many individuals. This is particularly so for people who have experienced severe forms of abuse, where the abuse was repeated, and for whom abuse was carried out in the context of disrupted or disadvantaged circumstances (Mullen et al., 1994: 1996; Nelson et al., 2002).

There is also evidence that such a history is the beginning of a pathway which leads to later contact with mental health services. Within outpatient psychiatric services, between 30–50 per cent of patients will have a history of sexual abuse (Briere and Runtz, 1987; Coverdale and Turbott, 2000; Lipschitz et al. 1996; Palmer et al., 1992) and it is likely that there is a higher incidence of such histories in people with more severe and enduring mental health problems (Beck and Van der Kolk, 1987; Briere and Zaidi, 1989). Amidst controversy, there are indications of an elevated prevalence of sexual abuse histories in patients with psychosis (Bebbington et al., 2004; Read et al., 2004) It is only recently, however, that psychiatric services have begun specifically to confront the issues raised by people with such histories. There are a number of reasons why this would appear to be the case.

First, the present structure of psychiatric services remains oriented towards particular diagnostic categories based on current symptomatic presentation (e.g. self-harm, eating disorders, substance abuse) where the successful outcome of such services may become symptom reduction and minimisation of risk rather than psychological well-being and a resolution of underlying issues. There continues to be a reluctance on the part of the statutory sector to develop dedicated services for problems arising from specific etiological factors (e.g. rape, bereavement, domestic violence), though such services are often kept alive by under-funded and under-resourced voluntary agencies.

Second, many mental health practitioners are reluctant to enquire about early histories of trauma, and in cases where histories of sexual abuse have been identified this may neither be entered into the patient's records nor be subsequently included in the case formulation. This process contributes to the apparent invisibility of CSA.

Third, in cases where a history of childhood abuse has been identified as being significant, there remains a lack of available psychotherapeutic resources. Where such resources do exist, waiting lists are often long and intervention brief. From many over-pressed mental health workers with multiple roles and large caseloads there may be a reluctance to engage in conversations with clients about issues for which they do not feel adequately prepared or resourced.

Finally, it is likely that the traditionally conservative and male-dominated psychiatric services will reflect the wider social and cultural norms in continuing to minimise the size and nature of the problem.

Given the above, it is not surprising that many women with a history of CSA should find themselves experiencing rejection, denial or silencing when they seek assistance. These experiences may in turn mirror the real or perceived response of adults at the time of the original abuse, and serve to confirm that what happened must remain hidden, secret and shameful. Clients' experiences of psychiatric services may then be one of re-intimidation and re-traumatisation (Jennings, 1998).

Case Study – Mary's initial presentation: Hospital

Mary was 28 when she came into contact with Adult Mental Health Services. She was admitted to the local accident and emergency department following an overdose. She was seen by the duty psychiatrist. He noted that six weeks previously she had separated from Mike, her partner of six years, and that she was finding it hard to cope alone with her two young children, Tom aged eight and Gemma aged four. She was currently living with a friend and had financial problems. There was a year-long history of excess alcohol intake, and for a number of years she had been an occasional user of amphetamines. He noted that she was the oldest of three children, her parents having separated when she was nine, as a result of her father's drinking and her parents' constant arguments. Her mother re-married two years later and Mary had little contact with her father thereafter; he also subsequently re-married. She did not enjoy school and had few close friends, leaving when aged 15 with no formal qualifications. She had a number of relationships and became pregnant with her first child when aged 20, following which she was treated for post-natal depression by her GP. She had experienced a difficult and tempestuous relationship with her partner.

Mary presented as being depressed and with low self-esteem. She was assessed as being of low suicide intent and subsequently discharged with the recommendation of follow up by her GP.

Comment

Admission to hospital for self-harm is three times more common in women than in men, and is the third most common reason for admission to hospital in parts of England (Gunnell et al., 1996). Approximately 80 per cent of people who die from suicide will have a previous history of self-harm. In one study approximately 70 per cent of people who took an overdose had a history of some form of CSA, 50 per cent of such cases involving attempted or actual penetration (Coll et al., 1998). In the same study it was found that people who take repeated overdoses have suffered physical, emotional and sexual abuse which was more likely to have been prolonged. For girls under the age of 13 who attempt suicide, over 90 per cent may have experienced CSA (Briere and Runtz, 1986).

A history of alcohol or substance misuse is not uncommon in people with the history of CSA (Brown and Anderson, 1991; Mullen, 1993). Similarly, many women with substance misuse problems are likely to have a history of CSA (54 per cent in a study by Loftus 1994: 33 per cent, according to Wallen and Berman, 1992). Some authors have suggested that this is in part an attempt to 'self-soothe' at times of significant stress (Briere and Runtz, 1993; Khantzian, 1997) and also an attempt to self-medicate in order to cope with traumatic memories.

With regard to Mary's background, CSA frequently occurs in the context of concurrent physical or emotional abuse and disruptive family backgrounds (Finkelhor and Baron, 1986; Mullen et al., 1994, 1996). Furthermore, there is evidence that it may be associated with a history of parental alcohol abuse (Brown and Anderson, 1991; Sheridan, 1995).

At interview it was noted that Mary suffered from a depressed mood. This has been identified as a common long-term consequence of CSA (Bifulco, Brown and Adler, 1991; Mullen et al., 1988). Similarly, low self-esteem has been noted as a long-term consequence in a number of studies (Fleming et al., 1999; Herman, 1981), with specific associations between the severity of symptoms of depression and self-blame (Lange et al., 1999) and a negative view of the self (Muller and Lemieux, 2000).

Case Study – Mary's account of hospital

Mary could recall little of her stay in hospital. She did recall her mounting distress in the days leading up to her overdose, not knowing how to cope or what to do next. She remembered too her shame and anger towards herself for having got into this situation, and her keenness to return home to her children. She recalled being left alone for much of the time, and that although the visiting psychiatrist appeared kindly she experienced his questions as intrusive and therefore wanted to end the interview as soon as possible.

Case Study – Mary's second presentation: The GP

Two weeks later Mary saw her GP. He did not know her well and usually only saw her in connection with her children's normal illnesses. He noted that she was somewhat withdrawn and unforthcoming at interview. He found it hard to establish rapport. He had not received a letter from the psychiatrist, though he had been informed of her overdose by the hospital. On examination of her notes he recalled successful treatment of her previous episode of depression following Tom's birth with anti-depressants, and he therefore re-prescribed, requesting that she attend for a further appointment in four weeks. He took the opportunity to suggest that she see the counsellor who worked in his practice.

Comment

Most GPs have long lists of patients to see in the surgery, with only a few minutes available for each consultation. Unless a GP has a particular interest in mental health there is usually little time to get to know the patient well or for prolonged enquiry regarding the current situation. In this context it is perhaps unsurprising that 52 per cent of people in a study by Frenken and van Stolk (1990) found their experiences of GPs to be negative. GPs do, however, often have unique access to details of a patient's history which may not be available to others, and they are additionally able to access a wide variety of other services. The quality of their response to clients with mental health problems is, therefore, crucial.

Case Study – Mary's account of the GP

Mary was anxious about going to see her GP. She didn't know what help she needed, but she knew she needed help and had no one else to turn to. She was still finding it hard to cope and often found herself breaking down in tears. The children were difficult, and she often found herself shouting at them in order to get some peace. She also found herself thinking about the questions which the psychiatrist had asked in hospital, particularly about her past which she always tried to put behind her. Memories of her childhood began to surface and she started having nightmares. Her GP was kind but she could see he was in a hurry. He didn't really seem able to understand, but she was grateful for the tablets he prescribed to help her sleep and thankful for the arrangement to see someone to talk to, which was what she really wanted.

Case Study – Mary's third presentation: The practice counsellor

Five weeks later the practice counsellor met with Mary. He felt apprehensive about meeting his first client with a history of self-harm. Nevertheless, as the sessions progressed he felt that they had established a good rapport, and he found Mary to have many qualities which drew him to her. She described so much: an unhappy childhood both before and after her parents' separation, turbulent teenage years with a series of unhappy relationships until she met Mike when she was 21. In exploring this relationship he enabled Mary to talk about her devotion to this man and her fear that he would ultimately leave her, her increasing attempts to please him in the face of his violent outbursts, her sense of never being good enough or loving enough, and her despair when he finally left. He helped her to discuss her ambivalent feelings about being a mother, the crisis when her son was born, and the subsequent sense of constant failure in trying to cope with the responsibilities for which she felt too young and unprepared. By the end of six sessions Mary's mood seemed to have lifted and she did not appear to blame herself quite so much for her recent difficulties. The counsellor found that he wished to continue counselling Mary but restrictions on his contract prohibited this.

Comment

Many clients find benefit from short term counselling, but the aims are necessarily restricted for both the counsellor and the client. In this context it is not always possible for clients to disclose a past history of sexual abuse, either because they are not ready or because they feel there is not enough time available to address the issues. For similar reasons the practice counsellor, like GPs, may not enquire specifically about childhood experiences of abuse.

Case Study – Mary's account of the practice counsellor

Mary recalls that she found herself gradually able to open up to this man despite his being a stranger. The words came tumbling out. It was the first time she had found anyone to listen and to make her feel she was not to blame for everything that had gone wrong in her life: Mike's violence, her difficulties with the children, and her parents' separation. But she had avoided talking about what her father did, and the counsellor never asked. In some ways she wished he had, as increasingly the memories of what had happened were coming back to her. She recalled thinking that perhaps it could never be talked about and therefore resolved to try and forget about it once more, and anyway she felt uncomfortable when he asked her about sex, particularly after he had invited her out to meet in town one day.

Comment

Some women find it difficult to disclose to a female therapist who may be viewed as representing their mothers who failed to protect them, but it is more common for women to report difficulties with male therapists who may come to represent sexual predators. In this case, Mary's reticence may have been justified and based on reality, given that the counsellor had over-stepped the appropriate boundary between client and himself, by inviting her to meet him outside, given that approximately five per cent of clients are sexually exploited in therapy (Armsworth, 1989; Russell, 1993).

Case Study – Mary's fourth presentation: Hospital again

Eighteen months later Mary presented herself at the accident and emergency department where she required treatment for lacerations to her forearm. She subsequently informed the duty psychiatrist that she had been raped three months previously. She was markedly distressed when talking about this. She was suffering from nightmares and flashbacks, and was finding it hard to leave the house or care for her children. She was subsequently offered support from the Community Psychiatric Services, meeting with a sympathetic social worker with whom she was able to talk about her recent trauma. Despite a number of counselling sessions, the social worker was concerned that Mary's distress continued, as did her self-harm. The social worker became increasingly concerned with regard to the welfare of Mary's children, and shared her concerns with the local Children and Families Team, though they took no further action. However, on being informed of this, Mary subsequently felt her trust had been betrayed and she broke off all contact with the social worker. In the light of her continuing concern for Mary, the social worker requested that another therapist on the team offer Mary a further appointment.

Comment

There are indications that women with histories of childhood sexual abuse are vulnerable to episodes of further abuse (Messman and Long, 1996). Furthermore, there is evidence that they are more likely to suffer more severe symptoms of post-traumatic stress disorder following such incidents, a previous history of abuse serving to exacerbate symptoms of recent trauma (Andrews et al., 2000; Nishith et al., 2000). In addition, the converse also applies with the more recent trauma serving to re-stimulate thoughts, feelings and images with regard to earlier similar traumas. The overwhelming feelings may lead to regression, dissociation and a fear that one is 'going mad'.

Like many parents abused as children, Mary expressed concerns about her own children. These concerns were with regard to their difficult behaviour, her ability to be a good enough parent, and her ability to protect her children from others. Whilst there are indications that some people with a history of CSA may have significant difficulties in parenting (Banyard, 1997; Roberts et al., 2004) it remains a difficult and sensitive issue as to when and how particular concerns can be appropriately addressed in the best interests of both parents and their children. In the context of guidelines for the reporting of child abuse, it is not uncommon for parents to perceive the involvement of the child agencies as a breach of confidentiality, a threat or punishment, and unless there is a sufficiently strong working alliance, people such as Mary may withdraw from contact with all agencies. This is also the case when a mental health worker has knowledge of an alleged abuser in a relationship with their client which leads them to consider that other children may be at risk. Clients require considerable support in preparation for making a disclosure to police or social services, at which time they may be pressurised to make a formal statement. The pacing and timing of such work becomes crucial. Nevertheless, it remains essential for workers in the adult mental health context to be aware of the potential impact of a parent's psychological distress on children and to liaise with other agencies as appropriate.

Case Study – Mary's account

Mary recalls having felt worse and worse over the previous eighteen months. She had felt increasingly lonely and isolated. She continued to fight against the memories of what her father had done, yet they returned to haunt her, often by night but sometimes by day without any warning. She would see someone in the street who reminded her of her father and find herself shaking, feeling sick and having to run back home. She found herself increasingly dressing in ways that would make her less attractive, but she still felt that when walking down the street people would see into her, know what had happened to her and judge her accordingly. She said she felt safest with her children at home, and had found herself constantly worrying about whether her daughter would be safe now that she had started school. Tom, her son, was becoming increasingly difficult and she found herself losing her temper more often with him. She wondered if he would turn out like her father. Then she recalled the night when she was raped by the man downstairs. This had been just like Mike and her father all over again. She spent the following weeks at home, trying to block out what had happened. Several times a day she would bathe to wash away the dirt, often scrubbing herself until she bled. She started cutting herself to cut away the dirt and pain until the day that she panicked, finding that she could not stop the bleeding. She remembers enduring the humiliation she experienced in the hospital by pretending it was all unreal.

She remembers that she had initially liked her social worker. They had talked a lot about her recent trauma though she could find no words to describe the depth of her pain and shame, and no words to describe the memories of her father's assaults when she was no older than Gemma, her own daughter. So when the mental health worker told her that she had contacted social services because of her concerns for Gemma, Mary felt betrayed, hurt and confused. She would never allow her daughter to go through what she had done. It was as if she had not been understood after all.

Case Study – Mary's therapy

In accepting the social worker's offer of a referral to another colleague, Mary was subsequently able to meet with a female therapist for eighteen months. In the knowledge that there would be time and space, in the awareness that she was seeing a skilled worker, and in her readiness to engage in therapy, Mary was able to tell her story.

In therapy they discussed Mary's current situation and recent events, her contact with psychiatric services and her hopes for therapy. She was encouraged to use appropriate medication to help her sleep, lift her mood and cope with anxiety. Slowly she was able to discuss her past. In doing so she became aware of further memories of what her father had done, each memory resurfacing with renewed feelings of horror. Sometimes these memories would return in the form of recurrent dreams, and at other times they would be haunting images at the edge of her consciousness. It was not unusual for her to re-experience specific events, the pain, the taste and smell, so that increasingly it became possible for her to understand what it must have been like for her as a young child, living in the state of perpetual fear. In the knowledge that she was not to blame, Mary was able to understand that many of her subsequent difficulties were a normal response to such abnormal circumstances. She was increasingly able to explore the ways in which her abuse had distorted her sense of identity and her ability to relate to others, both men and women.

She was encouraged to write, draw and paint as a way of clarifying and expressing her feelings. With the aid of self-help manuals she was able to explore and challenge the range of negative beliefs she had about herself which had originated in childhood and been perpetuated in adulthood, all of which she had assumed to be self-evident truths.

After a while, Mary felt able to attend a group where she met other women who had been through similar experiences. Here she gained strength from hearing other people's stories and sharing her own in the context of people who understood. The theoretical knowledge that she was not a lone victim became real as she talked with others face to face, and with them she became able to celebrate herself as a survivor.

With the conclusion of therapy Mary had a clearer idea of the life which she could now choose to live as opposed to having to endure the one that she appeared to have been given. Like many women who have a good experience of healing through therapy, Mary was able to see herself now as a survivor rather than a victim. But nevertheless she continued to wonder: why had her father done it and why had her mother not protected her? Why, despite repeated visits to the doctor, had he not suspected anything and why, despite having told her teacher, had nothing been done to stop the abuse?

Comment

Mary was finally able to find a therapist who was able to help. There are now an increasing number of texts available for mental health workers on the counselling of abuse victims, which serve to prepare them for some of the specific issues they may be required to address (Sanderson, 1995). Regrettably, though, not all clients will have shared Mary's ultimately positive experiences of therapy. In one recent study many clients are found to have experienced multiple episodes of therapy, with 30 per cent of episodes being unhelpful and ten per cent positively harmful (Dale, 1999). Similarly, Frenken and van Stolk (1990) found 35 per cent of clients with a history of sexual abuse had negative experiences of psychotherapists.

One less than helpful aspect of Mary's contact with professionals may be common to other survivors. This is the *number* of professionals with whom she had contact, an experience that has been described as the 'the long march through the consulting rooms' (Frenken and van Stolk, 1990). In their study of 50 women, the average number of professionals consulted was 3.5, and when abuse was reported 30 per cent of professionals reacted to their story with disbelief, 38 per cent belittled it, and 38 per cent put the blame on them as victims.

In part Mary's ability to begin to resolve her difficulties thus relied on a skilled worker who could accept her and 'bear witness' to her story, enabling her to retrieve the forgotten fragments of her past and piece them together to make a new, coherent and meaningful narrative. This process is necessarily about loss and bereavement as well as liberation, involving as it does the letting go of beliefs and fantasies about the nature of families, parents, relationships and one's own self. Throughout this process the therapist's ability to contain the client's feelings of grief and abandonment, together with their ability to provide a secure base to facilitate recovery, are crucial to successful outcome.

Whilst much of Mary's therapy was past-oriented, enabling her to work through early trauma and its historical consequences, she was also encouraged to challenge some of her current ways of being in the world and to test out a range of alternative possibilities in the here and now based upon a newly emergent self-identity. Thus the past, the past-in-the-present, and the present each in turn became the focus of therapy. (For a review of outcomes in individual therapy, see Price et al., 2001.)

In addition to other aspects of her individual therapy Mary was aided by the more straightforward educational component. Information with regard to the nature of child sexual abuse and the range of consequences can be of significant value in helping to re-attribute blame and responsibility. Such information given in therapy is often helpfully accompanied by reference to self-help material (Ainscough and Toon, 1993; Bass and Davis, 1994). These resources can enable clients to place their own experiences in the context of other women's lives, gaining strength and encouragement from a diversity of ways in which others have been affected and have subsequently succeeded in overcoming the legacy of their pasts.

Similarly, specialist groups such as the one that Mary attended can be helpful in reducing isolation and alienation by offering a context for the collective empowerment of individuals as survivors. Such groups can often be a powerful catalyst for the transformation of secret and internalised shame, where an individual's story can be shared in a context which both explores the ways in which women have been silenced and explicitly encourages the reattribution of blame in the context of personal and social inequalities (Watson, Scott and Ragalsky, 1996; Westbury and Tuttey, 1999).

Challenges to the System

Mary's case is not untypical of many people seen in adult mental health services, though there are many more people known to psychiatric services whose abuse may have been more severe or prolonged or for whom its consequences may have been more extreme. Many others will be continuing their 'long march through the consulting rooms', having not yet found a place where their needs can be addressed. It is thus evident that there continue to be significant challenges to be confronted by service managers and providers in order to meet the needs of female psychiatric patients in general (Sayce, 1996; Gadd, 1996) and CSA victims in particular (Harris, 1998). These challenges focus in particular around the provision of adequate training and supervision for staff as well as the provision of facilities, including therapeutic residential facilities, that are perceived to be safe by patients. There is a strong argument for the formation of specialist teams who are able to take responsibility for training and supervision, joint agency liaison, research and audit, as well as the provision of a range of specialist individual and group therapies (Llewelyn, 1997).

Whilst we are obliged to improve our existing services for the direct benefit of individuals seeking help, there are also statutory and ethical responsibilities placed upon us for the identification and protection of vulnerable people, children in particular, who may be at risk of abuse. Yet many mental health workers feel inadequately equipped to enquire after or monitor the welfare of children, to discuss issues of parenting, or to participate in a multi-agency protection arena when necessary. This is despite the evidence that parents of children on child protection registers have high rates of mental illness, that some people will continue to perpetuate the cycle of abuse, and that many of our clients' abusers may still be a risk to children.

These challenges require us to take a pro-active stance in relation to the prevention of abuse through multi-agency work, and in this respect we may also contribute to finding an answer for one of Mary's unanswered questions: 'Why did no one do anything?' In one recent study only 50 per cent of adults abused as children had felt able to disclose their abuse; in over 70 per cent of these cases the person informed did nothing, and in only 18 per cent of cases had the statutory agencies been notified (Usher and Dewberry 1995). There clearly remains an inability to listen to children and thus protect them, both in cases where children may be afraid or ashamed to disclose, and also in cases where help is actively and explicitly requested. It is likely that timely and appropriate intervention, both in terms of stopping the abuse and addressing the psychological needs of the child at this time, may well prevent the development of further problems in later life. The case of Sarah below illustrates this.

Case Study – Sarah

Sarah was referred to the Practice Counsellor by her GP. She was 23 years old, single, and living at home with her mother. She presented as a quiet, thoughtful and reserved young woman. She explained that she had always lacked confidence in herself, that she was afraid of meeting people in social situations, and that she therefore seldom left the house without her mother. She had worked in the past but was currently unemployed. She had not known her father, her parents separating when she was two years old, leaving her mother to look after her and her two older brothers. When she was eight, her mother's new partner and his son came to live with them. She recalls beginning to enjoy the sense of being a family, coming to accept her mother's new partner as a supportive father figure. When Ricki, her new step-brother, kept coming into her room at night, when she was ten years old, she was able to tell her mother. Shortly after this, Ricki and his father left their home. She and her mother met with a social worker on a number of occasions to talk about what had happened, always being reassured by her mother and the social worker that she was not to blame.

Comment

It required only a short period of counselling to help Sarah to clarify her thoughts around her relationship with her mother, and to help her find ways of maintaining their closeness whilst at the same time not sacrificing her own autonomy. Increasingly she became able to consider her own independent future.

Sarah's mother's original response to her daughter's disclosure had enabled her to maintain a good relationship with her mother, but had also left her with unresolved feelings of guilt associated with the part she herself had played in her mother's loss of a partner. This was the focus of Sarah's request for help: a much narrower focus than that presented by many adults who have experienced sexual abuse as a child. Moreover, the original intervention when Sarah was a child, which had sought to leave her feeling believed, protected and free from blame, had prepared her for the possibility that another intervention from a professional might be helpful. All that was required, therefore, was for her to find a therapist who was sensitive and well enough informed both to listen and to understand. This therapist Sarah found. Sadly, many others continue to be less fortunate.

Men: the Invisible Clients

Both the preceding case studies highlight the needs of women who have been sexually abused as children. What about the men who have had the same experience, fewer in number certainly, but still significant in their own right? Despite some research in this area (Durham, 2002; Etherington, 1995; Mendel, 1995) our understanding of the impact of abuse on men remains a neglected focus of attention. Although 13-23 per cent of males who seek help may have a history of sexual abuse few appear to present themselves to the adult mental health services in this guise (Hagar et al., 1998). This may be because men find it even more difficult than women to admit that they have been the victims of childhood sexual abuse, and, even when they do so, are less likely than women to see the answer as lying in the opportunity to talk about it. When women are victimised they tend to internalise their anger, becoming withdrawn and depressed and thus evincing symptoms that are recognisably ones of mental ill health. Men, on the other hand, tend to externalise their anger and are more likely to find themselves presented to the prison authorities or the probation service, whose workers have only recently begun to be trained to recognise the possibility that the experience of sexual abuse in childhood may lie behind their aggression. The environment to which these men are subsequently exposed may often be the source of further trauma and abuse.

As illustrated, adult mental health services have begun to recognise and meet the needs of women who have been sexually abused as children, although for such women there are gaps in the service and the path to help can be a tortuous one. On the other hand, men who have experienced sexual abuse as children stand less chance of accessing appropriate therapeutic help. The reasons for this gender bias are complex and represent a challenge for the future.

Conclusion

Abuse has very serious consequences for victims. It also requires much use of resources, only some of which are targeted at the reason for presenting problems. Primary and secondary care workers need active support, therefore, to investigate a history of abuse, so that skilled and dedicated therapists can be of assistance earlier in the care path. And it can work!

3.7 Individual Work: Conclusions

Paul O'Reilly

The young people speak volumes! Their stories are moving and exhilarating. We meet them as badly damaged young people who through the patience and endeavour of their therapists move to being able to have a different view of self. They no longer think that they are bad or mad, and can begin to develop positive and helpful relationships with others. It is clear they have suffered grave emotional and psychological harm irrespective of the form of abuse. That is so for most young people who have been abused. It is our view that planned, premeditated, and persistent abuse of a young person – whether physical, sexual, emotional or through neglect – leads to the same outcome in terms of their experience of being bad young people and of being damaged and not worthwhile.

There is clear formal evidence in the research literature that working with young people can be effective (Monck, 1997; Kazdin, 1994). Moreover, it serves a serious and calculated preventative process which cannot be underestimated, both in terms of lessening the likelihood of further abuse to the young person concerned and in terms of preventing the establishment of a cycle of abuse. There is clear acceptance that the endeavour is worthwhile and essential if the ever increasing referral rates of children and young people to mental health services is to be reversed (Audit Commission, 1999; Mental Health Foundation, 1999).

The task, though, is a challenging one especially for the therapists who require good training, the capacity for personal and professional maintenance, on-going resources and the ability to foresee and plan round sabotages that might exist in the young person's context. Supervision and consultation are also important, as without such, any therapeutic endeavour is likely to be much less effective.

It is important too that the abuse of the young person has been acknowledged and that protective systems are in place so that the therapy can be of the greatest possible assistance. The examples in this chapter show that there is also a balance to be achieved between idealism and realism. The more that any therapist adheres overly rigorously, even fanatically, to a particular therapeutic system or view of the world the less likely they are to be significantly helpful to young people who have been damaged. It is necessary to maintain a critical perspective so as to discover which types of intervention with young people are most effective and efficient.

Section Four: **Working with Groups**

4.1 **Introduction to Group Work**

Ann Catchpole

Introduction

Although group work was not originally specified for the remit of JACAT, it soon became a small but important part of its activities. Now it is a high profile part of its work, producing a steady string of referrals and providing a valuable way of offering on-going support to families. This has not, however, been achieved without some difficulty.

The first two groups arranged by JACAT were for pre-adolescent children, and spanned an age range of three years. Though these early groups were clearly successful in enabling the children to explore in a safe environment their thoughts and feelings relating to the abuse and its aftermath, it has proved very difficult to get more such groups off the ground. This is despite the regrettably high number of children who are known to have been sexually abused within JACAT's catchment area. It is possible to surmise the reasons for this: the natural desire of parents to help their children bury the abuse and move on; and the emphasis of professionals, whose involvement in the family tends to be short-lived, on child protection issues, disclosure and possible prosecution. By the time the parents realise that their child is not able to move on without help, the professionals are long gone and they do not know to whom to turn. In practical terms, too, there are particular difficulties about running groups for children. Developmental differences are more marked, the younger the age-group under consideration, so that the age band covered can only be fairly narrow. Groups can only be mixed up to the age of about nine years, and when they are mixed it is important that there should be a reasonable balance between boys and girls. It is also hard for both carer and professional to be sure that a young child is ready for such work and wishes to participate in a group. As a result of all these difficulties JACAT has over the years been able to run few groups for pre-adolescent children.

It will be apparent from the description of the two different types of groups which follows that adolescent groups suffer from some similar difficulties to those of younger children in terms of assembling sufficient numbers at any one time. Here, too, there are pitfalls for those who attempt to mix too great an age range. The difference between those who are still at primary school and those who have moved into senior school is much more marked than the single year age gap would suggest. It is only in groups for adults, where developmental considerations are not related to age, that the age of the client does not matter.

Although the two groups which are represented in the following two chapters have different clientele, one being for adolescents and one for adults, the similarities between them have been marked. Both produced material each week, derived from the family life experiences of the members, which tested the group leaders to their limits and at times threatened to make work with the group impossible. Both relied heavily on the provision of a safe, therapeutic environment which made it possible for group members to share experiences and feelings in such a way as to assist in the healing process for all concerned. Indeed the feedback from both types of groups indicated that it was the reduction in their sense of isolation, brought about by mixing with others who had had similar experiences, which brought them most relief. One may add that the demands of each group were such that running them with a single leader would have been dangerous — hence our decision that there should always be two colleagues working together in this role.

Logistical Problems

Despite the fact that JACAT was set up to work therapeutically with children who have experienced all types of abuse, it has only been possible so far to run groups for those who have suffered sexual abuse. However, the nature of sexual abuse is such that emotional abuse is always an accompanying component. In many cases, too, the prevalence of domestic violence, where sexual abuse is known, means that many children will have experienced or witnessed physical violence too, and frequently also have suffered physical deprivation and neglect. Nonetheless, it is, perhaps, surprising that JACAT has never run groups for children whose primary experience of abuse was other than sexual. The reasons for this are mainly pragmatic. JACAT receives a much higher proportion of referrals for work with children who have been sexually abused than it does for those who have experienced any other type of abuse. All the difficulties experienced in gathering sufficient children of the right age and gender at any one time for a group on sexual abuse, would have been multiplied by the small numbers of referrals for other forms of abuse. Without adequate referrals the formation of groups is impossible.

However, it is apparent from those groups that have been maintained over a period of time that there is another factor at work here. When JACAT appointed a specialist worker to look after adolescent groups it was recognising and responding to a need. It was also giving permission to one of its members to concentrate much of her therapeutic energies and time on that particular area of work. Similarly when another member of the team expressed an interest in taking over the regular running of groups for the mothers of children who had been sexually abused and was permitted to take this commitment on, another area of group work was given priority. It requires the presence of a worker with the appropriate skills and commitment, and the recognition of a team as a whole that such a concentration of time and energy is justified, before groups can both get off the ground and also become a regular feature. Moreover, it seems that referrals only arrive in adequate numbers when field workers realise that groups are on offer on a regular basis so that they can offer them to a client and be sure that that client will not have to remain too long on a waiting list. It takes time for the word to go out and be believed. In the meantime busy workers may find themselves preparing for and offering groups for which there turn out to be too few clients.

Running groups can never be an easy option, either in terms of time and energy committed or in terms of expense. To be safe, groups have to be labour intensive with two leaders per group, and more if young children are involved, proper supervision, provision for the needs of the carers of children and young people, and support from workers in the field. This is illustrated by the time-consuming nature of the practice for primary age children. Such a group ran for 26 weeks. There were pre-group meetings with referrers, then with schools, and finally with carers. A carer's support group ran in parallel with the children's therapy group. There was a mid-group review with referrers, schools and carers, and a final review. A report was prepared for each child, with recommendations for future work. However, such output is justified, for groups have a dynamism which even the best of individual work seems unable to achieve and are able to bring about change in the most unpromising of circumstances.

4.2 Group Work with Sexually Abused Adolescents

Anna Flanigan

Introduction

Adolescence is a crucial stage of development, a period of transition between childhood, and adulthood and a time of considerable change. The main focus of development according to Erikson (1968) is the search for a personal identity, the attainment of individual competence and socialisation. The stereotypical image of adolescence is one of rebellion, moodiness and conflict with adults. However, more recent research suggests that most adolescents cope well and maintain positive relationships with adults and each other. In his focal theory of adolescence Coleman (1974) suggests that each person concentrates on a different aspect of the necessary developmental changes and tasks at different times, rather than trying to deal with everything at once. In other words, issues go in and out of focus according to need and experience. The ones that recede into the background do not necessarily disappear but become of less significance and importance. Difficulties arise when there are too many issues to resolve at once. Young people who have been sexually abused are dealing with myriad difficulties including low self-esteem, feelings of helplessness, anger, depression and suicidal feelings. It is not surprising that they are often in need of professional support and treatment at this time. Group work is one of the treatments available. This chapter will look specifically at the benefits of group work with adolescents in the context of a group for young women who have been sexually abused.

Why Group Work?

We all grow and develop in naturally occurring groups such as family, friends, school and work. It is one of the central tasks of adolescence to perceive oneself as, and to become, part of a peer group. These groups can be mixed and often have an informal and changing structure. Within them young people can make friends, take risks and experiment, practise social roles and responsibilities, learn about sexual behaviour and interpersonal skills, and begin to challenge adult and parental authority. This sense of belonging and of mutual support plays an important part in the development of personal identity and the necessary individuation from their parents and family of origin. This can be a difficult time for a young person who is unsure of themselves or lacking in confidence. It is even more difficult if that person has been the victim of traumatic circumstances such as abuse where proper development is interrupted and compromised.

Group therapy can reproduce many of the benefits of ordinary peer group interactions but in a safe, secure and structured environment. Much of this depends on the skill of the therapists involved and their handling of the parental and authoritarian role. There is more discussion of this later in the chapter.

Groups can provide the young person with:

- Reduced feelings of isolation because they realise they are not 'unique in their wretchedness' (Yalom, 1975).
- Feelings of acceptance and support from others who have had similar experiences.
- A chance to explore and learn new ways of coping, to attain new skills, and to develop a sense of mastery over situations.
- The opportunity to give to, as well as to receive from others in the group, support, reassurance and suggestions.
- The chance to develop self-confidence through the recognition by, and validation of thoughts and feelings provided by, the group.
- The acceleration of learning through feedback from the group.
- A chance to make new relationships, and practice and develop social and interpersonal skills.
- The provision of a safe, predictable and regular environment away from home.
- The chance to express difficult and painful feelings in a supportive environment.

For many troubled adolescents their experience of family life is at worst abusive and distressing. But more frequently it can be unsupportive and uncomprehending. They may have poor models of family relationships. Groups can resemble families in many respects. By experiencing adults behaving in a safe way and by joining in with the therapeutic culture of the group, the young person may be able to begin to build a new symbolic 'family': one where wishes and needs are taken care of and worries and fears can be worked through and resolved.

Of course some of the benefits listed above also apply to individual therapy, but the particular advantage of group work is well described by Blaustein and Wolff (1972): 'The stresses experienced by the adolescent in the one-to-one situation seem to diminish in the group. Intensity is diffused, demands on the individual patient are fewer and therefore there is less need to defy for the sake of defiance'. The young person has the chance to be a spectator and sit outside the main focus of the action in the group. This has the double benefit of taking the attention away from the individual and giving the chance to learn by observation and imitation. Although there has been limited research on the efficacy of group treatment, particularly with children and adolescents, it is perceived to be more cost effective than treating the same number of people individually. However, in this area of work clients need to be seen in relation to their family, and it is often necessary to provide simultaneous support for parents and carers. Group work is only a part of an overall treatment programme involving individual and family work.

Victims of Sexual Abuse

The sexual abuse of children and young people is a serious and widespread problem. It is difficult to obtain reliable figures of the number of children and adolescents who are currently victims of sexual abuse, as evidence usually comes from retrospective studies. Current research suggests that 7–36 per cent of women and 3–29 per cent of men world-wide, have childhood sexual abuse histories and that 1.5–3 times as many women as men are sexually abused. In one recent Canadian study 40 per cent of the women interviewed reported some form of sexual abuse (Westbury and Tutty, 1999). The perpetrators of sexual abuse are still predominantly male.

The short- and long-term effects are well documented. In 1985 Finkelhor and Brown proposed a traumagenic dynamics model of the damaging effects of child sexual abuse on the victim. At JACAT we find this model helpful in informing our practice. It focuses on four main areas:

- traumatic sexualisation
- betrayal
- stigmatisation
- powerlessness

Traumatic sexualisation

In sexually abusive relationships the child is forced or coerced into sexual behaviour inappropriate to their age. This is often linked by the perpetrator to affection and attention, or to negative emotions and thoughts. Abusers are 'concerned with denying the fear and misery of the child and substituting the abuser's own sexual excitement and power' (Hunter, 2001). This confuses sexual contact with love, and care with intimacy, and is highly disturbing for the child. Some children then sexualise all relationships in the mistaken belief that all adults need to be pleased that way. Conversely, children may avoid any sexual or intimate contact. They may also find it difficult to separate physical and emotional responses to sexual stimulation. Because the body responds in a particular way this does not imply liking or consent to being touched. Sorting out this confusion is often one of the most problematic and intransigent obstacles for children and young people in therapy. The adverse effects of early sexualisation are long-term and persistent, resulting in problems with adult sexuality, the forming and maintaining of relationships and, for some women, difficulty in ordinary vaginal childbirth.

Betrayal

Children and young people are usually sexually abused by someone they know and trust. Children are inherently vulnerable and dependent and need care and protection by adults. When adults abuse their position of trust by violating this social norm the child experiences a deep-seated sense of betrayal. They are left struggling with irreconcilable emotions, which results in feelings of loss and confusion. Judgement about the reliability of others becomes impaired as well as trust in their own decision-making and intuitive abilities. Children are easily misled by the use of language by powerful and influential adults which is intended to deceive. For example: 'This is how I show you I love you. It happens in all families. You are my special girl'. This can have profound effects on interpersonal relationships, both intimate and casual. The feelings of loss can lead to anger, resentment and extreme sadness which become manifest in either anti-social and aggressive or withdrawn and dependent behaviour. This all has a potential for the child to become even more vulnerable to further abuse and exploitation. In adulthood this particular kind of vulnerability may lead to a higher risk of the victim's own children being targeted by potential abusers.

Stigmatisation

Sexual abuse occurs in an atmosphere of secrecy and is often accompanied by taunts, derogatory statements and threats by the abuser. Blame for what is happening is put on to the victim, which compounds the feelings of betrayal and confusion described above. The victim feels tainted, dirty, guilty and so 'bad' about themselves that they assume they are worthless and disgusting. They can believe that they are transparent and everyone else can see their 'badness' or, conversely, that their shameful selves are so well hidden that if anyone did discover the truth it would result in immediate disgust and rejection. They feel shame and embarrassment at what has happened and blame themselves for their gullibility in letting it happen. Such stigmatisation leads to feelings of being different and isolated from their peers. This profound loss of self-worth and self-esteem is manifested in self-harm and attempted suicide, anxiety and depression, drug and alcohol abuse, eating disorders, and criminal behaviour. These problems are both short and long term in nature.

Powerlessness

When children are sexually abused, someone who is usually physically and emotionally stronger than themselves overpowers them. They are beset by a web of lies which manipulates them into the abuser's power and control. The abuser who uses coercion, emotional pressure and deception to get their own way invades their personal and physical boundaries. The abuser ignores their feelings entirely. In an atmosphere of fear and secrecy children are unable to change or stop what is happening to them, either by doing something themselves or by telling someone else who could stop it for them. Children often need to disassociate in order to reduce the feelings of powerlessness. For example, they may put themselves into objects in the room like a lamp by the bed, so that they can persuade themselves that the abuse is not happening to their actual self, which is preserved elsewhere. Thus they gain some sense of control over what is happening. This coping strategy works well as long as it is not permanent. In therapy children often do not want to talk about what happened for fear of re-experiencing the abuse, or they may talk about it graphically with a marked absence of congruent emotions. If a reintegration of the self is not possible there are serious ramifications for the individual's future mental health. More common sequelae are anxiety and panic attacks, nightmares, sleep disorders, phobias and depression, resulting from of a loss of self-efficacy. This strong sense of powerlessness can be revisited in later life if an individual is faced with any situation, no matter how apparently insignificant, in which they feel out of control. Some children deal with their need to be in control of their environment by identifying with their own abuser and in turn becoming abusers themselves.

Anyone contemplating running a group must be familiar with the effects of sexual abuse on children. This, combined with knowledge of the dynamics of group work, will form the theoretical base that informs the format and content of the group.

Preparation

It is necessary to plan and prepare carefully before the start of the group. Time taken at this stage to consider the practical, professional and theoretical issues involved is crucial to the overall success of the group both for participants and therapists. Below are the issues necessary to consider when running any group. Their particular relevance to groups for young women who have been sexually abused will be shown. It is by no means exhaustive or prescriptive.

Selecting a co-therapist

Running groups is an arduous task, so it is preferable to run a group with another person. Not only can the tasks of being leader be shared and eased, but the couple relationship can provide a useful model of adult behaviour for the participants. It is important to have someone who is sensitive to the distinct needs of the group. It is preferable for both to have similar status but it is not necessary to be from the same profession. Yalom (1975) suggests that co-leaders should also have the ability to be close to, but not similar to, one another. Hall and Lloyd (1989) recommend that co-therapists examine their own feelings about sexuality and sexual abuse before starting the group so that any issues are confronted and resolved. In practice, when working with a new therapist, time is set aside to check out personal views and feelings over such issues as attitudes and beliefs about adolescent sexuality. It may be necessary to share any personal history or experience of abuse. To a degree, the choice of co-therapist will be dictated by the nature of the group. One with an educational model could include professionals or therapists from backgrounds other than mental health, whereas one run on a group analytic therapy basis will need suitably qualified and experienced therapists.

The gender of the co-therapists is a potentially controversial issue. In group work with young women who have been sexually abused, it can be argued that a male presence is not indicated. However, having male and female co-therapists can offer the young women an opportunity to develop solid and sensible relationships with both sexes. A male worker can provide an alternative model of male behaviour and act as a focus for the negative feelings that participants have for their abuser. However, he will also need to remain sensitive to the impact of his behaviour generally, not always assume the lead therapy role, and accept help and support from his female co-therapist, if he is to offer a positive role model to the young women.

It will also be necessary for the co-therapy couple to be sensitive to any sexual attraction between them and the impact which that may have on the participants (Gottlieb and Dean, 1981). It is also more likely with a male and female therapist partnership that the participants will try to split the couple and ally with one and then the other (Furniss, Bingley-Miller and Van Elburg, 1988). The co-therapy relationship is best summed up in a quotation from Maclennan and Dies (1992):

> When co-therapists are working together . . . they must learn to know and accept each other, be comfortable with their different styles, and take time to process together what goes on in the group. Co-therapy is like a marriage; leaders should enjoy working together and be able to serve as models for group members in terms of how they work out any problems between them.

Group format

In the literature of groups there are a variety of formats, such as solution-focused and skills development (Kruczek and Vitanza, 1999), art activities, role-plays and self-esteem activities cited in the literature review by Kitchur and Bell (1989), and an integrated treatment approach advocated by Giaretto (1981). Giaretto combines professional and self-help strategies with some therapeutic and educational elements. Furniss et al. (1988) describe a model which views child sexual abuse as a symptom of family disturbance, and groups are offered as part of a whole family package. This concentrates on psychotherapeutic change but also considers educational material and the recognition of responsibility. Such an approach is developed by Lindon and Nourse (1994), who advocate a multi-dimensional model which incorporates a skills component, e.g. social skills training and problem solving; a psychotherapeutic component, e.g. recognition of feelings, identification with others; and an educative component, e.g. self protection and sex education.

This latter is the nearest approach to the one used at JACAT, which could be broadly described as an integrated model. It is also a model that is commensurate with a joint agency approach. It takes account of the different therapeutic emphases in both agencies. In social services emphasis is often on the skills and educative components associated with future self-protection and improved social skills which will help families function more safely and better in the community. Within the health service the emphasis is more likely to be on the therapeutic component in order to facilitate the way back to non-abusive relationships and personal growth.

Generally our groups are closed, and run weekly for one and a half hours for a minimum of twelve sessions, again using a task-oriented model. However, we have experimented with a workshop format. This involved 6 two-hour sessions with a specific focus each week, and relied heavily on a task-oriented activity model. The rationale for this was the short time span available to both therapists and participants and the long gap since the last group offered by JACAT. What made it work therapeutically was the fact that the four young women referred had done a lot of individual therapy prior to the group. They also wanted to work on the specific issues, already identified and extensively dealt with in their individual work. They were keen to have the opportunity of exploring these issues in relation to others in a group.

Selection of a supervisor

This is an important part of the planning stage of the group. The supervisor should be chosen by the group therapists and not the other way around. This can be a tricky concept, particularly when hierarchical supervision is the norm and a supervisor is designated rather than selected.

JACAT practice is always to have a supervisor, usually drawn from within the team. This means that expertise and experience in both the field of abuse and group work is available. However, this has important consequences for the overall workload of the team. Account has to be taken of the strain on existing schedules, and the group should be timed, where possible, to accommodate them.

In choosing a supervisor the following need to be borne in mind:

- The supervisor should have some experience of working in groups.
- The supervisor should be aware of group process and dynamics.
- The supervisor should be someone you trust, whose work you admire, and by whom you can feel inspired.
- It is possible to use someone who has not run groups before as long as they have acknowledged expertise, enthusiasm and the experience to offer helpful and challenging insights into this area of work.

It is always helpful to meet with the group supervisor before the sessions begin, so that their input and ideas can be introduced at the planning stage, and a contract for future supervision sessions can be made.

The aim is to have one or two sessions before the group begins and then one supervision session for every two group work sessions, with a longer session for a reflection of the whole process after the group has finished. It is important to prepare for the supervision by writing up notes on the content and process after each session, and by keeping any relevant material. At JACAT we tell the group participants about the supervisor when confidentiality is discussed at the group interview.

Case Study – Supervision

In a recent group run with another senior occupational therapist one session had been particularly difficult with a fierce challenge to me from a young woman in the group. This had resulted in the two of us 'wrestling' with some art materials in the group, much to my consternation, irritation and discomfiture. My co-leader and I felt we rescued and resolved the incident for the benefit of the individual young woman and the rest of the group at the time. However, I was left with some personal unresolved issues regarding a lack of understanding of what was going on and feelings of irritation that I should have found myself in that situation 'with all my experience'.

In the subsequent supervision session I was able to discuss the incident at length. I was able to recognise where I had made inappropriate interventions, to understand the underlying meaning of the young woman's behaviour, to plan appropriate strategies for next time, and to accept the rational and unbiased opinion of my supervisor. Perhaps most importantly I felt enlivened and restored by the session and therefore able to contemplate the next group work session with less trepidation.

Seeking members for the group

There is a dilemma here. One possibility is to advertise the group and see what referrals are received. The alternative is to keep a waiting list and run the group when you have the requisite number of possible participants. At JACAT we have done both, and a mixture of the two, none of which has guaranteed the requisite number of referrals. A mixture of the two is preferred. Nevertheless, it took over four months to get enough referrals to begin the interview process for the last young women's group. In general the advertisement should contain the basic details about the group and the contact information. We back this up with two leaflets, one for prospective participants, in a question – and answer – format about groups in general, and the other for prospective referrers, with brief details of their responsibilities as well as about groups in general. It is useful to have a referral form to collect the basic information with a section on reasons for referral, particularly whether or not the young woman has been informed of the referral. Frequently, prospective members have no idea that they have been referred and find themselves contacted by an agency of which they have never heard, or with which they may not want to be associated. The word abuse in our title leaves no doubt about the nature of our work. It is important when working with adolescents in therapy that they have a sense of control over what is happening – all the more important with an adolescent who has been abused. The process of engagement in a group will not be successful if the young woman feels she is being sent or compelled to attend. Some may choose not to work on the abuse at the time the referral is made, and this wish must be respected.

We advertise to all the statutory, voluntary and independent agencies, who deal with young people in our area. We also keep a waiting list for referrals in between groups. Those clients in the specified age range are contacted about a prospective group and added to the referral list or deleted from the waiting list as applicable.

Selection of participants

Each young woman who expresses an interest in joining the group is interviewed by both group leaders with their parent or carer and the referrer. The aim of the interview is for the young woman to gain an understanding of what will be involved in the group and so to enable her to make a well-informed decision about attendance. It also allows the group leaders to make a judgement as to the young woman's suitability for the group. Below are the criteria we normally use, not necessarily in order of importance, but with young people, perhaps motivation to attend is the most crucial:

- *Motivation:* how willing is the young woman to attend, or is she coming only to please someone else, e.g. a parent or a social worker?
- *Age:* in groups for young people it is advisable to keep the age range within a narrow band, usually about two years; it also rarely works to mix middle school and secondary school pupils or secondary and further education college students.
- *Geography:* it is pointless offering a place to someone who cannot get there, so make sure you know if there is suitable transport available.
- *Support of parents and carers:* even though you do not want the young woman to come merely to please their parents or carers, it is crucial that the young woman attends in the context of a supportive environment – otherwise, sabotage at an unconscious or conscious level is possible.
- *Type of abuse:* while all the young women will have been sexually abused it may be necessary to differentiate further, i.e. intra or extra-familial. For example, it would present difficulties if only one of the young women, in a group of six, had been sexually abused by, say, a schoolteacher, while all the others were abused by their fathers: this might only serve to increase the first young woman's feelings of isolation and difference.

It is difficult to assess whether the young women chosen will interact well as a group. Although observing the above criteria will help, the final choice is more a matter of intuition based on experience of running similar groups and other previous clinical experience.

Other practical considerations

- *Venue:* the room needs to be private and friendly and not associated with other forms of treatment, i.e. not somewhere where the young woman has previously been for family therapy. It is helpful if there are kitchen facilities. If the group is timed to take place at the end of the day most young people are ravenous!
- *Timing:* bear in mind the time of the day and the time of the year. Is it better after school? Avoid the months up to GCSEs or A-levels as this may cause conflicts of interest and loyalties, and increase the anxiety of parents or carers that participating in the group will adversely affect academic attainment.

- *Transport:* this is vital. How the young woman arrives at and leaves the group is critical to the success of their participation. Any escort, and driver should be consistent and reliable, and preferably female. Escorts should know how to assist the young woman by being supportive and not intrusive, and by being able to withstand some strong emotions especially on the return journey. A parent or carer may not be the best choice in spite of a willingness to be helpful. It is best if the organisation of the transport remains the responsibility of the referrer, thus leaving the leaders free to concentrate on the needs of the group and allowing confidentiality to be protected.
- *Support for parents or carers:* it can be perplexing and lead to a sense of exclusion for parents and carers to have their child in therapy. The aftermath of sexual abuse affects all family members, and the adults are likely to be struggling with their own set of difficult and painful emotions. They may witness their child's behaviour deteriorating at the outset of the group, giving them a feeling that they are left to cope alone with challenging and unfamiliar situations at home. The leaders' wish to be separate in order to foster confidentiality and trust in the group may be interpreted as hostile. In order to minimise these effects we offer support to parents or carers. This can be either in the form of a group run by another member of the team for a number of times throughout the life of the young women's group, or regular contact by that team member by telephone or home visit to check on how things are going or to sort out concerns. Both have worked well and have contributed positively to the overall outcome of the group. We produce a leaflet for parents/carers at JACAT entitled Helping your Child through Therapy, which deals with the issues outlined above.

Case Study – Practical considerations

One of the young women, Karen, aged 15 years, was living in a local residential home. Due to staff rotas the same member of staff was not available each week to organise transport and check on attendance. Karen was consistently late, which was proving disruptive to other group members and kept her on the outside of the group. While there were personal issues for her to address within the group, we felt we could not do this without the proper containment of the situation on the outside. As group leaders we were feeling hostile to the staff of the home. Karen was a young woman who managed her anxiety by playing one adult against another, so it was vital that we sorted this problem out.

We asked the person supporting the carers to intervene. She visited the home and discovered that our hostility was mirrored by the staff there, who were coping with increasingly worrying and challenging behaviour from Karen and were beginning to blame this on her attendance at the group. They felt her experience of being in the group upset and provoked her every week and they were left to pick up the pieces for the next six days. They agreed that they might have subconsciously sabotaged her attendance in order to make their life easier. The support worker was able to work with them on our behalf. Karen's level of attendance improved immediately. The residential workers and ourselves were less hostile towards each other and could better appreciate our individual, but complementary, contributions to Karen's treatment.

- *Liaison with referrers:* it is helpful to keep in touch with referrers or referring agencies, particularly if they are involved with arranging transport. This can be done by the group leaders or by the support worker. The role of the support worker is outlined in the section on support for parents and carers earlier in this chapter. Referrers are always invited to the evaluation interview when the group sessions end and a short report is sent following this meeting. In a long-term group of 26 weeks in which I was co-leader, a mid-term meeting for all referrers was arranged in order to maintain contact.

As in individual work, a knowledge and appreciation of the personal and professional context in which the young person comes to the group is vital. A partnership between both parents or carers and the referrer must be established in order to best facilitate the work.

Referrers who may have little experience of therapy can be very suspicious of, and feel intimidated by, group work, which may appear to be shrouded in an even greater veil of mystery than individual work. They need to know that the workers involved are competent and reliable and that the young person's involvement will not create extra work for them. The majority of referrers are social workers. We have witnessed the gradual dis-empowerment of their profession in recent years, particularly in respect of the time and opportunity to be involved in active therapeutic work. The pressures of the job in relation to child protection and the investigation of possible child abuse mean that any prospect of more work, through further disclosures, for example, can appear overwhelming and may militate against referral to the group. A sharing of information and ways of working and thinking can be helpful here. One of the problems of communication between agencies is 'the contrasting backgrounds, terms of reference and operational practices' (Reder and Duncan, 2003). Good working relationships are based on mutual trust and respect for other professionals' perspectives. In a study of serious case reviews in 2002 by Sinclair and Bullock it was found that practitioners 'lacked an understanding about issues of confidentiality, consent and referral practices' and that 'an uncertain knowledge base therefore impacted on interprofessional communication' (Reder and Duncan, 2003). We try to minimise any difficulties by holding evening seminars on group work, by attending social services team meetings in order to advertise the groups and answer any questions or worries first hand, and by disseminating the information via team members who are also in local frontline teams.

The Group Sessions

It is an important tenet of our group work philosophy that we begin to help the young women put their experience of having been abused into the context of their whole life; that we enable them to begin to recognise and appreciate the other aspects of their lives that have meaning; and contribute to a psychological definition of themselves as functioning human beings.

As stated earlier, the sessions are for one and a half hours and are structured around a number of themes related to the aftermath of being sexually abused. These are themes identified from the initial interview, from an agenda set at the beginning of the group by the young women themselves, and from existing literature and the clinical experience of the group leaders. Very often the leaders' anticipated list of themes harmonises with those identified by the participants. The list is likely to include some or all of the following:

- Feelings about having been abused, including powerlessness, disgust and isolation.
- Issues of trust – in themselves and others.
- Feelings about, and attitudes towards, the abuser.

- Family issues, including family break-up and feelings about the non-abusing carer, often the mother.
- Sex, including sexual orientation, intimacy and the mechanics of sex.
- Peer relationships – same and opposite sex.
- Behaviour problems, particularly control of anger.
- Psychological problems, including anxiety and eating problems.
- School-related problems, usually involving non-attendance or poor exam prospects.
- Fears about the future, including fears of abusing their own children or not recognising that their child is being abused, fear of not being able to make good personal relationships, fear of whether or not they are 'normal'.
- Confusion between what is ordinary adolescent behaviour and what is prompted by having been abused.

Each session tends to follow a similar pattern. It starts with a ritualised introductory exercise. This provides a sense of continuity, predictability and safety. It is also a way of making a link from the outside world to the group room, and grounding each of the young women in the real experience of their everyday life. Such an exercise can promote self-esteem because everyone has the experience of being listened to and valued for their individual contribution.

This introductory exercise is followed by work on the theme of the week that dominates the middle section of the session. The ending is also ritualised as a way of reversing the process at the beginning of the session: that is, it is a way of marking the transition back into the outside world by delineating the end of the group session in a predictable and consistent way.

Case Study – Dealing with the abuser describes in detail a complete session. I have chosen as an example a session that focussed on the theme of 'the abuser'. I have used a version of this session on several occasions. Each time it has been a profoundly moving and powerful experience for me and for the young women involved. It has often been the session that has been cited as 'the most helpful' in verbal feedback and evaluation after the group sessions have finished. I usually plan this session at around the halfway point when the levels of safety, trust and commitment are likely to be at maximum. The Case Study described here was the second of two on the theme of 'the abuser' and was the seventh of a total of eleven sessions in all. The group therapists were myself and another experienced female-group therapist.

Case Study – Dealing with the abuser

In the previous session the focus had been on recognition of and expression of feelings about the abuser. Individuals had become aware of previously hidden feelings, particularly their anger and guilt. They began to recognise how these negative feelings about the abuser were often displaced on to others, including themselves. They all agreed they would like to be relieved of some of those feelings and place the responsibility where it belonged – with the abuser.

In session seven we began in the usual way by saying one good thing and one bad thing about what had happened during the week. The content varied from a description of a new boyfriend to prospects of a new work placement and future college plans. Links were made to the previous session by reminding everyone of its content by sharing again what had been said or written.

We then asked each person to make an image of their abuser, using the art materials available. Given the physical limitations of the room we were restricted to paper, paint and pens. Where possible I think it would also be good to use clay or other modelling materials in order to make a three-dimensional image. Group members were asked to write down any feelings to accompany the image or any messages they would like to give to the abuser. They were then invited to dispose of the image in any way they chose.

The initial response was mixed. One young woman was reluctant to begin, saying she could not draw very well. She seemed overwhelmed by the aggressive and violent images being created by some of the others. Gradually she was able to share that she had ambivalent feelings about her abuser. She experienced both hostile, and warm and tender feelings, especially when she remembered happy family holidays spent with him. We encouraged her to try to express this ambivalence in her image. Eventually, she managed to write something positive about him but also drew him as a pile of excrement – a metaphorical image repeated more than once by other group members. In contrast, another young woman drew a vivid picture of the slow, painful and sadistic torture and death of her abuser in the form of a storyboard. She thought carefully about each image and worked hard to get it just right. Soon the others were joining in with suggestions and her image became the focus of attention for a while, providing an outlet for the more violent fantasies of how to reek revenge on the abuser. We noticed how well the group members were working together and how trusting and confident they were in each other to be able to share potentially distasteful and shocking thoughts, and how accepting they were of the similarities and differences between them. We the therapists no longer had to play a very active role, as in the first few sessions, for they the participants now had the confidence to discuss things together as a group.

When asked how they wanted to dispose of the images they all immediately chose burning. It was fortunate that the premises we were using had a garden, which meant this could be done safely and privately. Once in the garden, the young women quickly organised themselves. They stood in a tight circle and piled the images in the centre. They all took a match to ensure the paper would be properly set alight. Once it was burning they held hands and danced around the fire shouting abuse and spitting on the images as they burnt. My co-therapist and I were rightfully excluded, and stood apart, but stayed watchful, mindful of physical safety and containment issues. The young women remained aware of our presence. They demonstrated this by checking us out from time to time. It appeared important to them that we were there as witnesses. As part of our safety precautions we had a bowl of water ready to douse the fire if necessary. As the flames began to die down, one of the young women noticed the bowl and asked if she could use it as she wished to drown her image 'just to make sure'. As she picked up the bowl the others wanted to join in and they all carried it to the fire and threw the water on to the embers. They waited until no trace of the burnt paper was left, and it was only then that they were prepared to return to the group room. There was a palpable sense of relief, and they stayed physically close to each other as they made their way inside.

The group session ended in the usual way with a round of each person expressing a feeling or statement they would like to leave behind in the room. They showed relief at being able to confront feelings of guilt and responsibility, and enjoyment at the sense of power they felt at having 'destroyed' their abuser. However, it was clear that many other issues had been raised by this session. Usually at the end of each session the young women waited together for their respective transport to arrive. This time, two of them decided to remain in the group room while the other three went outside. The two shared ambivalent feelings about their abuser as described earlier. The split was indicative of the difference present in the group. It was as important to nurture this difference as it was to celebrate the shared feelings displayed earlier in the session.

This session illustrates well the integrated model. The young women were able to effect some psychotherapeutic change:

- By recognising, confronting and expressing feelings.
- By being able to identify strongly with other members of the group and reduce feelings of personal isolation.
- By having the opportunity to be listened to and valued in a non-judgmental environment.
- By problem-solving and experiencing mastery over situations and consequent feelings of personal power.
- By learning that adults can allow freedom of expression without crushing or abusing it.

In this way they learn more about themselves in relation to others and they develop new coping skills, both of which are vital to the success of interpersonal relationships in the future:

> *There is an important psychological moment in that struggle to move out of a state of isolation and begin defining oneself through connection to a group.*
>
> (Frankel, 1998)

Evaluation

This is usually done in an informal and unstructured way and consists mainly of verbal feedback. In the final session each participant is asked to compare the aims they set in the first session with the achievements they feel they have made by the end of the group meeting. The therapists are also able to give feedback, and everyone's experience of attending the group is discussed. In a study of a previous JACAT group, Hughes (1992) found that the most helpful aspects of the group were sharing experiences and therefore reducing the sense of isolation, having a sense of belonging, talking about the abuse, talking about relationships, the expression of feelings, and having an increased understanding. This is in line with the verbal feedback given by the young women in subsequent groups.

After the group sessions have ended, each participant is interviewed again with their parents or carers and referrer. This is our opportunity to hear any feedback from the adults and to discuss future therapeutic needs. A short report is written to the referrer, any further work is undertaken by JACAT, or a referral to another agency is made.

JACAT has never undertaken any formal follow-up, with questionnaires, say after six or twelve months, though this is something we intend to make part of the programme in the future.

Issues Arising from the Work

There are some specific issues that single out group work in this field:

- The pacing of the work in the group.
- Matters of confidentiality and disclosure.
- The effects on the group leaders.

The pacing of the group

In my experience, it is noticeable how different the pacing is from other groups with young people. In sexual abuse groups one is confronted with the issues from the first session. There is no ambiguity about the known thing each participant has in common. In general, the choice to be part of the group has been active and elective, which enhances the wish not to prevaricate. The young women involved have often spent many years feeling overwhelmed and consumed by the abuse. The issues are very familiar in their head and heart even though they may never have verbalised them. In a way, all the issues connected with having been sexually abused are weighty and potent. In other words, there is no way of easing yourself gently into the minor issues before tackling the major ones. The story of the abuse needs to be told in the first session. If it is not, everyone is frantic with curiosity and there is a covert message that the undisclosed information is unbearable for all concerned, particularly the therapists, and that, somehow, the young person has been deceived and tricked into attending with a promise which cannot be delivered, and that their abuse still needs to be kept a 'secret'. This parallels part of the process of the abuse with the adults in the powerful and duplicitous role. This is not to say that the familiar and expected nervousness at the beginnings of all series of group sessions is not present. Participants will be wary of each other and of the therapists. 'Trust, the capacity to rely on an internal experience of love and protection, is shattered by trauma' (Briggs, 1998:). Although it can be rebuilt, the process is likely to be slow. Given this knowledge about the survivors of sexual abuse, the fast pace of the group can be unexpected and take even the most experienced therapists by surprise.

Confidentiality and disclosure

Setting the boundaries of confidentiality is crucial in establishing any therapeutic alliance. 'Therapy should not be a cloak for collusion nor an excuse for therapists not to shoulder ordinary adult responsibilities in relation to children' (Hunter, 2001). When working with adolescent survivors of sexual abuse who have already had their personal and physical boundaries disregarded and invaded by adults it is critical for the therapist to be clear about the extent and limits of confidentiality. The perpetration and continuation of abuse relies on secrecy and the actual or implied threat of what would happen if the victim tells. The group members will all have had experience of the process of disclosure. Of course, the effects will be mixed but there is likely to be confusion between the concepts of confidentiality, privacy and secrecy. Dealing with a disclosure made in the course of a group session is complicated by group dynamics. It is vital that the group leaders have an agreed policy about what to do in the event of a disclosure as well as the awareness that these issues warrant more in-depth discussion throughout the course of the group.

Comment

As in individual work, therapists working in groups with young people who have been sexually abused have a duty of care to carry out that therapy in a 'very clear framework of child protection and in the best interests of the child' (Hunter, 2001). We are bound by local child protection guidelines, but the issues are more complex, and less clear-cut, than in individual work. Inevitably more than one other person hears any disclosure made within a group. Personal information and similar life stories are being shared all the time. There is the concern that other members of the group may have influenced any disclosure by putting ideas into another person's head. For this, among other reasons, the Crown Prosecution Service (CPS) does not approve of group work as a pre-trial therapy. If any disclosure should be made during a group it is unlikely to ever reach court. It can be difficult to maintain the balance between emotional containment within the group, by preserving privacy and trust, and not over-burdening a young person with all the responsibility for whether or not to pass on information. Again a good working relationship with colleagues who can appreciate your dilemma in the context of their own agency's objectives is important.

The Effect on the Group Leaders

It is difficult to describe adequately the complexity and severity of the difficulties experienced by adolescents who have been sexually abused. Both adolescent and therapist will be dealing with powerful and disturbing emotions. There are strong interpersonal processes inherent in the child protection and child abuse systems which affect the way professionals work individually and together, such as mirroring, false optimism and professional envies and jealousies (White, Essex and O'Reilly, 1993). Given the prevalence of sexual abuse, it is likely that many of the professionals in the field of child abuse will themselves have been abused as children or adolescents. In my experience of groups for young women the question of whether one or both of the therapists have been sexually abused is always present. This may or may not be verbalised, but it is a matter for the adults to consider carefully at the planning stage. It is important to agree on the levels of self-disclosure with which each of you feels comfortable, and is appropriate. The young women will need to feel emotional containment in the group in order to take the necessary chance with their own risky emotions. They may feel this is only possible with therapists who themselves have experienced abuse. The projection of these anxieties on to the therapists may make them feel that they have to justify their position as group leaders by stating whether or not they have been abused.

Comment

In fact such disclosures are not essential, and may, indeed, be counterproductive if mishandled in any way. What the young people are searching for is containment. This is supplied by the evidence that each group leader is able to hear about, discuss and empathise with their abusive experience without descending into powerlessness.

Working with adolescents in general is one of the more challenging areas of therapy. The relationship between adults and adolescents is a complex one. Adolescents hold both positive and negative symbolic meaning on behalf of adults such as hopes for the future or loss of potency. Adolescents usually have conflicting emotions about adults: they are dependent on them, but want to be separate from them. Adults can find themselves behaving in unfamiliar and ambivalent ways which can leave them feeling de-skilled and useless, as any parent of a teenager will testify. This is the working domain of the group therapist. It is complex and difficult but rewarding. It is important that therapists remain aware of their own needs and feelings and seek the appropriate ongoing support.

Conclusion

Group therapy makes an important contribution to the treatment of childhood sexual abuse as it has the potential to meet both the developmental and the therapeutic needs of adolescents. The positive outcomes include reducing the sense of isolation and shame, promoting self-esteem and trust, facilitating the recognition and expression of feelings, increasing the range and scope of coping strategies, and increased awareness of themselves and others.

Adolescents are more likely to accept comments, criticisms and ideas from their peers than from adults. Groups can offer a less intense environment than individual therapy where the focus is entirely on one person and any silence can be threatening, frightening and more noticeable. Groups also take a lot of time to plan and execute, involve a large number of professionals and can expose a therapist's personal and professional limitations and vulnerabilities in a way that individual work does not.

Perhaps the last comments should come from the young women themselves. The following is an amalgamation of the feedback from one of our groups:

I looked forward to every Tuesday because I knew I could come somewhere I felt safe and say what I wanted ... I know it's not just me now that feels like this ... I feel more confident and feel things are changing but I don't know how yet ... I want to understand more about what has happened to me ... It was good to talk to other people. I think I've made some new friends.

Recommended reading list

Benson, J.F. (1987) *Working More Creatively with Groups.* London: Routledge.

Dwivedi, K.N. (1993) *Group Work with Children and Adolescents. A Handbook.* London: Jessica Kingsley Publishers.

Evans, J. (1998) *Active Analytic Group Therapy with Adolescents.* London: Jessica Kingsley Publishers.

Friedrich, W.N. (1990) *Psychotherapy of Sexually Abused Children and their Families.* New York: W W Norton & Co.

Lane, D.A., and Miller, A. (Eds.) (1992) *Child and Adolescent Therapy. A Handbook.* Buckingham: Open University Press.

4.3 Group Work with Carers of Sexually Abused Children

Ann Catchpole

The duty

In 1989 the United Nations adopted the Convention on the Rights of the Child. Article 39 of this states that parties 'shall take all appropriate measures to promote physical and psychological recovery and social reintegration of a child victim of: any form of neglect, exploitation, or abuse; torture or any other form of cruel, inhuman or degrading treatment or punishment; or armed conflicts. Such recovery and reintegration shall take place in an environment which fosters the health, self-respect and dignity of the child.' At JACAT we believe that we should play our part in this essential work.

The Need

Some years ago the members of JACAT recognised that it was proving impossible to work with some children who had been abused: either they were failing to turn up for appointments or, when they did so, they showed a marked reluctance to engage with the worker in any useful way. Moreover, more recently, it became apparent that there was another set of children, equally worrying because of their obvious distress, where it would be extremely unwise to begin work with them because their home circumstances were such that they might have been placed at further risk had we attempted to do so. In neither situation was it a case of malicious or thoughtless adults preventing their children from receiving help, but rather a case of adults so traumatised by what had happened to their children that they found it impossible to create a climate in which such delicate work was possible.

This apparent impasse was frustrating to professionals, faced with distressed young people for whom no help seemed to be available, and to their parent or parents who desperately wanted their children helped to disclose what had happened to them. Particularly vulnerable to a sense of helplessness, and prone to incapacitating feelings of guilt, were those parents who had been themselves the victims of sexual abuse. Many had vowed that they would make sure that their children would never endure the same fate. They had assumed that they would be better able to protect their children than most parents, and yet the unthinkable had struck again in their family.

For some children it was the overwhelming anger shown by a family member, not only their father or an older brother but frequently their mother as well, that made them sense that a full disclosure would not be safe. Given that in our experience therapeutic intervention often leads in the short term to children's being more distressed and more likely to act out that distress in ways which make them more difficult for their parents to handle, it was obvious that left to their own devices such parents would never be able to cope if therapy were attempted.

The need for therapeutic intervention was clear in many cases. Though by no means all children who have been sexually abused will develop mental problems in later life, for some that is indeed the case. The coping mechanisms adopted by children may be influential in determining their health in both the long and the short-term. Whereas, in the short-term, avoidance techniques may provide a temporary cushion against excessive and unbearable distress, they may also in the long-term lead to mental illness. The experience of sexual abuse had left many of the children referred to us with their self-esteem shattered, their sense of identity warped, and their anger unmanageable. They showed their distress in a number of alarming ways, some of which would in turn add to their vulnerability to further harm. At the extreme end we saw teenagers engaged in self-harming behaviour: drug abuse, attempted suicide, self-mutilation, food-refusal, self-neglect, promiscuity and criminal offences. In the case of other children, often those in the younger age range, we sensed that the damage being done to them was not the direct result of the abuse itself but rather a result of the reactions of the adults in their lives to that abuse. These children often lacked the confidence to go out, regressed in their behaviour, became clingy and demanding, and suffered wide mood swings. Both age-groups were lacking in confidence and had a low sense of self-worth. It is, of course, possible that this characteristic may have been present before the abuse, since offenders tend to target children in this category because of their obvious vulnerability.

Recent research establishes a correlation between the ability of children to remain in therapy and the attitude and functioning of their family. Indeed, whereas research into adults who drop out of treatment shows a number of influential factors, such as the attitude of patients, the characteristics of therapists, and environmental and demographic differences, this appears not to be the case with children who drop out. Research (undertaken by Tingus et al., and quoted by Horowitz et al., 1996) found that one of the important factors in the attendance of children for treatment was the belief by the mother that the family needed therapy. In a study, covering 81 sexually abused girls between the ages of six and sixteen, it was found that the prime reason stated by the mother for putting the daughter into therapy was a desire to help her. This was cited by 61 per cent of the participants (cf. Horowitz et al., 1996). All this led us to believe that there could be many advantages in starting work with the parents even if work with the children might be required later.

The Means

Having made the decision to intervene through the parent or parents in the first instance, several options were possible. In some cases individual work with one or both parents seemed to offer the best starting point, but for others this seemed unlikely to be productive. Group work appeared to offer another, perhaps better, alternative. First, it was likely to provide faster results than individual work. Second, it had the advantage of providing an antidote to the isolation that plagued so many of the adults. Third, it offered the hope of on-going support, provided by the group members for one another, once the formal group was over. Fourth, it was attractive because it appeared to be economical in terms of time and personnel. However, as this chapter will show, groups are, in fact, both time consuming and, if they are to function well, require a good deal of support from other professionals not directly involved in running the group.

When we first mooted the idea of such groups and discussed their composition the most pressing need seemed to be to provide help for mothers, since in almost all cases it was mothers who had to bear the major responsibility for child care within the family. Indeed, in many families they were the sole remaining carer. Even in those families where a male non-abusing partner was present he was often not the father of the children but rather a later partner who had arrived on the scene after the abuse had been disclosed. We were already running groups for children who had been sexually abused, and had at the same time provided a support group for their carers. In most instances it was mothers, grandmothers, or female foster carers who attended these support groups, demonstrating the fact that they were either the sole carer of the young person who had been abused, or saw themselves as having the greater responsibility for care. In making the decision to work with mothers we were also acting on our belief that many mothers of children who had been sexually abused were subject to such levels of distress that they would find it very difficult to assist in the recovery of their children unless they received a great deal of help themselves. The conclusions of the *Report of the National Commission of Enquiry into the Prevention of Child Abuse* (1996) supports this approach. In the section on the traumatisation of parents it confirms that 'mothers were vulnerable to experience secondary traumatic stress because of their role as the primary support for their abused child' (Manion et al., 1996).

Many years of working as a field social worker with families in which sexual abuse occurred had served to convince me that the ability of the child to heal, and the family to emerge intact from that experience, hinged upon the robustness of response from the mother. Sadly many mothers, because of the abusive experiences they themselves had suffered, were not in a position to offer such a response.

In making the decision to offer groups for women only, we were also influenced by conversations with other professionals who reported that in many instances the women with whom they were involved were so influenced by their child's experience of an abusive male that they were quite unable to work with a male professional. That being so, it seemed unlikely that they would find it possible to tolerate the presence of men within the group. So that is how we began: a group of women carers working with women professionals.

Group Size

Group size was of considerable importance. Too large a group would inhibit quieter and more reticent members from speaking as well as allowing too little time for each person to contribute, while too small a group would leave its members feeling exposed and even pressurised into contributing, an effect which would be exacerbated if attendance were unreliable. The rule of thumb seems to us to be that the type of group you hope to have must determine its size. Large groups can be fine if their prime purpose is educational and the style of the teaching didactic. We, however, were looking for something different. We wanted to create a group in which it was possible for the members to share their common experiences, learn from each other and draw strength from their common purpose. We calculated that this meant that the group should be no larger than nine nor less than six in number. We felt that this would allow for a viable group even if two people were absent at any one time. In fact we discovered the hard way that smaller groups do pose the difficulties which we had anticipated. Against our better judgement we agreed to run one group for just four participants in order not to disappoint those who had been waiting for some time. It was enormously hard work from the start, both from the point of view of the members who, in such a small group, had nowhere to hide when they felt like listening rather than talking, and from the point of view of the leaders who felt they had to do much more of the talking than they wished. When the inevitable happened and one member ceased to attend, the problems were accentuated. It was not long before we were reduced to a week in which only one member came. Eventually the group was disbanded by mutual consent as it had ceased to operate as a group.

Our recent experiences with groups has proved, however, that a group of four can be viable where the four are sufficiently committed to the group that their attendance is as near to 100 per cent as circumstances permit. Indeed groups of that size provide a closeness and bonding which is greater than that seen in larger groups. However, it is probably unwise to start with less than five as the level of commitment is very difficult to gauge at interview, even by experienced practitioners. Indeed, it is likely that the women themselves are unable to predict it because, without experiencing the group, they have no means of testing out its appropriateness for them. 'Group life' has to be possible, and relatively easy to nurture.

Group Composition

When we began to run these groups in 1991 the prevailing wisdom was that one should not try to combine work with mothers whose children had been abused by a family member with those where the abuse was committed by someone outside the home. This was in line with the policy of social workers and police alike, which was to hold combined interviews where the abuse was intra-familial but to involve the police alone where it was extra-familial. The assumption on which this policy was based was that the latter was likely to involve fewer child protection issues. There was also a feeling that the abuse itself was likely to cause less distress because it did not involve a family member. Accordingly our first few groups were run for mothers of children who had been abused by someone from within their own home. We soon ran into a practical difficulty, however. On the waiting list at any one time were mothers whose children came into each of these categories, but there were never enough of a single category to constitute a group without an inordinately long waiting period. This had two disadvantages. Firstly, mothers who had requested help, or whose children were needing help, did not want to be kept waiting too long. If they were, they sometimes lost heart, or felt that the time for intervention had passed. Secondly, the professionals working with them lost heart, too, and in some cases ceased to refer parents to us for help. So, for pragmatic reasons in the first instance, the decision was taken to try out a group with mothers of children who came from both categories. This immediately stopped the long period of waiting and increased the demand.

The distinction between extra- and intra-familial abuse is in any case much more blurred than used to be thought. Finkelhor (1984) drew attention to the fact that there was a great body of abusers who did not come into the category of members of the immediate family but who were sufficiently attached to the family to fall outside the category of stranger. In a sub-section of chapter five of his book, headed *No Distinction Between Intra- and Extra-Familial Abuse*, he writes:

> *Much prior theorising about sexual abuse has revolved around either (1) the psychodynamics of sex abusers or (2) the family-systems model of father-daughter incest. However, a great deal of sexual abuse falls in neither category. Many children are abused by members of their*

extended families who are not paedophiles and not fathers: for example, brothers, uncles and grandfathers . . . Many other children are abused by baby-sitters and neighbours who are also not paedophiles.

Our referrals at JACAT indicated that many of the children of the women who were seeking to join our group were neither abused by a family member nor by a complete stranger. They were abused by men who were well known to the family, either as friends of the family or as friends at work. These men were not family members but they were certainly not strangers. Indeed the way in which they were able to gain and maintain access to a child was by making themselves welcome within the family by such actions as baby-sitting. Thus, their acceptance by the adults within the family meant that many of the feelings present in the parents of children who were victims of intra-familial abuse were also present for them: guilt at inadvertently exposing their child to danger, consternation at their lack of judgement in letting such a person into the family, worry that they had not seen what was going on and also that their child had not felt able to confide in them. It is noteworthy that in all the groups I have run there has not been a single incidence of a child's having been abused by a stranger.

There were, however, other matters to be considered in respect of the composition of the group. The most important of these was to ensure that no one was isolated within it, particularly in terms of the age of their children or the type of abuse their children had experienced. A range of ages seemed quite acceptable, indeed even beneficial, but we would not have liked to have had a group in which the members' children were all, for example, of pre-school age except for one member who had only teenagers. We could not, of course, rule out all differences. In fact the groups' diversity was often their strength. We found, for instance, that it was possible to work with women with widely varying intellectual ability, incorporating within a single group a woman with acute learning difficulties and another who had experienced higher education. The area of difference which was most influential seemed to be the length of time since the abuse was disclosed, though even here there were exceptions to the general rule that progress was greatest among those who had known about the abuse longest. The women said they struggled most with the varying views of group members about the veracity of the disclosure. Leaders should be aware that failure to believe her child, or even an ambivalent attitude, may make a woman unacceptable to the group. So also may too lenient an attitude towards the abuser, though in groups where one of the mothers has a son who is both victim and perpetrator such a view is better tolerated. It is, I believe, arguable that complete disbelief that her child has been abused should disqualify a woman from joining such a group. Often, however, the position is less clear-cut than this, and the risk of inclusion may be taken.

Case Study – Disbelief

Mary came to the group and at the end of our first session admitted to me that she was far from sure that her child had been abused, though she understood the concerns of the professionals that this had happened. Gradually, as a result of conversations within the group, Mary became convinced that her child had, indeed, been abused and by week five she reported back to the group that she had made a phone call on her way home from the previous session in which she had informed her ex-husband that he could no longer have unsupervised access to their child.

Group Leadership

It might be possible to run this type of group on one's own, but there would be many disadvantages into doing so. The nature of the issues is such that the sessions are, at times, distressing for participants and leaders alike. It is also essential to keep a careful eye on all the members, something which is not easy if one is also planning one's next intervention and watching how the time is progressing. When there are two leaders the situation is markedly different. To give one example, it is possible for one of them to leave the room or return late from a break if a member needs comforting away from the rest of the group. There are other advantages, too. Having two leaders gives an opportunity for more diversity of background and allows a less experienced worker to learn from the example of the other. Moreover, on a practical level, should one leader be absent unavoidably through illness, it is still possible for the group to go ahead. However, the biggest advantage of all comes from the support that one leader is able to give the other. This is particularly important because of the way in which strong feelings of anger, guilt or despair can easily be transferred from group member to group leader, leaving her feeling overwhelmed by a sense of powerlessness. If those who run the groups feel safe in doing so then so will those who participate in the groups.

Case Study – Numbers

Recently a group which began in a very promising fashion, with members sharing information freely, and seven people present, took a serious turn downhill with attendance becoming erratic and numbers often reduced to two or three. The effect on the two of us was demoralising, and it was difficult not to let this spill over into the sessions with those who remained. Had there been only one of us I feel we would have given up. As it was we persevered and managed to stabilise the numbers at three and in the end concluded that the group had been beneficial for those who remained.

We have been able to exploit to the full and in a very special way the diversity made possible by having two group leaders. On one occasion I was able to co-lead a group with someone who had herself been a member of one of our early groups and was contemplating undertaking social work training. This gave an added dimension to the leadership, and was most appreciated by the women who attended. They saw the distance she had travelled, and they took heart at the thought that they might do the same. On other occasions I have worked with secondees to JACAT from both health and social services as well as a member of the Child and Adolescent Mental Health team.

JACAT's belief is that we all work very much better when supported and assisted by each other. We do not have a hierarchical system and therefore no formal system of supervision, but our team meetings at which consultations, referrals and on-going work is rigorously discussed by all one's colleagues, provide informal supervision, and each substantial piece of work that we undertake is open to the possibility of supervision by a colleague. Groups are no exception. Accordingly, when we decided to run our groups for mothers we asked an experienced colleague to act as our back-up. This meant that she would participate in the setting up of the group and in the preparation of the programme, and that she would provide on-going support for us, its leaders. This she did by meeting with us regularly throughout the course to discuss its progress and to enable us to off-load our concerns. She proved invaluable in helping us to identify matters that were holding the group back and in encouraging us to persevere when the going was difficult.

Course and Session Length

The length of each session has varied according to who has been leading the various groups, but the variation has not been great. None has been shorter than one and a half hours or longer than two. This seems to allow sufficient time for sharing, discussion and teaching and, with a short break in the middle, does not exhaust people's powers of concentration. For the leaders, whose involvement is extended by about an hour on either side of the group, by preparation and post mortem, it still means that it can be concluded in half a day. Course length was determined largely by pragmatic considerations, though we also felt it essential to avoid having large gaps between sessions. As our mothers have children who are at school, child-care considerations dictate that we break for half-term and avoid holding groups in the holidays. Accordingly groups run broadly in conjunction with the school terms, which means that they are about twelve weeks long.

Preparation of Participants

Although we relied on our referrers, who were all professionals, to ensure that those they referred were ready for such a group, we nonetheless believed that it was important to meet each potential member of the group before making our final selection. Referrers themselves varied in their understanding of what the group had to offer and also in their knowledge of changing circumstances within the life of the person they had referred. The latter was particularly the case when their involvement in the case had not extended beyond the investigation of the abuse. So every potential group member was met by one or other group leader to try to ascertain their preparedness for the group. Matters such as the level of the support they might expect from friends and family were checked out, their current attitude to the abuse and the abuser talked over, and the extent to which it was possible for them to discuss these things explored. It was clear that if they could not talk to us on an individual level it was most unlikely that they would be able to do so in a group situation. Some of those to whom we spoke felt most concern about their ability to hear about other people's pain without its adding to their own burden so much as to make it unbearable. We could only acknowledge that this was a very real dilemma: one of which we were aware and with which we would do our best to assist, but one about which, in the end, they would have to make a judgement. We could only point out that the support offered by the group, and the strength they would be able to gain from each other, were likely to outweigh the disadvantages. In practice this has proved to be the case, almost without exception, but I believe that our constant reiteration of the difficulties women will experience in the weeks before the group coheres has paid off and resulted in very high attendance rates.

Case Study – Attendance

The one group which experienced difficulties in maintaining attendance appeared to do so because so many of its members experienced major life changes very early on in the course of the group. One member developed what she feared to be womb cancer, one member's daughters disclosed sexual abuse by a family member on top of the abuse by a neighbour which was already known. Two members had traumatic court cases that did not go well. One member had to contend with her son's undergoing a serious operation and another moved house.

The meetings before the group began were also an opportunity for checking out that the infrastructure which would make attendance possible was present. Regular attendance, which brings the most reward, is hard enough in terms of the commitment and courage it requires, without practical difficulties adding further complications. We needed to make sure that those who had pre-school children could find alternative care for them on group days, and that transport to meetings of the group was available. This is particularly difficult in rural areas, such as Devon, where buses may be infrequent or even non-existent. Few of the women had cars or friends with cars, and even if they had, they might need help with the cost of petrol. We did find that, where there were car owners, they were extremely willing to help out with picking up other group members even when they were complete strangers before the group began. Where any of these practicalities could not be solved by the women themselves it was time to enlist the help of their referrers. It is, in these circumstances, a distinct advantage that JACAT does not take referrals straight from the public but only from professionals such as doctors, health visitors and social workers. The support of social workers and health care professionals was absolutely essential in ensuring that the mothers could attend the group. Some needed help with child-care, some with transport arrangements and some needed the actual presence of their social worker to ensure that they reached the first meeting. We found that most of the women did not have anyone else who could help them with either the practical or the emotional difficulties of attending.

At the same time as checking out these practical matters we also took the opportunity to explore the basic details of their family structure and the facts of the abuse. Though we did not probe, it gave the women a chance to alert us to any particularly delicate areas for them with which they might struggle within the group. Information concerning their own abuse was often forthcoming, bringing in its wake much additional pain and an increased sense of guilt.

Case Study – Peer pressure

One woman who applied for an early group and whose children had all been taken into care, though she still had contact with them and was working towards their return home, admitted to me her fears that the group might be antagonised by these facts. Nothing could have been further from the truth. The group was well able to understand the pressure she had been under from the children's abuser which had led her to doubt her children at first.

We had members of later groups with the same anxieties but on no occasion were their fellow members antagonistic to them, always demonstrating a high level of sympathy and understanding of the difficulties that must have led to such an event.

In addition to the other advantages of meeting beforehand it was beneficial both to us and to them to know some people within the group from the very beginning. I am sure that it made attendance possible for some who would otherwise never have come. In one or two cases we were able to alert their referrers to the fact that they might need the extra encouragement of being physically brought to the first meeting. Occasionally even this was not enough.

In trying to ascertain why some groups stay together when others disintegrate we came to the conclusion that one material difference between the two was timing. Though the difficulties experienced by group members during the life-time of the group were similar in kind and severity in every group it was much easier for them to bring their difficulties to the group and to experience its support if the group had been functioning for a few weeks and had attained a corporate identity. In those groups where a particular member faced a particularly difficult new situation or development, before the group had established its identity and was offering a strong degree of support, it was possible that she would choose to leave the group.

The Programme

The programme for these groups has to be carefully thought out but also sufficiently flexible to take account of the group's own agenda which will be revealed as the weeks pass. Our prime objective, as already indicated, was clear. We wanted to make it possible for the mothers to offer their children the support they needed and to provide for their children the sort of home environment in which they could be healed. In some cases this might mean that their children would be able to accept therapeutic help for the first time. To do this we felt that it would be necessary to help the mothers to look at their fears and feelings as well as their own patterns of behaviour prior to and after the abuse. We also hoped to help them learn more about the possible causes and effects of abuse, including how those effects might be addressed and reduced. Thus we were looking to create a group that was therapeutic in atmosphere while incorporating a certain element of teaching. We understood that group dynamics would ensure that much of the work was done by the group itself, providing we succeeded in establishing the right atmosphere.

We anticipated that many of the women would arrive each week burdened by the past week's events. We determined, therefore, to set aside sufficient time at the start of each group to allow for the sharing of news. These we called our 'good news, bad news' sessions. We also assumed that the women would need help in establishing an atmosphere of trust and in beginning to make personal relationships. We were aware, too, that there might be some who found it almost impossible to speak out in front of the whole group but who might manage better on a one-to-one basis. We tried to cater for all these eventualities by incorporating into the early sessions at least one item which involved talking in pairs. Later this item could involve feedback to the group which helped the less confident members to begin to share things more widely. The middle part of each session was planned as the meat in the sandwich. This was the time when the topic of the day could be covered in some depth. We believed that it would be necessary to help the group unwind before going home, especially since some of the sessions might have been gruelling and might have stirred up unhappy memories or strong feelings. Sometimes this winding down exercise could double up as the pairs exercise in order to save time. We were conscious, too, that many of the women were likely to have had their self-esteem severely diminished by what had happened to their family, so we attempted to include some activities which might bolster this again.

When we met to make plans for the first few sessions we decided that one of the most important things on our agenda must be to try to establish the areas which the group itself wanted us to cover and then to incorporate these into our future planning. Accordingly we did not set out to plan in advance more than the first two sessions in detail.

We felt that we could encourage the learning process within group members, as well as allowing them to explore in more depth topics in which they were particularly interested, by making available to them some of the books from our extensive and specialist library. These could be brought up week by week and signed for when they were taken out. In this way we were able to supply material concerning topics such as divorce, domestic violence and the effects on children of constant disruption in the home. These were all likely to be relevant to the group but might not be central to the issues for all of them. Similarly we were able to provide photocopies of relevant articles and material that we had found helpful when working with abused children which they could also borrow. We provided both adult and children's books on a variety of subjects, mostly but not exclusively related to abuse.

The Group Experience

Many of the assumptions we had made about running the groups were borne out in practice in our first ever series of groups. The time which we had set aside at the beginning of each meeting for the sharing of news proved invaluable. However, we had seriously underestimated how much time would be needed in each session. On some occasions the nature of the material and the number of issues it raised was such that the whole of the first hour had to be dedicated to exploring it. This was never wasted time. Apart from its obvious therapeutic value for the women themselves, most of whom had very inadequate support systems outside the group, many topics were covered at these times that would have had to be raised later anyway. If we had needed an illustration of the ripple effect of abuse on all those who are touched by it we would certainly have found one. It seemed to reach every part of their lives. In the first group alone, within the first three meetings, much was said about the worries which they each had about the behaviour of their children, of their own new relationships breaking down, and of the difficulties caused by access visits made by the children to their abusing parent. In later groups members spoke of impending court cases, of interviews with the police, of difficulties experienced in trying to sell the family home, of sexual problems, of children in trouble with the law, and of many of their children's difficulties with school work and with peer-group relationships.

The need for time spent in one-to-one discussion seemed to vary from group to group. One group found it very helpful in cementing relationships.

Case Study – Peer support

One of its members, whose mood was dramatically lightened after such a discussion, was able to comment on this in the following session. During the giving of her news she attributed this improvement directly to another group member. This member's idea of encouraging her to write down her thoughts and feelings in a notebook had proved most helpful. Her comments about the assistance she had received were, in turn, helpful to the member who had given that help.

Other groups have found it quite impossible to stick to the formula and have reverted to speaking together as a whole group almost immediately. In recent groups we have dropped the use of such one-to-one sessions, while bearing in mind they may be needed in future sessions.

There has been some discrepancy, too, in the feelings of the different groups about the benefits of the winding down sessions. One group found these necessary and helpful, whereas another group invariably sabotaged our efforts. On those rare occasions when we did appear to have succeeded in ending on a low-key note they would continue to talk after the session had ended and thus wind themselves up again. In fact we made an adjustment in our practice in order to try to accommodate this group's need to continue discussions after the session had ended. They used to meet in the corridors or outside the front door, neither of which provided a confidential environment, so we offered them the continued use of the room for a short time after the session was over. The provision of the room allowed them to conduct their own winding down sessions, which in fact they did effectively. However, if this devise is used it is important to make sure that everyone knows that the group is officially finished, the leaders off duty, and all are free to go home.

The Effect of Having a Clearly Identified Theme

We had been ready for the rapid progress that group work often engenders but not for the speed with which these groups were prepared to discuss difficult issues. Our intention was to conduct matters in a gentle way, taking our pace from the group and not pressurising anyone into making a contribution before she felt ready. We had expected that the more difficult topics would take weeks to surface and that, in some cases, they would only do so if we took the initiative. This proved to be far from the case. From the first day some members were able to share some of the most intimate areas of their lives with the group. Feelings of anger and guilt were aired early on, too. In fact it became one of our most pressing tasks as group leaders to try to ensure that people did not overstep the mark in a way that might make them feel vulnerable later. The members of one of the most vociferous groups showed themselves aware of this danger. However, the group with which we have had most difficulty, about which I have already written, in the Case Study – Numbers, probably suffered from erratic attendance in part because of our inability, as leaders, to prevent them from sharing deeply personal material, in great detail, on their first meeting. Nevertheless, such revelations are part of the group experience and are not usually a problem.

Case Study – Showing personal material

On one occasion when a group member did not turn up for a session, having revealed quite a lot about herself the previous week, the rest of the group were anxious lest it had been that which had kept her away. At their request we sent her a card saying that we missed her and hoped she would be returning the following week. She did, making clear that her absence had been for quite another reason.

The open acknowledgement by the group leaders at the very start of the first meeting of our reason for being there, and indeed before that, in our individual meetings with the potential participants, was of vital importance. However, in itself it would not have been enough. We had to make sure that the members themselves brought the topic to the fore from the beginning. Thus every person, at each group, is asked to tell the group her name, the names of her child or children, and which of them had been abused. They are also asked how long ago the abuse happened and how recently it was disclosed. The nature of the relationship of the abuser to the family, if any, is also requested. All this information is carefully recorded on a flip chart and makes a useful focal point as well as an *aide-memoire* for future sessions. Many women volunteer considerably more information than this, some of which they ask to be written up. In some instances this includes the name of the abuser which they have not uttered in public before. For many this is the first time that they had spoken in such a way about their experiences, and it is obvious what a relief it is to be able to do so.

It seems likely that it was the common agenda of abuse of which everyone was aware, and which was present as a topic from the start, which may have been the reason for this phenomenally quick venture into topics at depth. However, it is imperative that group leaders are aware that the pace has to suit everyone, and some may not be ready for too much revelation too early.

The Impact of Isolation

In our early deliberations about the benefits of running groups, rather than working with individuals, we had identified the opportunity of ending the isolation induced by abuse as one of our prime targets. Indeed, it seems to be the case that social isolation is often a factor which makes abuse more possible, as well as being a possible result of it. In an interesting study undertaken in Australia recently, which was aimed at identifying the risk factors for child sexual abuse, social isolation was found to be a significant indicator, particularly in children of under twelve (Fleming et al., 1997). There was plenty to confirm that this was a common factor throughout the groups. A poignant incident illustrated this clearly.

Case Study – Personal isolation 1

One week one of the women reported the fact that it had been her birthday the previous week. She was asked if she had had a lot of cards. She replied that she had had just one, and that she had bought that one herself so that her four-year-old daughter could give it to her. There was a stunned silence in the group after she made this statement, as the degree of her isolation struck all of us.

Even those who, on the face of it, appear to have people in whom they could confide, do not in fact do so. Many women who have formed new relationships are reluctant themselves to involve their partners in matters relating to the abuse. It was noteworthy that, in the first group, in all cases but one, the women had separated from the father of their child. This was true even for those families where the abuse was committed by someone who was not a member of the family unit. It continued to be the case for the majority of women in future groups. Indeed, in most groups fewer than half their members had a partner at all. Also few women had a wider family circle which could be described as really supportive. Some had had to leave their wider family behind as they fled to Devon to escape from domestic violence. Some were totally alienated from the rest of their family. When this was the situation they seemed to be carrying the blame for the effect that abuse had had upon the family as originally constituted. This was particularly likely to be the case where the abuser had been another family member.

Case Study – Personal isolation 2

In an early group a woman reported that her daughter's abuser had been the child's uncle, her own brother. She and her children were left isolated because the grandparents sympathised with the abuser, rather than the victim, and blamed their granddaughter for the spell he had to spend in prison. She was particularly devastated by the loss of support from her own mother, not only on her own account but even more on her daughter's account.

Often the women in the groups reported considerable pressure from other family members who wanted them to show sympathy to the offender and to welcome him back into the fold. This only added to the pain they were already experiencing as they faced up to the part played by an erstwhile beloved family member. They could, in most cases, appreciate the dilemma faced by their parents who loved both their children and saw one of them spending time in prison. For some women the dilemma was only too painfully obvious as they struggled to come to terms with the fact that one of their own children, not necessarily the one known to have been abused, was beginning to show sexualised behaviour which bordered on the abusive.

Though the women obviously found the group experience beneficial we, nonetheless, had to fight against the tendency to try to deal with particularly difficult matters with individual group leaders rather than within the group itself. It is, of course, impossible to brush someone aside who comes to you in obvious distress requesting a few minutes of your time. However, we felt it was important to encourage the group member to bring to the group, on her own, or with our help, matters which we had been discussing one to one. This, in most cases, they were able to do most successfully, and it contributed hugely to the group identity's remaining intact. Where this was not possible, or where further help was needed, we felt it necessary to suggest that help be sought elsewhere for individual problems which were outside the scope of the group, either because of their content or the attention they required.

Expressing Feelings

We had identified the need for the women to be able to recognise and express their feelings if they were to benefit from the group. This was a useful exercise in itself, but it also had the merit of helping them to identify the feelings of their children and to begin to see from where those feelings came. They were quick to spot the mirroring that takes place between mother or parents and child, and to understand that this had ramifications for their children's ability to heal. Only if they could come to terms with their feelings of guilt and anger, sometimes misdirected internally and leading to acute depression, or dealt with inappropriately by a retreat into drink or drugs, could their children learn to do the same thing. They began to see tangible evidence that movement in their lives could bring about movement in the lives of their children. The very fact that they had come to the group had, in some cases, been enough to alert their children to the fact that they were taking some action to try to improve their circumstances. Then, when they began to take books home, some for themselves and some to share with their children, it became even more apparent to these children that abuse was no longer a taboo subject. There were reports of children talking about the abuse willingly for the first time, or about the possibility of having discussions about other family matters which had been barred before.

We did, however, find it necessary at times to keep a curb on some of the feelings that were being expressed, as these threatened to overwhelm the group. This was particularly the case in the first few sessions of most groups, when anger, towards the police, and towards social workers, and towards society, for what they perceived as their failure to get justice for their children, raged around the group. Such anger was not surprising in view of the catalogue of crimes committed and the paucity of action taken, let alone conviction secured. Out of the thirteen women who attended the first two groups only one reported that the perpetrator had served a gaol sentence, and he had been convicted following his own admission of the offence. In one other case the man had been gaoled for another more serious offence, having abused her child while out on bail. She had been told that he could not be tried for the offence against her child. There were also immensely strong feelings present against the men who had abused their children. In some cases threats of vengeance were made, often in the form of murder. Many women were clearly frightened by the strength of these feelings. The absence of a trial, let alone a conviction, added hugely to their sense of grievance. Seldom is there more than one successful conviction within the group, and sometimes there are no instances of court proceedings at all.

Case Study – Strong feelings

One spoke of the fear she had of any man whom she saw riding a motorbike, because that was the form of transport chosen by her partner. When she analysed this she realised that she did not fear what he would do to her but rather what she might do to him. She used to find herself getting up close to such men and staring into their visor to check out that it was not her ex-partner.

We employed several devices to help the women look at their feelings and attempt to analyse their depth and the extent to which they were being helped or handicapped by them. They seemed to find it helpful when we were able to do this pictorially or in chart form. Using the flip chart, we asked them to place themselves on the railway-line of life. This was a helpful metaphor for it enabled them to place themselves in tunnels, on bridges, at stations or faced with inclines or declines. It provided a very graphic description of where they felt themselves to be. By doing this near the beginning of the course, and then looking at it again at the end, it was possible for them to see what progress they had made. Throughout the sessions we deliberately employed some methods of working which we might use when working with children. We identified these and explained that we were using them, both because they were useful tools in their own right but also so that they might gain some insight into the ways in which we worked with children. This, in some cases, gave them the inspiration to be more adventurous in their ways of communicating with their own children. This had the added advantage of adding to the element of fun in the group. One week, for instance, instead of going round the room telling people the news we all took it in turns to *draw* our news. On another occasion we mimed it. Since neither of the leaders was good at either acting or drawing this caused much mirth.

The Link between Physical Violence and Sexual Abuse

In recent years it has come to be recognised that men who sexually abuse their children are often physically violent towards their partners. Recent studies in Australia and in this country have indicated that domestic violence is very common in families where the man is sexually abusing the children. When talking to women who had been sexually abused as children, researchers (Fleming et al., 1997) discovered that 'the strongest predictor of CSA was physical abuse, with those girls subjected to physical abuse having an odds ratio of 11 for CSA. In addition physical abuse remained the strongest predictor for CSA that began both before and after the age of 12 and for familial and non-familial CSA.' Several instances of such violence were reported within our groups. In some it had been accompanied by physical abuse towards their children, too. In others, where this was not the case, it was apparent that it was this very violence towards themselves that lulled the women into a false sense of security where their children were concerned. They believed that by taking so much punishment they were protecting their children. It was devastating for the mothers in our group to discover that their endurance of violence from their partner had not, after all, protected their child, as another form of abuse had been going on all the time. Sacrificing themselves had been in vain. The fear of vengeance led to their postponing the time when they left their partner and extended the time during which their children could be abused, for their children were unable to reveal what had happened to them while the abuser was still in the house. The propensity for the threat of violence towards mothers to lessen their ability to protect their children is attested in a book by Marianne Hester, Chris Pearson and Nicola Harwin, who write:

> Both Hooper (1992) and Forman (1995) argue, on the basis of their studies concerning mothers of sexually abused children, that the sexual abuse of children could be seen as constituting domestic violence or abuse in relation to the mothers. The violence to the mothers also served to distance them as a source of support to the children, so that the men could more easily continue their sexual abuse.
>
> (Hester et al., 1889)

The recognition of all this only added to their sense of guilt. Thus it was not surprising that these women needed many weeks of help from the group before they could allow themselves to look at the damage that had been done to them by that violent relationship with their partner. Assurance had to be given over and over again that this was not only a reasonable thing for them to do but would also benefit their children in the long run. Dong and his colleagues (2004) offer a useful study of the co-occurrence of various types of abuse and domestic violence.

Health Matters

A subject which provoked much discussion and for which we had not bargained was that of the women's physical health. We had anticipated that there would be referrals to the group of women with quite severe mental health problems, and this proved to be the case. We had also assumed that there would be others whose depression was masked and for whom the group might prove the cause of its revelation, but we had not anticipated the extent to which their physical wellbeing would be threatened. It is, perhaps, significant that many of their physical problems were gynaecological. Moreover, without exception they were experiencing real difficulties in taking these problems to the doctor or in following up the doctor's advice for further tests or treatment. Some had put up with painful and distressing symptoms for many months without even reporting them. Again this seemed to arise in part from their sense that it was improper to focus on their own ills when their children had suffered so horribly and, in the case of those who had been abused themselves as children, from a fear of intimate examinations, especially by a male.

As well as the gynaecological problems experienced, most of the women complained of difficulties in sleeping, often associated with night-fears and night-mares, of headaches, stomach ache and back ache, of a tendency to over-eat or to starve themselves. Although at least one member of each group was referred by a mental health worker and had a diagnosable mental health problem, generally depression, the rest of the women fell outside the remit of the mental health service though they suffered considerable mental distress.

Sexual Abuse and its Impact on Sexual Relationships

Before we began the groups, we had assumed that there would be some women in the groups who had themselves been child victims of sexual abuse. Indeed there were. However, it was noticeable that they were extremely reticent about bringing up the matter even when talking about other sensitive issues in their lives. In one of the groups we ran it was not mentioned at all and in another it only surfaced late on in the sessions. Again there was possibly an element of feeling that what had happened to them was unimportant. However, it seems likely that they were mirroring the difficulty that children experience in disclosing. Their fragile self-esteem would have taken another blow if they had revealed their own abuse. Those who were able to talk about it, instantly made apparent the necessity for doing so. They were able to admit that the abuse their children had experienced had brought memories of their own abuse flooding back. Feelings which they believed to have been dealt with long ago surfaced again, and the whole experience served greatly to reduce their capacity for handling their children's grief.

In view of the presence of a number of women within the groups who had been sexually abused it was, perhaps, not surprising that another common theme was their difficulties with their own intimate relationships. It is rare for a group member to be in a relationship with her original partner, even if her children have been abused by someone other than a family member. Some women do form relationships but many of these are problematic. Their children's exposure to sexual abuse seems to have impaired their trust to such an extent that it is not surprising their relationships are affected. For some this impairment is so complete that they cannot contemplate ever allowing a man near them again. More than half of all group members are alone with their children. Their distrust is not directed principally towards men but rather towards themselves. They reason that if they have chosen so poorly in the past, how can they be sure that they will not do so again? This is a theme that surfaced again and again, causing many of them to suffer considerable unhappiness as they saw themselves condemned to live without the support of an intimate relationship. Those whose relationships were causing them concern looked to the group to give them strength to contemplate their termination. In some cases this happened.

The distrust which the women felt towards their new partners was directed in particular to their partner's relationships with their children. Almost all of them found it difficult to consider them in the role of father and tended to keep the parental duties firmly in their own hands. They reported their unease about leaving their children with their partner, and said that they found themselves looking at quite normal games and activities with suspicion. If their partner treated the children kindly, they thought he must be grooming them for future abuse. If he chastised them for wrong doing, they felt resentful because of all the children had suffered. In some cases they felt unable to take their partners into their confidence over matters relating to their children's abuse. This must have led to great confusion on the part of their partners, especially when their homes were invaded by police or social workers, some of whom were still on the scene long after the event. The women's attendance at the group was also not always explained to their partners. Not surprisingly, therefore, they found those partners less than adequate in their support. We used a video called The Other Victim, which highlighted the plight of other family members who were also deeply affected by the abuse, to illustrate how their husbands, partners or sons might be feeling. It had a tremendous impact upon most groups, forcing the women to look realistically at the experiences of their partners and to think of ways in which it might be possible to include them more in their children's lives.

The prevalence of such difficult themes, and the request of the women themselves, encouraged us to offer an advanced group to those members who wanted to attend. It was more usual for women to explore their sexual difficulties within this second group. Although these groups were formed from some members of each of the previous two starter groups and, therefore, had to create a new group identity, this took place very quickly. By the end of the second group the members would have spent more than twenty-four sessions with half the group and twelve with the other half. This seemed to give them the confidence to look more closely at difficult issues.

Difficulties over Contact

In setting up the groups we had anticipated that the subject of contact between the child and the abusing parent would arise frequently, and in this we were correct. Most of the mothers were able to understand that their children should see their father if they so wished, though it went against the grain to allow them to do so. They felt the need to keep some control over this so as to protect their children, but found it difficult to adopt a strong line and insist on their taking a supervisory role, and they were not happy to allow their partner's parents to take this role. For most, contact was a constant source of worry to the mother, and anxiety and distress to the child. This was so even when the arrangements had been determined by the court. Several of the women felt that they had been too intimidated by a violent partner to argue for the pattern with which they would feel comfortable. In some cases they felt strongly that contact should stop altogether because of the adverse affect it was having, but felt powerless to prevent it. A complicating factor for many of them was their resentment that their child should still want to see someone whom they now considered beyond the pale because of the abuse he had committed. For those mothers who felt that they had a poor relationship with their daughter this was especially distressing, as they experienced their daughter's anger and resentment directed against them instead of against the abusing parent. Paradoxically these were often women who had, in earlier days, fallen foul of the authorities because of their unwillingness to accept their child's disclosure and, therefore, their opposition to co-operating with the plans of social services for the safety of their children. In some cases this had cost them the support that they needed.

Nurturing the Group

In planning the programme for our groups we bore in mind that the women we were working with were likely to be suffering from low morale. It seemed sensible, therefore, to try to introduce some group activities that they might enjoy, and which might indeed reveal hidden talents. Accordingly we experimented in some of the early groups with the use of painting as a medium for self-expression. We were not very confident about handling its introduction but found that, after some initial uncertainty, all the women participated readily and seemed to find it fun. They were able to use their pictures to explain their feelings to the group and, in some cases, to take their work home and share it with their children. This, in turn, enabled them to open up a worthwhile conversation around the topic of abuse and feelings with their children. We also encouraged group members to share with the group as a whole anything which they had found helpful: some brought a book or a poem, others a picture or a plant, others still a favourite tape. More recently we have asked them to use collages as a way of sharing information and demonstrating their feelings. However, groups have varied enormously in what they have found beneficial.

As part of our nurturing programme we made sure that the facilities were comfortable, that there was a plentiful supply of coffee, tea and cold drinks, and that the biscuits were chocolate! For those members of the group who were trying to lose weight we also made sure that fruit was available. At the beginning of the course we supplied them all with notebooks and pens. The group rapidly adopted a similarly considerate attitude to one another. This was particularly noticeable when anyone was absent for any reason, or when someone was known to be going through a difficult time.

Case Study – Sisterhood

One member had to leave the group unexpectedly as she went to care for a sick relative in a different part of the country. We kept up a weekly correspondence with her until the end of the group which both she and the group appreciated.

We believed that the way in which the groups ended would be just as important as the way in which they had begun. We used different techniques to mark them as special. With one group we took photographs and gave them each copies. This seemed to be particularly appreciated, as it was a tangible reminder of the group's membership. We distributed certificates of excellence to others. This was partly a fun exercise but there was a serious aspect to it as well, because all the compliments were rightly earned. Each group took away messages from all the members. On one occasion we used large sheets of paper, one for each person, and asked everyone to write a message for every other member. Later we refined this by using cards for everyone, which had the advantage of being more easily displayed and kept. The group leaders were included in this activity. It was very moving to read the words of encouragement that they had for one another and for us as leaders.

We had understood that it would be difficult for the women to finish the group and, as well as making the ending as memorable as possible, we had thought hard about some way of enabling members to remain in touch with each other once the group had ended. Several weeks before the end we began to discuss the possibilities ahead of them. The first group was adamant that there were matters that they wished to explore in greater depth, and requested that we consider running a follow-up group. As we were committed to running another 'starter' group it was not likely to be possible to do this until the following year. So they opted for two reunion meetings. These were set for the end of the summer holidays and Christmas. They were to take the form of a buffet meal to which we would all contribute and which would be held in our usual meeting place. To our surprise these were very poorly attended. Accordingly we did not expect that there would be many takers for the advanced group. This proved to be quite wrong. When it came to doing the work we had almost 100% attendance for the follow-up group.

The second group opted for a different means of continuing support, though they also indicated that they would like to participate in a further group if one became available. They chose to try to run an informal support group of their own, meeting in each other's houses on a regular basis. They, too, struggled with getting this off the ground. Only three of the seven group members attended the planning group, and few further meetings took place.

As a result of seeing the way in which all the groups had struggled to provide on-going support for themselves, we decided that the time had come to offer something ourselves which might fulfil this need. Accordingly at the end of 2000 we agreed to run an on-going support group, a follow-up group (known affectionately as FUG) which would be open to all group members from then onwards. It would meet four times a year at JACAT, offering lunch and an opportunity to share news and discuss problems, progress and achievements. It has met for nearly five years now and attendance continues to be good.

Attendance

Once the first three weeks of the starter groups are over, during which time people tend to be erratic in their coming, it is our experience that attendance is exceptionally high. There are occasional absences but these are always for unavoidable reasons, mostly ill health on the part of themselves or their children.

The first few weeks have posed a problem in almost every group that we have run, with some coming on the first week and then missing the second and others joining only on the second or third week. Absences early on have meant that we have had to work hard to create the group identity, which has led to some unavoidable repetition of material. Two things seem to be crucial here. The first is to let the group members themselves be the final arbiter about the possibility of starting late. They have been more relaxed about this than we might have been as leaders, and they have shown the capacity to carry it off. The second is to encourage the group itself to determine how much of the ground which we have already covered they want to share with latecomers. Again they have been prepared to repeat material which is both personal and painful. This magnanimity seems to spring from an understanding of just how difficult it is to make the initial move to join the group, and a wish for others to have an opportunity to participate in what they regard as a worthwhile venture.

As group leaders we have felt it necessary to ask that everyone stay to the end of each group meeting unless it is quite impossible to do so. We realised that there would be times when other engagements, such as doctor's appointments, would have to take precedence but we have not been prepared for anyone to join the group who has had to leave early on a regular basis. We did, however, by mutual agreement, tinker with the times of starting and finishing in order to accommodate group members.

Messages for Other Professionals

Work with these groups has helped to highlight a number of matters that could be of relevance to other professionals working in the field of child abuse. It might be helpful to summarise these here.

Much of the early child protection work centred on the threat posed by strangers. When some research was undertaken to test how effective this work had been it found that 'traditional stranger-danger education concentrates on warning children against strangers making offers, and the evidence suggests that, although the older children are beginning to get this message, too many children at all ages seem unaware of the risks of complying with an approach from a stranger' (Moran et al., 1997).

Most children are sexually abused by someone they know, even if not by someone within their immediate family. The concentration on 'stranger danger', therefore, which still remains prevalent, particularly in schools, can be a red herring or even potentially dangerous, since it may allay the child's fears in relation to those who are not strangers.

The message that someone may harm you who is not a stranger, and is in fact a trusted adult, is obviously much more difficult to get across. If it is to be effective it must be accompanied by a change in the way children are brought up, so that they understand that it is not axiomatic that adults are always right and must always be obeyed. Children must be taught that they can and should complain if any adult hurts them or treats them in a way that is not acceptable. The study on stranger-danger referred to above commented that 'adult educationalists must remain alert to the potential conflict children may experience in learning to keep themselves safe from harm and a socialisation process which exhorts them to be kind, helpful and obedient' (Moran et al., 1997).

Much research has been undertaken on the factors that might make a child at risk of sexual abuse. One study highlights the following predictors in the case of intra-familial abuse:

- physical abuse
- having no one to confide in
- having no caring female adult
- having an alcoholic father.

The risk factors for extra-familial abuse were similar:

- physical abuse
- social isolation
- the mother's death
- having an alcoholic mother (Fleming et al., 1997).

The combination of drink, violence and a mother disabled, whether by social isolation, personal ill-health or fear, which is so commonly found in families where there is social work involvement, must raise the awareness of professionals to the danger that child sexual abuse may flourish in such circumstances. Where one parent is dis-empowered and the other dis-inhibited, children are at risk. In every group that we run we would expect to find: women who have been abused themselves, either sexually as child or adult, or physically by parents or partner; women who have abused drink or drugs or whose partners have done so; and women with mental health problems. Despite all these factors they have still managed to come to and benefit from a group.

The findings of recent research, and our own experience in working with these women's groups, both emphasise the critical part such groups have to play in breaking the cycle of abuse. They also demonstrate the beneficial effect that sensitive and timely intervention, by way of groups such as ours, can have upon the general wellbeing of the women and upon their sense of being able to influence events and outcomes as far as their children are concerned. In the detailed questionnaires, which we ask group participants to fill in at the end of every course, many emphasised the improvement in their relationship with their children. Our experience suggests that the support of other professionals before, during and after the group, can also be crucial in making attendance possible and in maximising the benefits.

Putting scarce resources into supporting and educating women carers of children who have been sexually abused is clearly worthwhile. At the beginning of our groups, many of the women had all or most of these feelings: 'self-blame, loss, helplessness at their inability to prevent or change what had happened' (Manion et al., 1996). At the end of the groups, many were making decisions involving their children and themselves which would clearly make a radical difference to future outcomes.

Conclusions

Working with twenty groups of mothers whose children have been sexually abused within the space of ten years has only served to convince me that, though this is difficult and demanding work, it is infinitely worthwhile. The signs of personal progress and change within the women themselves, and the way in which they grew in confidence and understanding, offered the hope that their children would not only survive the experience of abuse but, with the help of their mothers, be able to prosper emotionally in the future.

Along with this progress, however, was the sense that much still remained to be done. The women themselves were crying out for on-going support once the groups ended. They, and we, knew that they would be returning to lives which were often isolated and devoid of the personal support they so desperately needed. Moreover, in some cases, their children were still presenting major management difficulties through their behaviour in the home. Often acting as lone parents, or with unsympathetic or uninformed partners, the mothers carried the burdens alone.

The offer of an advanced group to mothers who had experienced an initial group was one way in which we responded immediately to the need. This has become a regular feature of our work. We hope that the more recent support group, or follow up group, FUG, which is open to each past advanced group member and meets four times a year for four hours over lunch, will provide on-going support for as long as it is needed.

A further area of work, which is clearly a very pressing one, is with the partners of women whose children have been abused. From the information given to us by such women, the men in their lives are often puzzled and disturbed by what has happened. They are also having to cope with women who have been greatly distressed by what has happened to their children, and whose reaction may be to distance themselves from their partner in a way which must be very confusing to him. However, if the children in the family are to make a full recovery the attitude and behaviour of the father-figure in their lives will be of great importance. They have already been given a very skewed picture of what men are like and of what men require of them if they are to please, and this needs to be offset by a normal, healthy, non-abusive relationship with their mother's partner. Such groups are difficult to set up, given the notorious reluctance of men to engage with their feelings and given the inherent suspicion of all men, even their own partners, by the women in question. However, it is essential work, as the above study goes on to say: 'Clinicians need to expand their treatment forms beyond the child victims to the traumatised families and to normalise the potential of all close family members to be vulnerable to experience adjustment difficulties.' (Manion et al., 1996) At last, in 2003, I was given time to pursue the task of setting up groups for non-abusing fathers and stepfathers. My previous colleague and another group member have taken over the current group for mothers and, along with my colleague, Brian Johnson, I have the responsibility of running groups for men.

As expected we have had to work very hard to reach the men in need, and to persuade them of this need. This has entailed visits to their home from both leaders, obtaining the support of their wives and encouraging professionals to keep fathers in mind. Though more than half the men who have attended groups have been working, it has been possible to run one group in the day time as the men were able to negotiate time off work, or to juggle shifts, in order to attend.

So far the groups have indicated clearly that they appreciate having the opportunity to meet and discuss with others matters relating to the abuse of the children for whom they care, just as the women have done. The participants show the same signs of social and personal isolation, symptoms of guilt and sense of helplessness as the women do. We hope that the perceived difficulties in convening men will not prevent professionals from bringing their names forward to us.

The decision to expand the number of groups on offer to women, and in particular to offer on-going support beyond the life of the two initial groups, in a structured way, has not been easily reached and remains a source of some contention among some colleagues. None of them doubt the need for such work or its worth, but they recognise that it does soak up a good deal of our resources which arguably might be more profitably directed towards children themselves. Similarly the offer of groups to men could incur the same criticism. However, it remains my belief that, if it is possible, the best way to heal children who have been sexually abused is through their parents.

If anyone still doubts how worthwhile it is to work with women whose children have been abused, let me end with a direct quotation from a member of a recent group:

I feel the group has been of great benefit to me. My visits to the group have helped me to release the feelings of guilt and anger that have been eating away at me.

I met other women who shared my feelings. I think it helps a lot in times of crisis to know that you are not alone and to have other people that understand what you are feeling, having experienced similar things themselves. Because I listened to what others had experienced and could see that no fault lay on their shoulders, (only on the perpetrators), I then had to, in turn, release myself from blaming myself. I think the activities in the group helped me to understand my own feelings and those of my daughter. She now feels more able to talk about her abuse without the obvious feelings of discomfort she suffered previously.

I feel all my relationship skills have been improved due to the things I have learnt at the group.

(Group member)

I am immensely indebted to her for allowing me to include her words in this chapter, and am grateful to all the members of the groups for allowing me the privilege of sharing with them their thoughts and feelings about issues which were often painful and distressing. This applies equally to the men who have attended groups, though this work is still in its infancy. I take two abiding memories from the work that I have described here: one is of tears and despair, the other of laughter and hope. Laughter and hope will prevail. Indeed our experience in running these groups would make us echo the conclusion that:

... vulnerability arising from non-optimal social attachment history and current social environment can be mitigated by groups that provide a secure protected opportunity for nurturing and social contact. More time-limited groups can also provide a context for specific therapeutic work that may be more productive and less stigmatising than individual therapy. Alternatively, groups can provide a forum for self-help and empowerment and growth.

(Natinal Commission of Enquiry into the Prevention of Child Abuse, 1996)

My colleagues and I hope, and believe, that the groups for mothers, and for fathers, of children who have suffered abuse have been able to do all those things.

4.4 Group Work: Conclusions

Ann Catchpole

The experience of running groups for a period of over ten years has highlighted their effectiveness as a form of therapeutic intervention. This is particularly noticeable in the case of JACAT groups because of the narrow focus of their brief and the experiences common to all group participants. Thus the period normally taken for joining groups, establishing ground-rules and developing trust is, despite the sensitive issues constantly under discussion and examination, and the strong emotions present, considerably reduced compared with groups that have a wider focus. This allows more time for key issues to be explored. The experience of sexual abuse, either at first hand or through another family member, is both isolating and stigmatising, so the presence of others who have been through the same things is extremely helpful in reducing this sense of isolation. However much an individual may know intellectually that they are not the only person ever to be abused it is often only when they meet another victim that this knowledge can be internalised.

The running of such groups requires a commitment from group leaders who will find the work exhausting as well as rewarding, and similarly from other team members, as it removes a sizeable piece of time from other areas of the work. It is by no means an easy or a cheap option. Groups need a high ratio of leaders to participants, especially when they are being run for young children; their leaders need supervising, and the carers of participants need support. In the case of mothers' groups, some individuals who have no adequate support systems of their own may need the on-going involvement of a JACAT worker, working on a one-to-one basis, prior to the formation of the group, while it is in being and afterwards. Attention to all the practical details, too, is time-consuming but essential.

Initially only one group was offered to all categories of participants, and no groups at all were available to males. However, group leaders rapidly recognised that much remained to be done at the end of the initial mothers' group, which became known as the starter group, and a second group, known as the advanced group was instigated. During the latter, mothers were encouraged to look in detail at their own childhood and upbringing and the influence this had had in their parenting of their own children. Women who have participated in both these groups now have the option of joining the Follow Up Group, which meets four times a year, and offers a chance to stay in touch with both leaders and members, and to receive on-going support. Members of this group are themselves participating in the healing process for others as they meet by request with women who have asked for contact with another mother whose child has been the victim of abuse.

As far as the work with men was concerned it had long been recognised as a gap in our service. It was felt to be important that this group should have both a female and a male leader, but it was some time before a male leader became available. At the time of writing (September 2004) the first two men's groups are completed, and they have proved to be just as necessary as were the groups for women. The groups were small but attendance was at a high level despite many day-to-day occurrences which could so easily have kept the members away. Plans are now in place to make these as regular a part in the service as groups for women already are. Men's groups are also leading the way by offering the same service to adoptive parents as well as natural parents.

So, despite some success in this area, JACAT is only too aware of gaps in its groups service. Physical abuse, emotional abuse and neglect all can leave children with a legacy of poor self-esteem, angry feelings which may be externalised or internalised, and possible mental ill-health in the future, yet there are no groups for parents of such children or the children themselves. Much remains to be done in the area of group-work development as in that of so many other areas.

Section Five: **Working with Families**

5.1 **Introduction to Family Work**

Paul O'Reilly

It is established practice now, that family work is undertaken when child abuse is suspected or disclosed (Dale et al., 1986; Bentovim et al., 1988; Bentovim and Jacobs, 1988; Bentovim, 1992). While family therapy (systems-informed practice) has been the primary theory underpinning work with families, other ways of theorising intervention into family life have been developed. In recent times major developments in the way that family therapy is described (White, 1995) mean that social constructionists or narrative approaches have predominated. In addition, social psychological theories have influenced working with abuse in families (Howe, 1989) and the feminist critique of practice has also had great impact (Burck and Speed, 1995).

What is meant by the term 'family' is in itself a complicated matter. 'Family' is both an idea or ideal notion and a lived reality for people in our society (Muncie and Sapsford, 1993). The dominant ideal notion is of two adults, a heterosexual pair, coming together, making a commitment to each other in a marriage ceremony, and deciding to have children for whom they care. Roles are defined, though recently there has been some crossover of gender-based roles. It is assumed that the adults will be very skilled in nurturing each other, extremely confident in their parenting skills, and therefore able to deliver authoritative parenting. It is assumed too that each will develop themselves as well as performing the other tasks.

In reality there are a number of family patterns in our society. There are:

- Those who choose to remain single (an increasing number).
- Those who choose to be single parents (also an increasing number).
- Those who end up being single parents through divorce, separation or death.
- Those who choose to live in reconstituted or reformed families, following separation, divorce or death.
- Those who choose to live in same-sex intimate relationships and have children somehow.
- Those who live in extended communal forms (a decreasing number).

Further variety is added by the different races and cultures now represented in Britain. It is crucial then that we deliver services or interventions which are not only based on rigorous good practice and collaboration but also suited to the many types of possible families.

Nevertheless, the tasks for that group of people living together, the family, remain much the same as previously. There will be intimacy, loving sexuality, caring and nurturing parenting, the possibility of self expression, the hope of financial security, and the realisation of more straightforward matters such as going on holidays, and the acquisition of luxury goods. Integration with other systems in society, through liaison and networking, can be more easily managed from a family base.

Importantly for our work, there is also the dominant expectation that there will be privacy afforded to families (precisely on the basis alone of being a family); that the state and agents of the state will seek to refrain from interfering in family life as much as possible; that the adults, or perhaps one adult in particular (usually the adult male), will be predominantly in charge; that the children will be obedient and relatively powerless; and that there will be great wisdom in the development and implementation of rules and regulations for shared living.

The Children Act 1989 has been influential in framing the debate about child sexual abuse and in shaping practice, as well as trying to manage how the state will interfere in family life. The legal framework is much stronger in terms of both the criteria that have to be met and the arrangements following any settlement in court. This was deliberately constructed and embedded within the Act, with the intention that, as case law evolved, it would influence the practice of the relevant agencies. Unfortunately we at JACAT have observed the dis-empowerment of social workers and social services generally as they grapple with incidences of child abuse or suspected child abuse. The same social worker must represent the system within which they are based, at the same time as undertaking the specific intervention indicated in a particular case. Much of the difficulty centres on the requirement in the Act for social workers to form working partnerships with the concerned or involved parents who are assumed, despite the arena of child abuse, to be reasonable. There is an inevitable tension between trying to protect children and at the same time respecting the rights of parents. It makes sense then to set up an agency such as JACAT which can undertake the necessary interventions in association with colleagues who are forming the working partnerships which cannot simply be based on consensus. The differences between 'partnership' and 'therapeutic alliance' will emerge through this chapter as each issue is developed.

Undertaking family work in the arena of child abuse throws up another dilemma. There are two broad themes that are present in the literature. The first is rehabilitation, and the question of whether or not rehabilitation will be useful and helpful to all concerned. The second is the process of recovery for the victim at least, and the question of whether the perpetrator can or cannot be involved in the future arrangements for family life. The assumption in this chapter is that rehabilitation and recovery are to be held as possible outcomes and are not necessarily mutually exclusive. For some agencies and services the dilemma is resolved by focussing on one or the other area of concern.

5.2 Approaches to Family Work

Paul O'Reilly

Introduction

In the remainder of this chapter the various kinds of family work will be described with case examples. Family work itself can be thought of as consisting of the following five areas of work, each with its particular emphasis:

- family support
- family education
- family consultation
- family counselling
- family therapy

Naturally, these are not mutually exclusive, and they all require similar skills of the worker:

- The ability to convene families.
- The ability to join empathetically with family members in facing the reasons for attending (i.e. their distressing experience).
- The ability to engage with the family in a joint enterprise which stresses hopefulness and the probability of change.
- Skill in developing and maintaining a therapeutic alliance, enabling experimentation and a self-reflective healing process.
- The ability to promote experiences of competency and empowerment.
- The ability to consolidate.
- Finally to enable termination with the experiences of loss that occur.

Alongside there are the skills that are needed in interacting with other agencies and systems, that is, liaison and networking. Moreover, the therapist or worker must remain open-minded so that young people, in particular, can move towards recovery, beginning to travel forward positively again. In what follows, support, education, consultation, counselling and therapy will be described, as will general guiding principles for each form of work, all illustrated with the use of a particular case example from current practice.

Comment

Each member of the Joint Agency Team is expected to be able to work in any area of family work as required. However, the various ways of working with families will enable each member to work to their strengths in the beginning and, with support, to develop confidence in working in less familiar ways. A further expectation here is that doing direct work with clients, whether individual, family or group, is a sine qua non for each team member, whether or not they have a primary task in administration, co-ordination, training or representation. An obvious question is 'does this work?'. Some answer is provided in Section Six where team and service maintenance and development is discussed. The final chapter of this Section *Does it Work?* provides some further answers.

Family Support

The supportive family worker will be guided by the notion that it is important to control what you can control. This is an axiom which enables the worker to remember that small, supportive, and practical measures may enable families to develop a sense of empowerment. Acceptance is crucial in supportive work with families. The worker will need to offer their acceptance of the circumstances in which family members have unfortunately discovered themselves to be, and to discuss them without accusation. Such discussion will promote the family's acceptance of itself. The message that there is general acceptance of the nature of the problem and its consequences by workers in the helping and caring systems can in itself be empowering.

The importance of giving information is easily overlooked. Information may take the form of books, leaflets or pamphlets, videotapes, descriptions of self-help or other groups, contact points and telephone numbers. Each and all of these in themselves enable people to make decisions about how and when they might proceed. The family support worker will enable ventilation of feelings to take place, during which family members will be able to experience and describe their helplessness, their fury, their dismay, their guilt, their intense, and perhaps even murderous, feelings for revenge. They will often experience the attendant and difficult emotions of shame and disappointment. Throughout the ventilation process they will tend to minimise the nature of the abuse and the consequences. It is important to speak of that process of minimisation. There may be 'lifelines' that can be thrown to the family which may enable them to help themselves. Lifelines such as financial assistance, or advice about finances, help from other agencies, the possibility of re-housing, the offer of assistance in convening extended family or neighbourhood meetings, can be very helpful. When the abuser has sexually assaulted or abused a number of children in the same neighbourhood from a number of different families, it is useful to offer a meeting to all the involved families and young people so as to work towards a supportive neighbourhood culture for recovery. Finally, the supportive worker will meet with the family in various combinations (including meetings with individuals), in order to continue a process of maintenance of development as a result of support. The worker should also think with the family, in their own specific and particular circumstances, about the tactics they can employ for waiting. There is an inevitable urgency when a child has been abused to move quickly on, to forget what has happened, as a way of recovery. But the more that people can discover or develop tactics for waiting, to enable themselves to hold in mind their difficulties and problems, the more they will appreciate that time alone, especially combined with a thoughtful progress through time, will in itself be a healing agent.

Case Study – Family support

A family is referred by the General Practitioner because one of the boys in the family has told his brother about the physical and sexual abuse he has experienced from a relative. Their mother is extremely distraught about what has happened. Though a vulnerable person herself, in that she has a history of drug dependency, she has a volcanic temper and is prone to impulsive assaults on those she regards as enemies. She is worried about, and moved by, her son's distress. His father has a history of criminality. The couple have a tempestuous relationship, which sometimes means that they part for some days following verbal arguments which are generally unrestrained. They are suspicious of the professional systems which they encounter but, on the other hand, they are highly critical of the fact that they have had minimal assistance from all the agencies. It seems to them from what they know on the grapevine that much more input has been given to the perpetrator's family and the perpetrator himself than to their son who was abused. The victim was eight years old, the victimiser fourteen.

The abused boy shares a bedroom with his older brother (aged ten). Now that he has disclosed the abuse he has nightmares (similar to night terrors). Over the first few months of meeting with his family worker, the boys develop ways of feeling safe at night in their bedroom. They begin by tying string to the door and to the window and around their wrists so that they will know if anybody tries to enter their room at night, and they think that by these means they will also know in which direction to run. Such poignancy is common in post-abuse work. They move on to learning martial arts skills, then to developing personal confidence, and finally to trusting in their parents again.

The boys are supported in ventilating their feelings. They experience acceptance from the worker who shows respect for their competency and courage. The parents want information about the effects of abuse, and this is provided. Following that, they begin to help the boys feel safer. They contain and embrace the boys in the context of their experience of the dangers of the world. Responsibility for safety is transferred to the parents. Liaison with other agencies enables the possibility of lifelines to be considered, including re-housing and financial assistance. Positive conversations with the school and education system are enabled.

The family are extremely suspicious about therapy, given their view of what it might mean and their feeling that something will be imposed upon them. It is necessary, therefore, for the worker continually to repeat their position of support and collaboration. The family are able to be in charge of who attends, when they attend, and the agenda which will be followed through each meeting. The boys learn to keep a journal which they share, and into which they write their thoughts and memories. They express their feelings through drawings. They find ways to think with their peers about what has happened and why. (The extended neighbourhood in which they reside has come to know about the abuse and its consequences.) The parents individually, and as a couple, tentatively explore the possibility of counselling or therapy, and the supportive worker introduces them to other agencies and therapists as requested.

Meetings are convened with workers from other agencies as appropriate, sometimes with the parents present, and sometimes in their absence (at their request, or at the request of the worker). The children themselves are able to stop being aggressive at school, to stop challenging the teachers, to stop running away from school, to stop assaulting other children (sometimes in quite vicious ways) and to begin to feel less guilty about what has happened to them.

Eighteen months after first being referred, it becomes possible for the adults to request appointments for family therapy. It is their view that there are many issues and relationship struggles to be faced, concerns which are not related to the abuse of one of the boys.

Comment

The odds were stacked against the family moving into therapy. The parents were resistant to the idea of therapy, whereas some members of the professional network were equally enthusiastic about therapy being provided for all members of the family. These professionals felt that JACAT was withholding therapy. A mature joint agency system can manage such polarised views where one set of workers insists that there should be therapy and the other set feels that not enough has yet been done by way of protection and support to make therapy viable. In this instance it was possible to manage the difference.

It does not follow that it is a 'success' if a family moves on to family therapy. In looking forward to a successful termination it is likely that support will be needed at longer intervals, for instance, or a family may realise that they only need to consult from time to time depending on circumstances and events. Generally we find, however, that one or more family members enter a therapy process about a year after termination of the supportive relationship.

Family Education

The guiding principle with respect to family education is that knowledge equals empowerment. It is probably obvious what is meant by such a guiding principle. The more individual family members and the family together can learn and understand about abuse – who abuses, the relevance of history, the consequences, the particular issues, the victim dynamics and especially the importance of the question and consequences of domestic violence – the more it will be possible to develop a sense of some mastery and control.

Importantly, the family educator will probably have to begin with the matter of who perpetrators are and how they create the circumstances within which abuse can occur. There is also the question of why it is that perpetrators behave as they do. We have a good description now of how perpetrators might organise and plan their assaultative behaviour (Wyre, 1991; Elliott et al., 1995). We are able to give a reasonable psychological explanation of why there is emotional abuse or neglect. We can describe the perpetrator in terms of how and why they are so emotionally abusive and neglectful. We can describe the circumstances in which such a person has found themselves. The descriptions in respect of physical abuse are much less sophisticated than we might wish but are nonetheless generally satisfactory for families and victims.

The complex area of domestic or partner violence is beginning to be described and unravelled (Mullender and Morley, 1994; Jukes, 1999). In particular, the oppressive use of domestic violence to control a household, and the relationship of child abuse to domestic violence is well documented (Elliott et al., 1995; Kashani and Allan, 1998; McGee, 2000). We are more aware than we were of the association between child abuse and domestic violence. We are able now to give spouse victims, and child victims, good descriptions of their circumstances. We can describe the factors which have resulted in violence. We can even describe why it is that the violence has been tolerated over what may have been a very long time. Moreover, we are becoming increasingly aware of the grave impact that bullying has on victims. We are also beginning to understand that not all bullying happens in schools, that not all victims are children or young people, and that not all bullies are adolescent thugs.

The family educator is able to investigate the history of the family and its individual members, and can make that history relevant to recent and present circumstances. Explanations can be developed on the basis of history. More importantly, history can be used to remind people of their competencies. There are skills they themselves have developed in order to survive. The history is relevant also to the consequences of abuse for any one person. People express their distress in a variety of ways, often as a result of past experiences. We know that we can teach families that certain forms of behaviour are an expression of distress by a young person or an adult and not to be taken at face value alone. Sometimes it is self-directed and self-punitive. Sometimes it is directed outwards and is dangerous to others. It is possible too to assure people that they need not remain the victims of their history, and that abuse will not necessarily be transmitted through generations.

The family educator can describe victim dynamics in a way that elaborates the individual story of any one abuse victim. What is being managed and how it is managed in a particular, idiosyncratic way can be described. Such descriptions, with acceptance and understanding, enable both the victim and current carers of the victim to develop a repertoire of communication skills and help the victim move towards recovery and restoration.

Different family forms and structures bring their own range of issues. Through education an increased understanding of the dynamics of stepfamilies or reconstructed families, foster families and adoptive families, as well as single-parent families, can be attained. General and specific problems can be predicted. The knowledge employed and the type of intervention used in foster families and adoptive families have been described elsewhere in this volume (see Chapter 2.2 page 23). Stepfamilies or reconstructed families do have particular dynamics which may lead to specific difficulties and problems. There is the inevitable pressure to conform within the dominant ideology so as to look and behave like a nuclear family. Embedded within this, the two issues which arise time and again are the question of discipline and authoritative parenting, and the nature and quality of the relationship between the young people and the newly arrived adult partner. Relationships are even more complex when both partners bring children from previous relationships to the current partnership. Adult partners can presume too easily that the children will like their choice of partner. He, or she, is in love with, even entranced by, that new partner, but the children may be highly suspicious of them, especially if they have been abused or assaulted by a previous partner. It is likely that there will be an even greater presumption that the children will in fact love the new partner, and that they will do so rather quickly. This is a remarkably naive view of love, and an extraordinary dis-empowerment of children and young people.

It is generally the case that the newly arrived partner will rather quickly become involved in matters of authoritative parenting and discipline, and all before a relationship has been developed, and deepened, with the young people concerned. Again this can be a highly challenging and painful matter, especially when the young people have been abused and assaulted by a previous adult carer.

The family educator, in describing these matters to stepfamilies or reconstructed families, and in the process of helping the new family constellation to discuss these complexities, will promote the competent care of children in the context of the new relationships.

It is possible also to consider particular dynamics in single parent households so that the single parent or adult can be more empowered through a greater awareness of the likely outcome of the particular circumstances in which they now find themselves. One (or more) child may try to move into a partner position and attempt to develop into a 'parental child'; younger children may well regress and therefore become more difficult. Authoritative parenting by one person is not an easy matter. That one person will be encouraged by the family educator's descriptions of where resources may exist so that the experiences of others in similar circumstances can be drawn upon.

Many of these matters are difficult. They can cause strong feelings of anxiety in the various family members. Anxiety is a feeling which people find troubling or unbearable. It is all too easy to express it in aggressive ways. It is important therefore that the family educator helps family members to recognise anxiety and the consequences of such feelings.

Case Study – Family education

Sarah and her two daughters, Anna (14) and Nicky (11) are referred by the school counsellor. Sarah had recently left her partner of three years standing because she discovered that he was being emotionally abusive to the girls. He had been verbally violent and threatening towards them, though without actually hitting them. However, they thought he might well do so at any time. The girls had moved in with their mother and her partner some two years previously, following the death of their father, with whom they had lived since he and their mother had parted when Anna was seven years old. Their natural father had been a binge drinker. On one occasion, when drunk, he had fallen down the stairs at home and died. The girls do not talk about him other than to say positive things.

They are unable to say much about their experiences at the hands of Sarah's more recent partner. Nicky is generally silent and withdrawn at meetings. Anna is talkative but in a hostile and angry way. Sarah is concerned about the girls, especially that they do not talk about their father. Their resistance to discussing anything to do with their recently acquired stepfather is also a concern. She does not have any complaints about their behaviour at home, nor are there any difficulties at school.

Sarah had approached the school with a view to the possibility of one or both of her daughters seeing the counsellor about their grief. The counsellor thought the young people did not want to see anyone and recommended family work instead. In the first appointment it rapidly became clear that the young people, in particular, were very resistant to the notion of 'therapy'. They felt it meant that they were to blame for how they now were, or for what had happened to them, or both. When it was suggested to them, and to their mother, that it might be helpful for them to attend so that the family worker could help them learn more about grief, abuse, and the likely consequences of each, they all agreed to return for more meetings. The girls said they were puzzled and bruised by what their stepfather did. They wanted to know more about perpetrators of abuse. They liked the idea of thinking about what might be 'around' for a single parent household.

It was agreed that meetings would take place monthly – to give time for reflection, discussion, and further reading (all three were people who liked to read). A family member would ring in a week before each meeting with items to discuss at that meeting. They were all able to read leaflets, articles and relevant texts over the following year. By the end of that series of meetings they had covered alcoholism, grief, divorce, step families, single parent households and had started to consider family violence. Matters then became complicated because Sarah started a new relationship. Anna and Nicky were very cautious about her new partner, Michael. He was concerned about this. He thought it might be about their father rather than the abuse by their stepfather.

Occasionally all four attended together. But over the next year the young people gradually stopped attending and the adults came to meetings bringing various concerns, sometimes about the relationship between Michael and the young people, sometimes about the developing couple relationship. At the end of the second year it was agreed that it was no longer necessary to meet.

Some four months later Anna called up and made an appointment. She wanted to talk about her father and her previous stepfather (though she did not think of Michael as her stepfather): she said she would prefer to talk to a woman, and that was arranged. Six months after that call all four attended for a follow-up appointment. They were all living together and reported that things were going well.

Comment

The family educator who is also a trained family therapist may well have a good deal of difficulty in an instance such as the one described above. The temptation will be to adhere to a family therapy process.

This can involve consultation with other team members, which is extremely helpful in these circumstances. However, there must be mutual trust and respect. All four family members were pleased to hear of the idea of consultation with colleagues and, indeed, of the struggle the worker experienced in maintaining the agreed role. Eventually it became helpful to have the family come in to observe some consultations between the worker and colleagues.

Family Consultation

Family consultation as a particular variant of family therapy has been described elsewhere (Street and Downey, 1996). Families are offered two or three appointments with a follow-up some weeks later. Sometimes a résumé of the appointments is sent by mail. Family consultation, in the arena of child abuse, has a different meaning entirely, though it shares some principles with the model described by Street. By family consultation we at JACAT mean working collaboratively with family members over an extended period of time. The frequency of the meetings is determined by the family. The content of the meetings is determined by the family and worker together. The guiding principle employed is that *collaboration is strengthening*. Through collaboration family competencies will be rediscovered. Often the struggle to develop a collaborative process will in itself lead to feelings of competency and strength.

There are a number of key components to the consultation process:

- Listening is essential.
- Giving feedback is helpful and empowering.
- Discovering a direction through the development of a plan is necessary.
- Describing family competencies is extremely helpful, and a detailed description of the problem gives hope to a family in distress.

Through consultation the family can seek to understand how agencies work to carry out their tasks in the context of the particular culture of the agency. The consultant who actively listens is affirming of the family. The past, the present, and the anticipated future are all celebrated. The consultant is not listening to discover in what way people are dysfunctional. Listening occurs in the context of a co-created space which is helpful and containing.

Giving feedback is important. The family then has the power to decide how to make use of the observations and the interactions that occur amongst and between family members and with the consultant. The feedback can be as simple as 'I feel scared now', or 'You look sad'. It can be more complex. Conversations can be held between the consultant and professional colleagues to which the family can listen. Consultation appointments may occur infrequently, so direction needs to be established as early as possible. Through listening and feedback a plan is established to give the family a sense of direction. A description of the trials and tribulations that may well occur as they seek to recover from what has transpired is important. It gives the family members a chance to predict what may happen in the following months. With the consultant they can begin to work out how they may process difficult feelings of shock, dismay, grief, anger, desire for vengeance, and the inevitable enquiries that people have of each other for a better understanding of what has happened. Those enquiries are easily experienced by victims as accusations, since the asking of a series of 'why?' questions creates defensiveness.

Much has already been achieved by a family which has found itself a consultant. Much more will be achieved as they continue the consultation process. The competencies that are already there will emerge. Newly developed competencies will be important. It is extremely helpful to family members if the consultant describes those competencies, for such a description underlines achievement. This sense of achievement is essential if family members are to undertake difficult tasks for themselves. Being listened to, receiving feedback, establishing direction and remembering and discovering competencies – all these will give family members an increased experience of hope. The consultant will articulate that hope. Discovering that it is possible to be different and to recover will energise people even more. Morale will increase.

It is inevitable that there will be hiccups and problems for families through the consultation process and over time. Careful elucidation and detailed description of those problems will enable families to begin to look for solutions themselves. They can test those solutions with the consultant from time to time. Frequently such solutions will involve interactions with other agencies. The consultant should be able to describe how systems might operate and how an agency will conduct its practice in the context of its particular culture. It may be that the family consultant will invite colleagues from different agencies to join a meeting and to describe to the family their agency principles and philosophy. This modelling for the family – the consultant who consults – is in itself a strengthening process for them.

Sometimes families ask for meetings of professionals to be convened by the consultant and to include family members. Thus a fuller description of the views of the professionals can be delivered and the offers that they are making to the family can be presented. The family will be then in a better position to choose which offers to take up.

Case Study – Family consultation

Shirley, who is 30, lives as a single parent with her daughter Crystal (14). Shirley works in the care system. When she was approximately 12 years old she spent some time living in the care of the Social Services Department because of difficulties between her mother and herself. She never lived with Crystal's father, but has remained friends with him. Crystal has spent some periods of time living with him by agreement. Difficulties have arisen for Crystal, and Shirley would like some assistance. However, she knows about therapy and does not feel it would be helpful for her and Crystal to be in family therapy or its equivalent. She does not think that

Crystal will want to talk to anyone by herself. When Crystal was ten years old, they had been referred for assistance to a clinical psychologist and had found that helpful, mostly because the psychologist had listened carefully to her and had enabled her to talk to the staff at Crystal's school at a joint meeting. Now she was approaching the services again because it had emerged that Crystal had been physically maltreated by one of Shirley's previous partners, around the ages of six to nine. Crystal had also recently told Shirley that she had been bullied at school in a way which she had found extremely frightening and alarming; so much so that she had stopped attending school and Shirley had found it impossible to get her to start again.

Shirley was invited to a consultation meeting. She accepted, and attended alone in the first instance. She was very cautious at first, and challenged the consultant about 'how it all might go', and how similar or dissimilar her experience with the consultant would be to her previous experience of a psychologist. She was quickly relieved when the process of consultation was described to her. She thought that that would be most helpful, and that it would be easier to have Crystal attend as she felt necessary rather than as a therapist might require. Following the second meeting Shirley arranged with the education system for special education provision as preparation for Crystal to attend full-time school at some point in the future. Shirley and Crystal attended consultation meetings on a monthly basis, and Crystal was present for probably half the time. Between meetings they did a lot of written homework.

Crystal was a very scared young person. She wanted to be able to go back to school or to change to another school but was frightened that the bullying would happen again. She vividly remembered the physical abuse at the hands of her stepfather, and of course the images were re-evoked when she was bullied at school. The consequences of the bullying were similar for her. She felt isolated, to blame, guilty, friendless, and unable to tell her mother. She felt as if she had no direction in which she could go. She easily became confused and overwhelmed by her schoolwork, and found it extremely difficult to be in any group or context whatsoever.

Shirley invited Crystal's father to some of the consultation meetings which he attended along with his new partner, and at various times she invited members of other agencies to come along so that she would be clear about what might be possible for Crystal. Crystal attended some of those meetings and asked relevant questions herself.

Shirley and Crystal were always well prepared for consultation meetings. They would spend much time writing scenarios for themselves and thinking about the kinds of questions they would like to ask various people including the consultant. They generally made careful note of the answers they received, and continued with their self-imposed homework throughout. Shirley and Mike (Crystal's father) were concerned that Crystal might get pregnant in the relatively near future, as she was rising 16.

Meetings took place over a period of approximately two and a half years, but in the last year their frequency reduced to once every three months. The family themselves chose to stop consultation meetings, because it seemed to them that they had made great progress. They felt strengthened, could tolerate the fact of the abuse, rediscovered competency, had a sense of direction, had carefully described the problems they were encountering as well as those they were likely to encounter. They could recruit people to their cause as appropriate and necessary. They could think together about past events and rehearse tactics and strategies with respect to feeling scared and frightened, and were most hopeful about the future. At the point that they chose to set aside the consultation process Crystal was happily attending college and Shirley, having completed some further training, had been promoted within the care system.

Comment

The relationship with the consultant, which begins as a collaborative one, might easily develop into more of a therapeutic alliance. Partnership is difficult to maintain given the obvious differences between the position of the family members and the consultant. If the differences are experienced as inequalities, and the consultant does not have occasional consultation or supervision, then an increasing despondency on the part of the family may lead to a deepening dependency which has to be worked through into a therapeutic alliance. If family members do not agree initially to the development of a relationship then the dependency can generate dissatisfaction and lead to termination before it can all be worked through. The consultant must, therefore, be vigilant.

Family Counselling

For the family counsellor the nature and quality of the relationship they have with the family and its individual members is more important. They will need to make increased use of specific counselling skills and have an increased awareness of processes during the meetings both among family members and between the family and the counsellor. The counsellor will be making much more use of group work skills with respect to understanding and explaining the dynamics of the meeting to family members. The family counsellor will be concerned that the family receives a particular message, which is that *difficulties are surmountable*. It will be possible to move to a sense of competency and mastery about the effect of abuse on victims and their relatives or carers.

The usual stages in a course of counselling or therapy will take place:

- A referral made, and its meaning considered.
- The family convened.
- An engagement process undertaken with the therapist joining the family.
- A contract made, covering the procedures and processes.
- Some problem formulation undertaken.
- An end point can be agreed.

The counselling itself will be based on the family's agenda for each meeting, but the problem formulation and contract will be held in mind. There will be a period of consolidation after change has occurred, and then a period of termination leading to ending and closure. Generally a review appointment will be offered and a follow up appointment some six months following review.

The theoretical underpinnings of the practice of the family counsellor are important, because the working relationship between the counsellor and the family is regarded as crucial with respect to outcome. The counsellor should be able to describe how he or she is informed, and how their model of practice has limitations because of how they think. The family counsellor is likely to be a systems thinker, of a humanistic, behavioural or psychodynamic background and persuasion and informed about the politics of interaction between people. They will have a heightened awareness of the meaning and pragmatics of communication between people, and be sensitive to the ways in which discourse and language both facilitates, and limits, possibilities. (Full accounts of some of these issues can be found in Truax and Carkhuff, 1967; Box, 1978; Jones, 1993; Street, 1994; Dallos and Draper, 2000). Essential to these matters is that the counsellor is an interactionalist (see Langs, 1976) and is able to make use of matters of transference, dependency and counter-transference in the work with family members.

A particular tension is present at the beginning of the family counselling process, not unlike the tension present in other forms of counselling or therapy. This tension is about the engagement of the family in a working relationship with the counsellor, at the same time as formulating the presenting problems and making a contract about how to proceed. During this phase of the counselling both the non-verbal and the verbal communications are important. Non-verbal matters such as speed of talk, structure of the language used, posture, facial expression, interruptions, silences, and order of talking and turn taking, all inform the counsellor of the mood state of any one person and of the family as a whole and indicate some of the ways in which emotions are present and experienced. Such communications also enable the counsellor to comprehend more fully that not just verbal communications occur but also the impact that they may have on the family members as matters proceed. The interactions amongst and between the family members and with the counsellor are closely observed, historically analysed with respect to their meaning for the family, examined for current issues, and contrasted with the future as they imagine it to be. Family interactions are contingent and contextual, and it behoves the counsellor to understand the family's story or narrative about itself as fully as possible.

Formulation of the problem will focus on present difficulties and issues as compared with how the family or family members imagine the future. Insofar as this is possible, that desired end point or end state is described. The contract or agreement between the counsellor and the family can then be described. At the same time the procedure for the meetings will be agreed. The fact that the progress that occurs in meetings will be described, analysed and researched will also be made clear. The working relationship which develops between the counsellor and the family will be one that concentrates on, and illustrates for them, collaboration with respect to 'the art of the possible'.

It is easier if there is warmth and positive feelings between the counsellor and the family, but this is not an absolute requirement. A working relationship can still take place when there is conflict and hostility, disagreement and distrust. What is possible on the basis of such a difficult working relationship may be limited compared to other relationships, but much is still possible. The way in which the counsellor is empathic will enable a fine-tuning of the relationship to occur as time goes by and may make it possible for variations in tuning to happen from time to time.

A good deal of the conversation that occurs will be about 'imaginings' where possibilities, outcomes, and wishes will be discussed and described, as well as those things that are likely to make it difficult to realise these imaginings. A high degree of counsellor activity is likely throughout all of this. Such activity may be directly in the room with the family or indirectly, with the counsellor's spending time thinking about meetings and considering how to make use of their skills to be of assistance. Formal or informal tasks (homework) may feature highly at some periods of the counselling process. Formal tasks are those which the family and counsellor describe together that the family will attempt to undertake between meetings. Informal tasks are those which follow on from questions asked by the counsellor. They are simple questions but indicate much. Examples are:

- 'What did you make of the last time we met?'
- 'What thoughts have you had since then?'
- 'What things have you said to each other since our last meeting?'
- 'What things have you noticed as a result of what we talked about last time we met?'
- 'On reflection, where would you say you are now compared to when we first met?'
- 'If you were to be meeting me today for the first time, what would you say your difficulties or issues are?'
- 'I wonder what we'll talk about when we meet next?'

Another highly useful task question is:

- 'What would we be talking about today if we weren't talking about what it is you are now saying?'

There will be many crisis moments during meetings as counselling proceeds. The counsellor knows that difficulties are surmountable, and the illustration for the family of the ways in which it is possible to have conversations so as to manage disagreements and difficulties will give family members hope for themselves. Spencer (2000) gives an interesting account of how difference is inevitable with respect to supervisors and supervisees. The same is true with respect to counsellors and families. A contained and reflective space is offered by the counsellor so that differences and difficulties are seen to be surmountable. There is a wide range of possible differences. There are differences in life experience and family experience, education, lifestyle, age, race, politics, status, class, religion, disability, culture, gender, and sexual orientation. Some of them are particularly poignant in the arena of child abuse, especially for victims, and particularly challenging when the family members present are both victims and victimisers.

Case Study – Family counselling

Michelle, aged 38, works as a nurse in a local hospital. She has had a number of careers, firstly training and working as a teacher, then developing and expanding her own business, and more recently training on a part-time basis to be a nurse. She had qualified one year previously and moved into the area because of difficult memories and mixed emotions about where she lived previously. She has approached her general practitioner for family counselling because of her difficulties and her relationship with her daughter Kindi, who is eight years old. She describes Kindi as being oppositional, defiant, uncooperative, challenging, disrespectful and provocative. Michelle can get very angry with Kindi, so much so that she finds herself feeling murderously rage-ful and has on occasion punished her daughter too much, or hit her. The punishment has been to withdraw material or luxury possessions, including the withholding of pocket money or any treats that might normally take place during the week or at weekends.

Kindi's father is African, but she has never lived with him and her mother, nor does she have any contact with him. Michelle is in some contact, but it is contact which causes her pain and distress. Michelle has not been in another intimate relationship since Kindi's birth, other than to embark on two possible relationships slowly when Kindi was four and again when rising five. Kindi did not meet one of the men at all, though he was particularly important to her mother, who felt that she had fallen in love with him. The other one Kindi met only briefly. Neither man was able to remain involved in a developing and deepening relationship for Michelle. Both caused her anguish.

After two sessions, and following the counsellor's suggestion, Michelle agreed to attend a number of sessions over the following year. A contract was drawn up which stated that there would be discussion in the sessions about strategies and tactics in terms of being an authoritative parent, about single parent households and the issues and forces that occur in them, and about the psychological and emotional development of children. This would be undertaken in a detailed and hopefully empowering way. Following the contract, Michelle called the emergency social services team on the weekend previous to her next appointment and said that she had reached the end of her tether, that it was impossible to live with Kindi anymore, and that she had hit her over that weekend and thought that it would be dangerous for her to remain in the home. A Child Protection Conference was convened and Kindi was registered as having experienced actual physical abuse, and as being at risk of emotional abuse. When Michelle and Kindi next attended the contract was changed so as to begin with the issue of the physical abuse of Kindi and to concentrate also on the issue of the likelihood of her experiencing emotional abuse.

Michelle was an impatient and volcanic person herself. She had been abused by her mother when she was very young, her mother had died when she was six, and she had then been sexually abused by an uncle and aunt with whom she lived for the following five years. She had trained as a teacher at secondary level but had found it too difficult to continue and had then developed her own business. It was her view that she needed to learn nothing about child development nor did she want to know what was usual or normal with respect to how Kindi behaved, especially towards her. Moreover, she had no idea about the differences between authoritarian, authoritative and democratic parenting styles.

It seemed likely that Michelle would develop an attachment to her therapist which would promote a level of dependency which was unacceptable, given that it was important that she experience herself as empowered in leaving meetings rather than dis-empowered. Therefore it was decided that it would be most helpful if two therapists work together with her and Kindi, one a male and the other a female. This was arranged with the agreement of all concerned.

The teaching about child development made use of Kindi's life story to date. Kindi's time line was drawn and relevant matters inserted along it, and parallel to that was a theoretical time line with respect to the development of a child in ideal circumstances. Michelle rapidly began to be able to speculate about how things might have been experienced by Kindi and therefore why she might have behaved at times in her life in the way that she did. Michelle began to comprehend also why she sometimes felt so extremely negatively towards Kindi because she realised Kindi so resembled her father that she, Michelle, behaved towards her as if she were him. Authoritarian, authoritative and democratic parenting styles were described to Michelle, and she and Kindi were invited to role play various aspects of each. Though Kindi was not present for all of these sessions she thoroughly enjoyed being involved in role plays where she sometimes took the role of being parent to Michelle's daughter and sometimes role played herself in various situations involving her mother. The structure and dynamics of a single parent household were described to them both, and they went off to draw a series of cartoons about the ways in which they noticed single parent issues occurring for them during the following month. Michelle began to keep a journal for herself of her thoughts and ideas and experiences and was able to make use of that journal to reflect on how things used to be and how they had changed for her since attending counselling. Conversations took place with Michelle without Kindi about how to maintain herself as a woman in her own right, and about how it might be useful to behave and to handle things if and when she met someone with whom she wished to develop an intimate relationship.

Michelle began to develop humorous and creative ways of interacting with Kindi about issues such as bedtime, tidying and homework. She was delighted when it was explained to her that homework was the bane of every parent's life and yet had little or no significance to children who, on the whole, are minimal about homework and have little ego involvement in producing it for their teacher. The final two sessions revolved around the issue of collaboration and co-operation. Michelle and Kindi talked with each other and with therapists about what happened between them when collaboration occurred, as opposed to anything else, and when co-operation was present between them, especially with respect to Kindi's share of the household arrangements.

It is interesting to note that there was remarkably little difference in the way that Kindi behaved in the final sessions compared to the early ones, but that the impact of her behaviour on Michelle had changed dramatically.

Comment

The direction in which energy is aimed has now changed. The focus is now more on the family and on the nature and quality of the relationships. The agenda is very firmly controlled from session to session by the clients. Liaison with other agencies is minimal though, of course, all child protection concerns will be addressed. Paradoxically it can now be more difficult to involve statutory agencies. It is as if they are reluctant, or feel it unnecessary, to become involved once family counselling is taking place.

Family Therapy

The guiding principle for the family therapist is that change is both desirable and possible. Change may occur in the way people think; speak about matters; feel; behave or, sometimes, in all of these.

Family therapy itself is a relatively young form of therapy. It dates from the late 1950s and early 1960s. The Association of Family Therapy in Great Britain was formed as recently as 1975. There has been remarkable development and progress especially in the ideas and theories which inform practice. As is the case with other forms of therapy the rate of development has accelerated recently.

There are four key building blocks for the family therapist. They will be a systemic thinker (von Bertalanffy, 1968); will be informed by communication theories (Watzlawick et al., 1968); will hold the family life cycle in mind (Carter and McGoldrick, 1978) and the mimesis (the deliberate imitation of one group of people by another as a factor of social change) when the family and therapist form a newly functioning system (Minuchin, 1974). They will be committed to anti-discriminatory practice, will actively seek to work collaboratively with clients and families, and will endeavour to hold in mind the importance of the individual's internal world, the complexity of the familial environment and its influences, and the impact of existing social-political and social-psychological forces (see Goldner, 1998). Dallos and Draper (2000) give a good recent account of developments in the field and helpfully describe some of the practices which are associated with those developments. Carr (2000) also gives an illuminating account and comparison of approaches.

Moral and ethical dilemmas loom large for the family therapist in the field of child abuse. They are particularly poignant when the victim and the perpetrator are at the same family meeting. A number of ways of thinking about this have been developed by family therapists (see McCarthy and Byrne 1988; Madanes, 1991; Essex et al., 1996). Bentovim (1992) has been particularly influential in this country.

It is not easy to remain humane, thoughtful and relatively well balanced emotionally when faced with perversion, brutality, supreme indifference, murderous rage, and the objectification of children by their parents or carers. The difficulties and complexities have been described elsewhere (White et al., 1993) but in this section some particular issues will be expanded upon.

As in many other therapies, the family therapist facilitates individuals to 'speak the unspeakable'. It is more difficult when a number of people with different agendas and competing wishes are present. Nonetheless it is a central task for the family therapist. It may not be easy for family members to speak about feelings, thoughts, wishes and imaginings but that they do so is important. Strong negatives are the most difficult. For example:

- 'I imagine him dead.'
- 'I wish I was dead.'
- 'I wish I could kill him.'
- 'I'm so ashamed.'
- 'I still think he didn't mean it.'
- 'I still think my mum was pretty mixed up.'

When there has been abuse, everything is thrown into greater disarray than usual. The usual human confusions, mixed-up feelings, ambivalence, puzzlement, paradoxes and uncertainties all get attributed in such a way as to exacerbate feelings of guilt, shame, puzzlement and disordered thinking. The ability to distinguish between what is real and what is imagined lessens.

A great deal of fear will be experienced by family members and will, therefore, be present in meetings. The fear is important because of the limitations it may impose on progress and possibilities. And that fear itself may well be justified. We know that families are highly dangerous places for women and for children, and we know that violent or threatening men do take extreme actions. The mantra 'There is nothing to fear but fear itself' comes to mind frequently in family therapy sessions. But it is more likely to be the case that the therapist can be helpful to family members when they can accept that they are fearful. The issue is not about their being fearful but rather about what family members think or imagine might be possible given that they are afraid.

The impact of people's individual and shared histories cannot be overestimated. The way in which the past is made present is important to the family therapist as well as the way that individuals and families give accounts of their history. When family members tell stories about their past it is important for the therapist to be able to ask:

- 'What do you make of that now?' or
- 'In what way do you think that has helped (or hindered) with respect to the abuse, or with respect to what you can manage to do about the abuse at this point in time?'

Again:

- 'Is there a way we could together make use of what you have told me now to consider what might happen next or to think about what you will be able to do next?'

Once the family is engaged with the therapist it is highly likely that major transference issues will develop and possibly counter transference issues as well. Such transferences are poignant in the field of family therapy. It is not difficult to see that a family, or family members, may begin to behave towards the therapist as if they were a new parent, another mother or father, and to be fearful that they will behave as previous parents have done. It is easy to see that the therapist may become an imagined possible partner for a single parent, or even the source of sexual fantasies for adults or for children who have been abused. Such transferential phenomena are not difficult to manage and to work through with families so long as the therapist can remain calm and accepting. Patterns of interactions between family members and with the therapist will emerge and become visible through the intervention of the therapist. The family's observation of itself and its members, coupled with the observations of the therapist, will lead to illumination for the family so that it can begin to predict for itself what might happen or is likely to happen next week, next month, next year. It is not uncommon for family members to come to a session and, because of the conversations about the patterns and relationships amongst clients and workers, say:

- 'I have found myself doing it again during this week' or
- 'I managed to stop myself doing it again during this week'.

Finally the individual psychology of family members is to be respected. Individuals have their own metaphors and their particular meanings which they attribute to each other and to events in their lives. It is important that these are held in mind by the therapist and if necessary given due time and attention in a series of individual meetings with family members.

Case Study – Family therapy

The Martin family were referred because Tony (13) was on the Child Protection Register in the category of actual physical abuse. The family consisted of Mr and Mrs Martin (John Martin was Tony's stepfather) and Mr and Mrs Martin's shared child, Caroline (two and a half). They had started to live together when Kate Martin was pregnant with Caroline.

Any time that Kate came physically close to her son Tony she would hit him. She thought she had always been rejecting of him (perhaps not when he was a baby), feeling hostile and full of animosity about him, but when she and John started to live together her hatred for him increased even more and, after the birth of their daughter, she found herself unable to refrain from hitting him whenever they encountered each other. This had alarmed John who approached social services for assistance, and, eventually, following an investigation and assessment, Tony was registered as suffering actual physical abuse. Given that the family, and most especially Tony, insisted on living together, they were referred for family therapy.

At the end of three assessment sessions the family were told, and given in writing, the opinion of the therapist. They were then offered up to eight further sessions, which they attended, and following that a review meeting and, finally, a follow-up meeting some six months after the review.

From the first session it rapidly became clear that Kate Martin, who had probably experienced a puerperal depression, continued to feel extremely low in mood. John himself felt helpless and hopeless about this and had managed it all by working harder. The more he was around Kate the more he felt low himself, and the more he was angry about the way she was treating Tony. In the second session there was a long discussion about the appropriateness of using a male or female therapist, given the presentation by the family. This was a not uncommon gendered presentation, where the female partner is low in affect and the male partner is busily trying to compensate and defend himself. The more each takes his or her position carrying on regardless, the more the other is driven or depressed. Kate argued strongly that she would prefer a male therapist and though not able to give compelling reasons her wish was respected. It became clearer later why she chose a male therapist. A genogram showed that both Kate and John had had difficult and painful childhoods, and that Kate had been abandoned by her mother when she was seven years old. Tony's father, with whom there was little contact, had been violent. Kate had escaped from him when Tony was approximately three years old. She had lived quite reclusively thereafter until she had met John and rather quickly became pregnant. Fortunately for Tony they had lived in a small village where two sets of neighbours had effectively offered him alternative homes. They had cared for and nurtured him even though he remained living with his mother. He was a remarkably robust and sensitive 13 year old.

After a period of reflection the family decided that they would like to meet for further sessions and began to do so from three months after the third family session. We had established after the first session that Kate would not be violent to Tony when travelling to or from family sessions or during them. She agreed. It became clear that the family had developed a particular routine for living. Tony would get up first in the morning at 6.00 a.m. or so, waking John who would prepare breakfast for both of them. John would then leave for work at 7.15 a.m. and Tony would go next door to wait with his friend and eventually get the bus to school. On returning from school Tony would drop off his school gear, change and leave home. He would not return until 8.30 or 9.00 p.m. when he knew John would be there. In the meantime Kate would lie late in bed with her daughter and then spend a slow day doing little other than to play slow games or to draw and paint with her daughter. She cooked an evening meal for everyone but did not eat it with the others as she could not tolerate being with Tony. A version of the usual day occurred on Saturdays and it was only on Sunday that John insisted that Tony was home some of the time while he was there. Kate would then absent herself from any room Tony entered or, if he came close to her, hit him. When Kate hit Tony it was his view that 'it was a drag'. It was almost as if it was an accident that somehow or other he had caused and could easily avoid by being careful. Four of the eight sessions were spent with Kate and John alone, each listening to the other's story of his or her life and coming to some understanding of each other's strengths and weaknesses.

Kate felt awful as a mother. She had felt challenged by Tony all of the time, even from an early age. She experienced herself as hopeless and helpless in respect of how to care for him, nurture him and love him. At the same time she thought it would be impossible to abandon him, and she knew that if she tried to reject him wholly it would cause problems for John who cared for Tony very much. The therapeutic conversation was to the effect that while she might not be able to mother Tony herself, she would feel less guilty and less ashamed if she made good arrangements for someone else to mother him. That might be good enough both for her and for him. The more parents can be involved in the arrangements for substitute parenting the more it is helpful for them and for the young person.

In the following session use of a sculpt highlighted the challenge for the family. John's sculpt showed the family working closely together – mother, father and the two children. Kate's sculpt had mother, father and daughter in one corner of the room and Tony on the windowsill, the furthest away point, though she would have preferred outside the window. Caroline spontaneously moved between Tony and their mother, and experiments with different positions using the sculpt were attempted. It was only afterwards that Kate realised that she had not felt like hitting Tony throughout the meeting, unlike previous meetings.

John became much more supportive, much more understanding, renduced his work and they began to have conversations about how they might work together with respect to providing for Tony. On arrival for the eighth session they told the therapist they had made arrangements for Tony to attend boarding school. He would come home from there one day a week, on Sunday, and for some of each holidays, and the rest of each holiday would be spent with other friends and relatives. The review meeting and follow-up allowed them to describe how things had continued to work out. Tony had begun to be able to be at home overnight at weekends. On enquiring about the things that made a difference for family members the adults thought that it had not been attending that had helped so much but rather the fact that they had begun to work together. Tony said, 'I learnt through attending family therapy that it wasn't me. I was not the problem. I am alright and the difficulty my mother has is about her.'

Comment

Sculpt is a term used in Family Therapy and psychodrama to denote the making of a human sculpture by family or group members. This illustrates the internal experiences of processes or dynamics between members. It is a powerful tool which can be static (snapshot) or active (short film).

The Child Protection system was alarmed about Tony. Members thereof were very relieved that family therapy was offered and accepted. There was a good deal of tension at Child Protection meetings. Adult members of the family wanted their efforts recognised, and rewarded, by de-registration. The family therapist and the team agreed that attending for therapy was not in itself sufficient to indicate change. Partly as a result of this, the family therapy sessions were intense. However, most of the intensity was generated through the very painful conversations about self; self as mother, self as father and self as partner. The more the adults developed and remembered their competencies, tolerated vulnerability, and began to problem solve about their differences, the greater the initial intensity, but, quite quickly, relative optimism developed and tension declined.

The Family Worker

Much is required of the family worker. It will be easier for such a person if they can work closely with a team of colleagues, and some of the time at least with supervision. Live supervision enables the worker to consult with a colleague before, during and after a family session. It allows the worker and colleague to have conversations, while observed by the family, if that would be helpful. Video recording of sessions is useful for every one concerned. The family may want to watch the video of itself and may do so if it so wishes. (Surprisingly, extremely few families wish to take videos of family sessions home to look at.)

How then may one become such a family worker? In short, through training and experience. It is easiest to have a professional training first, as a social worker, a psychologist, a doctor, a nurse, or suchlike. It is then important to train in family therapy and systemic thinking. Thereafter the acquisition of further experience in the profession of origin, combined with experience in family therapy, and practice in the field of child abuse, will produce a very competent family worker. A personal therapy will be extremely helpful, of whatever form or orientation, and regular supervision and consultation is essential. It is probably advisable to be skilled in working with individuals, both adults and young people, before training as a family therapist or, indeed, a group worker.

A good working knowledge of people individually, in groups or families, and a good working knowledge of how organisations and systems operate is important, if not essential. It is necessary to be an autonomous practitioner and clinician. The confidence to act independently, at the same time as having the confidence to seek advice as and when necessary, is crucial.

A collaborative style of working based on interactional thinking, informed about the micro-politics of relating, and an open-minded curiosity will be of great assistance. It is important also to be able simply 'not to know'.

5.3 Does It Work?

Paul O'Reilly

There are at least two strands to the answer to such an apparently simple question. The first must be a consideration of the ethics of family work, and the second has to do with the pragmatics. Implicit within the case presentations throughout this chapter is the assumption that it is good to communicate about complex and difficult matters. Speech is only one means of so doing. This is underpinned by further operational assumptions: that a communicatively-based formulation of key ideals like justice, equality, anti-discrimination, fairness, respect and the importance of witnessing in the therapeutic world can be reflected by the workers and family members. Donovan (2003) describes this very neatly with her account of assumptions in the therapeutic domain ([. . .]* indicates my additions to Donovan's text):

> that all participants are allowed to initiate and take part in the discourse [or communication field]*; that everyone is allowed to question assertions made; that everyone is allowed to introduce any assertion into the discourse [as children and, especially young people, do with great effectiveness when they remain silent]*; that everyone is allowed to express their attitudes, desires and needs; that speakers [communicators[* will not be prevented by internal or external coercion or constraint from exercising these rights.

Implicit also within the case studies is the assumption that the abuse of children and young people has to be considered within the intimate and social contexts of victim and, perhaps, the perpetrator. Thus the first part of the answer to the question is an ethical response: how could we defend *not* working with the families or other context of the victims of all kinds at all levels?

The second part of the answer is more straightforward. There is increasing evidence in the theoretical and research literature of the effectiveness of family work or therapy. Shadish and Baldwin (2003), in a review of twenty meta-analyses, concluded that overall marital and family therapy was as effective as, and sometimes more effective than, other interventions. The effectiveness of work with parents and families where there are child and adolescent conduct and emotional problems is becoming increasingly established (Northey et al., 2003; Cottrell, 2003). It is also now widely accepted that family therapy is the treatment of choice in cases where there are eating difficulties in young people. There is evidence too of efficacy and cost effectiveness in the use of systemic interventions in helping adolescents and adults with drug and alcohol abuse problems. The interventions promote engagement in treatment, help improve family relationships, reduce drug dependency and help users maintain a healthier life-style (O'Farrell and Fals-Stewart, 2003; Rowe and Liddle, 2003). These findings are important because the presenting difficulties are strongly associated with abuse and its consequences.

Now that family work or therapy has become less technically-minded the feedback from family members, whether the presenting difficulty is in the adults, or in the young people, is generally positive.

5.4 Family Work: Conclusions

Paul O'Reilly

Neither we nor our clients need be the victims of our history. But in order that our clients may free themselves as much as is possible from the vagaries of personal history, and yet live within the complexities of personal development, empowering assistance may be required. We all have relatively limited internal worlds. We all live in complex social networks, or aspire to do so. There are great demands, therefore, placed on the client and the worker. It is crucial then that the worker is able to be self-aware and to be appropriately thoughtful. Such a capacity for reflection will lead the family worker to seek support as and when necessary and will enable the worker to offer various levels and kinds of contracted intervention to meet the needs of families. The worker should be concerned with maintaining and caring for himself or herself while allowing families to come to know that such self-maintenance is being undertaken and is important. Self-maintenance is much easier if the worker is a member of a team and embedded within a committed service. Optimistic intervention, and an optimistic stance generally, will be extremely helpful for the worker and for families, indicating the belief that recovery and growth are possible. We can develop a mastery about the present, and the future, especially if our current intimate network will also embark on a journey towards such mastery.

And a final comment

For workers, however, there are added difficulties. The systems in which we work are not always as supportive as they might be. As employees we are expected to fulfil certain requirements: to be of best value, to use effective interventions, proven through outcome studies, to audit our practices and procedures, to be involved fully in clinical government, or its equivalent, to assess and manage risk, to hear from our users, to maintain professional development, and all this within limited resources. Moreover the allocation of resources will be made by managers, of whom there is an ever increasing number, but who often seem inexpert in our field of work. Nonetheless, validated, collaborative and anti-discriminatory practice which can be scrutinised even in the challenging area of child abuse is rewarding and fulfilling work.

Section Six: **Research**

6.1 **Introduction to Research**

Alex McCahearty

During the normal round of JACAT meetings, formal and informal, much is done by way of analysis of our work, and its impact upon clients and those who consult us. The first evaluation of JACAT's service occurred fairly early on in its history (Whiteley and Alexander, 1990). The service was perceived as useful and helpful, and as a result its pilot status was removed and future funding assured. In 1992 Jane Hughes, a psychology student, investigated the participants' perceptions of the process and outcome of a group for young women who had been sexually abused. She discovered shared problems relating to sleep, and difficulties in relating to young men as well as a broad range of general distress. She reported that the biggest changes during the life of the group occurred within the first six weeks and that everyone experienced some improvement, though this varied in amount. Both therapist and clients found the sharing of general experiences helpful. The therapist, however, tended to put more emphasis on the importance of the techniques used, whereas the clients attributed change more readily to the content of the sessions.

In general terms the presence of secondees from health and social services, and latterly from a voluntary agency (Women's Aid) has subjected JACAT's work to a healthy scrutiny and necessitated the answering of many questions about techniques employed and decisions made. In 1996 questionnaires were sent out to all past secondees asking them their views of the service in retrospect. This, together with the report sent in by secondees at the end of their time with JACAT, made us look at how the project had been set up. As a result of this influence, the way in which the secondees' time at JACAT is organised has been changed. They now come for one half day per week, over a full year, rather than for a full day over six months. This not only allows them more time to learn the way in which JACAT operates but also permits them to participate in longer term pieces of work.

However, we had long had it in mind to undertake some more formal research. The opportunity for such a project occurred when Alex McCahearty joined our team in 1998 as an Assistant Psychologist. Though limited in scope, because of the small numbers of respondents to our request for information, the work that Alex did is nevertheless valuable for the more formal insight it provides into how JACAT is viewed by those who use its services. The report of the work is presented in this Section in a formal manner.

6.2 The Research Project

Alex McCahearty

Introduction

It is difficult to undertake research in a clinical setting (Iwaniec and Pinkerton, 1998; Monck, 1997). There are many forces that work against the possibility of collecting research data, analysing it, and then drawing conclusions from it. Even if research is defined in terms of what might be called an action perspective (Kiesler, 1971), that is, investigation based on the receipt of continual feedback, with outcome leading to service development, it is still difficult to persuade the busy and overloaded clinician to provide research data in any rigorous form. That is not to say that as clinicians in JACAT we do not believe we should be subject to public scrutiny, nor that we are unwilling to provide the data necessary for this to take place. Indeed we are fairly amenable to scrutiny by relative strangers, never mind by ourselves. Audit is to be welcomed, as is inspection of methods, procedures and policies.

Nevertheless the conversion of clinical impressions, clinical work and clinical data into something which is replicable, capable of analysis, and which leads to defensible conclusions is very difficult indeed to achieve. Rigour is required for clinical practice. This is clearly so, both in terms of the way in which we think about what we do, and in terms of what actions we undertake with respect to our clients and ourselves. There is also a requirement for rigour when research is conducted, but it is a different kind of rigour. Perhaps there is something essentially non-clinical and even inhumane about the requirements a researcher makes of clinicians. The clinician should always have an open mind, should make hypotheses, work on the basis of these hypotheses, and test them continually, refining and changing them, and offering them to clients in a collaborative enterprise which is rich and expansive. In contrast, the researcher wishes to punctuate; to translate complexity and detail into generalising approximations; to reduce a vast array of inconstant information into fixed terms, whether it be qualitative or quantitative. There appears to be little common ground for collaboration. The researcher is therefore regarded, at a primitive level, with some suspicion by the clinician. The other more actively conceived and somewhat paranoid issue for the clinician is the doubt and mistrust between managers who wish to collect data informed by research or audit, and the clinician who finds little of clinical relevance in management requirements (Whiffen, 1994). This is an issue which is compounded in human services systems, where the providers of the services regard themselves as sophisticated, experienced, skilled and emotionally-engaged practitioners, while the managers appear to the providers to be none of these. Indeed the managers themselves, especially in social services systems, are practitioners who have stopped working directly with clients. In the eyes of practitioners there can be a doubt about their motives in making such a move: was it because they could no longer tolerate working with clients, or because of issues of career progression? Clinicians generally think that it is the former rather than the latter. Such views are reinforced by the difficulty that clinicians have in presenting the stories of their clients to management, as opposed to the numbers of their clients. Similarly, difficulties may also exist in discussing the efficacy of their work with managers as opposed to the efficiency of their throughput.

At JACAT we are convinced, however, that at least a minimum amount of research or audit is required. We believe that if we can model for others that minimum, and maintain the minimum we expect of ourselves, then we may well be in a much better position, among other things, to argue for further resources, so that in turn more detailed and effective outcome research may be undertaken. This is clearly possible (Trowell, 1999) though resources and sponsorship are required.

As a minimum it is important to describe our work in terms of the proportion of time that needs to be allocated to the various tasks that as a service we undertake. A similar description of a related mental health organisation has been undertaken both locally and nationally (Audit Commission Report *Children in Mind: Child and Adolescent Mental Health Services*, 1999). A good deal can be learned from the description of the proportions of time spent on various activities alone.

Background to the Project

In setting up a research project designed to monitor and measure our work we set out to describe the general allocation of time. Time could be seen as devoted to each and all of the following:

- group work
- individual work
- family work
- consultation
- fostering and adoptive parent support
- staff development and administration.

We tried to take into account the amount of time spent on corridor or telephone conversations, the hidden time that people put into reading at home and elsewhere, and the time spent together in more social settings which is highly relevant to the work we undertake. In order to achieve this, basic statistics are required. These statistics tell us who our clients are, who our referrers are, what they refer about, what proportion of referrals concern which things, and basic matters such as waiting times, mean contact times with the service, follow-up times and re-contact times, if and when relevant. The collection of these basic statistics is itself unsatisfactory, as it is not possible to collect all the information that is necessary to be able to describe accurately all that happens. In addition to the activities mentioned there is liaison and networking time, attendance at meetings, attendance at child protection case conferences, evening and weekend telephone calls, and general staff support. There are, too, the inevitable and frequent 'corridor consultations'. Nonetheless we have been able to produce some basic statistics that have helped us in relationship to the current work.

Probably the most important issue in conducting this minimal research is the feedback that we collect from users, whether they be clients, referrers or colleagues in similar service systems. Such feedback helps us to know how people experience the services we offer, and whether or not they have felt these services to be helpful. This can then be compared with our own feelings about the level of helpfulness we were able to offer. The more they can tell us about their experience of our service the better. We have found it difficult to get referrers, in particular, to give thoughtful feedback. It is not uncommon, for instance, for the referrer to tell us, after one meeting only, that clients liked their experience of us. It is important that we have feedback from colleagues who attend for consultation and who make on-going use of the resources we provide. There is evidence (Rogers and Pilgrim, 1997) that it is difficult to hear from any constituency of users because any one person's feedback can be dismissed on the basis of particular circumstances. Nevertheless we endeavour to take account of all feedback, and the thoughts of any person in making predictions about future needs or things that should be changed. It is very helpful to us in changing the provision of services even if that feedback brings surprises in terms of its nature and quality. Of course we have to resist attributing expertise to users of the service mainly on the basis that they are users alone.

Undertaking the Research Project

In this chapter we will describe the work, presenting basic statistics, describing feedback from users, referrers and colleagues, discussing that feedback, and giving some estimate of the assessed outcome of our endeavours in the systems in which we operate. We will further describe the mechanics of how we endeavour to maintain team cohesion, thoughtfulness, maintenance and development. We will come to some conclusions about JACAT and the work we undertake. We will consider finally the issue of research and data collection generally in human services systems like JACAT.

Method

The data was collected from JACAT referral records for a period of one year, April 1997–March 1998. This information was shared with the relevant JACAT workers, who then completed any missing data that was not on record. The team was also asked to estimate the number of hours they had spent on each referral, and how they had made use of this time. Finally, the team was asked to rate – if possible – the outcome of each referral on a 5-point scale (ranging from very satisfactory to very unsatisfactory).

After this information was collected from the team, other people's views were sought. Different questionnaires were sent to clients, referrers and those who attended consultations, known in this chapter as 'consultees', to gain data regarding users' and referrers' experiences of JACAT. All this information was then collated and fed back to the team. The data, including a selection of questionnaire responses, are summarised below.

Results

Referral and team data

The total number of referrals during the period of the survey was 168: 103 male (= 61.3 per cent) and 65 female (= 38.7 per cent). In an age range from one to 18 years, the average age was about 11 years. It was known that 50 (= 29.8 per cent) were on the child protection register. Sexual abuse was the most common referral reason, accounting for 72 per cent of female referrals and 65 per cent of male referrals.

Referrals were managed mostly by individual work, one-off consultation, on-going consultation, or family work. Of note is that therapy is much more time-consuming than consultation work. For this reason it is important to protect consultation time; otherwise new referrals would seldom receive a service, and JACAT's work would grind to a halt.

Group work was, atypically, under-represented in this data. This was accidental. Some groups had just finished before the time period studied and time was spent in reviewing and planning for subsequent groups and development time for group leaders, an exercise that is necessary from time to time if new leaders are to be introduced and existing leaders are not to become stale. During most years two or three groups would take place.

Social service departments were the largest group of referrers with nearly 50 per cent of the referrals. Health services, the next biggest category with over 30 per cent, includes general practitioners, mental health services and paediatrics. The remaining category included self or carer referrals, education and the police service.

The JACAT workers involved with each referral were asked to rate the outcome for each case on a five-point scale and the most common rating was 4: that is, 'satisfactory'.

Client feedback

Of the 79 questionnaires sent, 13 were completed and returned (16.5 per cent). Most respondents had attended their first appointment at JACAT within the previous year. The average waiting time for an appointment was about 8 weeks, which just 9 per cent rated as unacceptable. The average number of appointments, ranging from 1 to 24, was about 10. Of those who responded, 85 per cent rated what they had received as 'acceptable' or 'very acceptable': 92 per cent felt that their situation had improved, either 'probably' or 'definitely'; 85 per cent said they would recommend JACAT to friends or family if appropriate; while 15 per cent were not sure.

Questions asked and answered in the questionnaire were:

Q 'What did you hope for?'

A Just to be able to talk and to help get the past out of the way enough to get on with the future.

A Answers to our questions, help, advice and a starting point to solve the problems we were having.

A Some advice on how to deal with the situation and support.

Q 'What do you think you got?'

A I got enough strength to get rid of the demons of my past.

A Not sure.

A Advice, support for me and the kids.

A Some help with my son.

A Understanding and support and someone who listened without bias, and gave us helpful advice.

Q 'What do you think of the person you spoke with?'

A Very nice, understanding, good listener, friendly and gave me hope.

A   Most professional and caring – easy to speak to, not feeling intimidated.

A   Helpful, but we need more help.

Q   'Was anything surprising to you?'

A   The informality of the interviews.

A   It was odd to have someone to listen to me and who understands.

A   The cost! We didn't expect to have two people focused on our situation at most meetings – a feeling of great support.

Q   'What has been the most helpful thing so far since this problem arose for you?'

A   School.

A   Knowing it's not my fault.

A   Speaking out – not bottling up.

Q   'What has been the most helpful thing about JACAT so far?'

A   Being told we were on the right track and not that what we were trying to do was wrong.

A   Having someone who understands our situation.

A   Books and information given.

A   Being able to have contact with experts.

Q   'Any other comments?'

A   Although we use JACAT rarely, it is a reassurance that if we do need advice, there is someone we can seek help from.

A   It takes a long time to get to see anyone for the first time, but you were really helpful and supportive to myself and my children – brought light into the madness – thank you.

A   The agreed phone calls were not returned.

A   Talking about the problems and getting praise for what we were doing enabled us to gain confidence in our ability to deal with the problems as they arose and to see a light at the end of the tunnel. Thank you.

Referrer feedback

Of the 35 questionnaires sent, 17 were completed and returned (49 per cent). Of these 35 per cent were social workers and 59 per cent were from health services. Twenty-four per cent had referred between two and six times before; 29 per cent had heard about JACAT during their training; 53 per cent through professional contacts (or 'common knowledge'); and 12 per cent through local JACAT meetings or seminars. For 75 per cent of respondents, knowledge of any action taken was within two weeks of their referral. Sixty-four per cent deemed this time either 'satisfactory' or 'very satisfactory', 12 per cent were 'unsure', while 24 per cent felt the waiting period to be either 'unsatisfactory' or 'very unsatisfactory'. For 71 per cent of those referred, work was offered, while for the remainder, advice was given to the referrer or a strategy meeting was called. Eighty-six per cent deemed this action to be either 'satisfactory' or 'very satisfactory'. The remainder rated the action taken as 'unsatisfactory' or they were 'unsure'.

All of those who responded said that they would refer to JACAT again.

Q 'Any comments?'

A It might be helpful to have some written notification of how soon a response can be expected, e.g. a priority or weighting system. Once these particular parents agreed to the referral, to maintain their interest, a quicker response may have been helpful.

A Sensitive and supportive approach with this particular lady who was very concerned about coming to a consultation, but who was very positive about the meeting.

A I found the support that JACAT gave very helpful. Having to travel into JACAT to discuss the family became quite time-consuming.

A A responsive, necessary service.

Consultees' feedback

Of the 43 questionnaires sent out, 15 were returned completed (35 per cent). Sixty per cent of respondents were social workers. The others were a parent, a teacher, a family support worker, a project worker at a family centre, a clinical psychologist and a school nurse. Sixty-six per cent had attended a JACAT consultation between once and ten times before (sometimes concerning the same case); 70 per cent attended previously for advice, and 30 per cent were requesting therapeutic work for their client. Respondents waited between 'a week or less' and two months for their appointment (averaging about two weeks). The wait for the previous consultations was regarded as acceptable for 89 per cent of respondents; 90 per cent rated their previous consultations as either 'helpful' or 'very helpful', while only one rated it as 'unhelpful'.

The average wait for the current consultation was about three weeks (ranging from one week to three months): 77 per cent felt this to be either 'satisfactory' or 'very satisfactory', while 14 per cent rated it as either 'unsatisfactory' or 'very unsatisfactory'. The remaining 14 per cent were unsure.

Of those who came for consultation, 62 per cent were seeking advice or support; 33 per cent were seeking counselling or therapy for their client; 79 per cent rated what they received as 'helpful' or 'very helpful', 14 per cent were 'unsure' and a further 14 per cent felt what they received to be either 'unhelpful' or 'very unhelpful'.

Q 'Any comments?'

A Useful to borrow books and discuss cases.

A Generally helpful – can be difficult to work through aspects of complex situations within the time limit. Also found traces of a JACAT line – wonder how the team deal with uncertainty and dissent?

A Generally supportive in clarifying issues.

A It is useful to enable workers to bounce their ideas and concerns off fellow professionals, and be given advice and direction.

Q 'How do you feel about what you got?'

A I was very pleased and have since been able to use this advice to support my recommendation for this child's future education.

A Very helpful – ongoing support with care, including JACAT attendance at reviews.

A Problems working with families where level of co-operation is negligible – but common issue to struggle with. Consultations need to maintain a joint agencies approach.

A Difficult to say as many of the key professionals were unable to attend.

A Permission to share concerns and a way forward for the client.

Q 'Any further comments?'

A Valuable service.

A There has been a long delay in offering appointments, but some responsibility lies with the family who have chosen not to accept some invitations.

A More publicity needed, as until recently I was unaware of the extent of the service as I'm sure others in education are.

A 'JACAT' not an easy name for families – doesn't promote partnership.

A In common with many services, probably a few more trained bodies would help.

A Very good service – if unable to help, advice given on where help should be sought.

Individual and team maintenance and development

A significant piece of data about the service provided is that which concerns individual and team maintenance and development. Both are multi-faceted and involve significant amounts of time, some of which can be quantified.

Maintenance

Currently (2005) there are twelve members of the team. In total they work 110 hours per week, the equivalent of 4.45 full-time workers. To protect each person from being overwhelmed, exhausted or both, and because of the nature of the work, no one works more than part-time for JACAT, and few pieces of work, apart from individual counselling, are carried out by one worker alone. JACAT workers make active use of peer consultation or supervision, according to their requirement, and intensive clinical supervision is available for individual long-term psychotherapy. Debriefing occurs as and when requested by any one worker or pair of workers, and occurs formally in the process of reporting back to the weekly team meetings.

Though the central core team at JACAT is stable, other workers join and leave the team on a regular basis. The process of caring for them, though time-consuming, is essential. It is important to be thoughtful about the ways in which secondees and others join and leave the group by such simple means as congratulating people on the contribution they have made and welcoming them properly when they arrive. Actively working together as family therapists is helpful for team maintenance in that the work of any one person, whether secondee or regular member, is scrutinised and helped by others. Autonomous practitioners are encouraged to be process-aware, and that process-awareness is maintained throughout the team on an ongoing basis. From time to time the team takes time out to spend half days or full days away from the base. Finally, we have an Advisory Group that meets twice a year. An overall estimate of the time spent per week on such matters of maintenance is in the order of 10 per cent.

Development

Most members of the team have, through personal choice, been in individual therapy either before they joined the team or during their team membership. This is not a requirement, but it seems to be the case that it has been extremely helpful. The therapy takes place outside normal working hours and is funded by the individuals themselves. Each individual member also receives input from the other settings in which they work part-time. A rich cross-fertilisation occurs between the other settings in which people work and JACAT. This is deliberate and actively sought. Individuals are encouraged also to go on training conferences and courses as necessary and relevant to their work and interests.

Team members are also encouraged to *offer* training and to participate in relevant training when requested by others (see above). This plays an important part in the growth of individual confidence and expertise.

Finally, from time to time external consultants are employed by JACAT to meet with the team on an 'away day' and to give the team the benefit of their observations and experiences. An estimate of the time spent per week on such matters is approximately 10 per cent (excluding time spent on individual therapy).

A clear focus on individual and team maintenance development has a number of outcomes, but the primary one is that morale is maintained, developed and promoted and is generally high. This is reflected in low turnover of staff, low absenteeism and low sickness rates, and in particular the acceptance of the scrutiny of others.

6.3 A Consideration of the Project and its Data

Alex McCahearty

Introduction

It has taken significant effort to collect the data presented here and yet it is limited in nature and open to criticism. Collecting information through the use of questionnaires alone has advantages and disadvantages. It is difficult to make questionnaires 'client friendly' and they may not be timely for clients, depending upon the stage they are at in their work with JACAT. The advantage of questionnaires is that clients can actively opt in to giving feedback, and can decide not to complete questionnaires without any consequences. The low response rate from clients compared to referrers and those who attended for consultation is disappointing. We have to be careful, therefore, in the use we make of the data and any extrapolations from it.

Cases seen at JACAT are not representative of those on child protection registers (DoH, 1998). National data states the percentage of children for each category of abuse in England: neglect 41 per cent, physical injury 31 per cent, sexual abuse 21 per cent, and emotional abuse 16 per cent. The data for the south west are similar. It should be noted however that only 50 per cent of the young people attending JACAT were currently on a child protection register, though many more would have been on it previously. Open-ended questions are difficult for any researcher to evaluate in a reliable way. However, qualitative responses can enrich any quantitative data by adding flesh to the bare bones of numbers alone.

A further limitation is that the researcher was employed by JACAT and actively supervised by a member of the team. He was not, therefore, a truly independent researcher. There were times when the work was clearly isolating, and he felt it to be so. At other times it was exciting to be involved in an activity that was so different from the work of the other team members. The researcher had difficulty in extracting information from staff members, who were already busy and over-extended, as he was reluctant to add to their workload.

What the Data Suggests

What then are the key features of the data collected? Firstly, individual therapy is a time-consuming process, and indeed all therapy offered takes up a good deal of time and energy. Second, a significant proportion of referrals can be managed in relatively little time, through the consultation process, in what appears to be a generally satisfactory way for JACAT, for colleagues who consult and for clients themselves (cf. the chapter on consultations). Feedback received indicates that consultation is perceived to be supportive and useful. Third, the vast majority of referrals are for children and young people who have been sexually abused. Fourth, there is little liaison with colleagues in the education services, though this may be partly related to the fact that the education system does not fund JACAT. That leads to the question of mandate – it continues to be crucial that services in the post-abuse arena are mandated by the relevant agencies. Fifth, the proportions of time spent on the various activities required of JACAT are informative and not surprising.

Changes to Practice

The research has led to a number of benefits and service developments. This is to be expected with an action research perspective, where the findings are fed back into the system so as to lead to changes which are then investigated, with further findings being fed into the system again. There is, thus, a recursive process of findings leading to changes in the provision and development of services.

A very significant benefit was that the data, though limited, confirmed the impressions of the team members about the usefulness of JACAT. It may not be surprising that team members estimated that for the majority of people there was a satisfactory outcome, but this was confirmed by the 85 per cent of people who felt that they had an acceptable or very acceptable service and by the 92 per cent of clients who felt that their situation was probably or definitely improved. While only 16.5 per cent of clients gave feedback we did enquire informally of clients generally about the poor response. Many replied that for them it was simply the case that the questionnaire was no longer a relevant matter. They were not in a position to recall easily how things had been for them when they first came to JACAT compared to when they were asked to give specific feedback. They were also unable to attribute the reasons for change or improvement in any meaningful way to JACAT compared to anything else. Very many did say that they would certainly have used the questionnaire to complain or criticise! Monck (1997) found similar issues in her more ambitious study. Another measure of satisfaction is that the rate of non-attendance at JACAT is extremely low (in the order of 3–4 per cent) and the rate of unilateral ending by a client of an agreed piece of work is also very low (in the order of 5 per cent).

There were other benefits in respect of services provided and questions arising about service development. The music played in the waiting area was changed so as to be more congenial for young people. The change was noted approvingly. Magazines were provided which were more age-appropriate. Toys were constantly replaced or updated. More formally we produced a series of new leaflets which we could disseminate to people. Among these were the following:

- *Information for Clients*
- *Information for Teachers*
- *Information about the JACAT Consultation Service*
- *Helping Children Through Therapy*
- *Management of Contact*
- *Referring to JACAT*
- *About JACAT as a Service.*

All of these are much appreciated by all users of the service. We made sure to seek more formal feedback from colleagues who attended seminars and especially from those who attended our conferences. A good deal of the feedback was not surprising; indeed it was rather bland in nature. However, some was surprising and therefore helpful. We continue to collect feedback whenever possible.

The research also raises questions about service development. The high level of referrals of young people who have been sexually abused compared to other forms of abuse raises concerns. It may be that this is a result of factors which are beyond our control, operating in the general context of child abuse and neglect, and stemming from the views of many practitioners in the field that sexual abuse is the most damaging form of abuse and the most difficult with which to work. Though young people are damaged by all forms of abuse a different level of concern may exist among professionals with respect to sexual abuse, hence our referrals. This has to be investigated.

The research itself (and the data from it) has been used to disseminate information about JACAT. The results were presented and discussed at a team 'away day' which was both invigorating and revitalising. Inclusion of some of the findings in the Annual Report and in this chapter itself maintains and develops a presence for JACAT and gives a higher profile to the services needed by abused young people.

The proportions of time spent on the various tasks (see Table 1) are in line with similar organisations such as local and national child and adolescent mental health services (Audit Commission, 1999).

Table 1: Showing time spent on each aspect of work per year

Direct work	30%
Support/consultation	15%
Maintenance (including training others)	20%
Administration (including team meetings)	15%
Travel	10%
Other (including case admin and chairing meetings)	10%

What then for the future? Direct therapy work with individuals, families and groups will continue to be needed and will have to be provided by JACAT or by similar organisations. The more that post-abuse work is offered and accepted by victims, the more likely that they will make some, or a good deal, of progress. They are then likely to make use of adult services in the future. It will be important to continue to support colleagues in the field, as there is a relatively high turnover rate amongst health and social services professionals working with individual clients and families. It will be important to develop closer working relationships with colleagues in the education system. Our leaflet Information for Teachers is a step. We must also ensure that they are aware of the existence of our telephone consultation service, should they have any concerns about any child or young person in their school system. We must continue to facilitate feedback about the service provided. JACAT must maintain a positive and high profile for clients, families and colleagues in order to facilitate the task undertaken for young people in the local community who have been the victims of abuse. Research, both qualitative and quantitative, formal and informal, will serve to promote the provision of the best possible therapeutic services to young people who have been abused and their carers.

Conclusions

While it is difficult to conduct research in a meaningful and formal way about the services provided by JACAT, some positive outcomes are still achievable. We can compare our services on an ongoing basis with research conducted nationally, and we can compare and contrast our services with those that are offered locally. Comparison indicates that the proportion of time we spend on each task is reasonable, and follows the requirements of our founding principles. However, it would be helpful and useful to be able to conduct a more formal research project which addresses more fully the experiences of clients on an ongoing basis so that we have some idea of how they are when they enter our service, how they are as time goes on, and how they are when they leave us. This calls for the provision of resources, which will take energy, and time, and finance. Now the research project is completed we may well be in a stronger position to seek those resources.

6.4 Research: Conclusions

Ann Catchpole

Reviews of JACAT's work, both internal and external, have continued to take place. Over many years our internal review took place in the form of an annual report. This gave statistics about referrals, and reported on general trends. Pressure of work has meant that this practice has ceased for the time being but it would be useful to reintroduce it, if possible. In 2003 JACAT was subject to a joint review conducted by the health and social services. As a result of this, suggestions were made for the expansion of the service to two further parts of Devon. In January 2005 JACAT accordingly established a satellite branch in Newton Abbot, to cover the Teignbridge area, and another such expansion is planned for North Devon. At the present time an audit is taking place of the service offered to mothers of children who have been sexually abused (see Chapter 4.3). This public examination enables accountability to our funding bodies and gives us the chance to see how effective we are in reaching out to children and families where abuse has occurred and to those who work with them.

References

Ainscough, C. and Toon, K. (1993) *Breaking Free.* London: Sheldon Press.

Akister, J. and Canever, N. (1980) A Year in the Life of an Adolescent Group. *Journal of Adolescence.* 3: 3, 155–63.

Andrews, B. et al. (2000) Predicting PTSD Symptoms in Victims of Violent Crime: The Role of Shame, Anger and Childhood Abuse. *Journal of Abnormal Psychology.* 109: 1, 69–73.

Armsworth, M. (1989) Therapy of Incest Survivors: Abuse or Support? *Child Abuse and Neglect.* 14: 4, 541–4.

Audit Commission (1999) *Children in Mind: Child and Adolescent Mental Health Services.* Oxford: Audit Commission.

Baker, A. and Duncan, S. (1986) Prevalence of Child Sexual Abuse in Great Britain. *Child Abuse and Neglect.* 9: 4, 457–69.

Banyard, V.L. (1997) The Impact of Childhood Sexual Abuse and Family Functioning in Four Dimensions on Women's Later Parenting. *Child Abuse and Neglect.* 21: 11, 1095–107.

Barker, R. and Price, M. (2005) Working in Collaboration: A Therapeutic Intervention for Abused Children. *Child Abuse Review.* 14: 1, 26–39.

Bass, E. and Davis, L. (1994) *The Courage to Heal.* New York: Harper Collins.

Bebbington, B.E. et al. (2004) Psychosis, Victimisation and Childhood Disadvantage: Evidence from the Second British National Survey of Psychiatric Morbidity. *British Journal of Psychiatry.* 185: 3, 220–6.

Beck, J.C. and Van der Kolk, B.A. (1987) Reports of Childhood Incest and Current Behaviour of Chronically Hospitalized Psychotic Patients. *American Journal of Psychiatry.* 144: 11, 1474–6.

Bentovim, A. (1992) *Trauma Organised Systems: Physical and Sexual Abuse in Families.* London: Karnac.

Bentovim, A. and Jacobs, B. (1988) Children's Needs and Family Therapy: The Case of Abuse. In Street, E. and Dryden, W. (Eds.) *Family Therapy in Britain.* Milton Keynes: Open University Press.

Bentovim, A. et al. (Eds.) (1988) *Child Sexual Abuse Within The Family.* London: Wright.

Bifulco, A., Brown, G.W. and Adler, Z. (1991) Early Sexual Abuse and Clinical Depression in Adult Life. *British Journal of Psychiatry.* 159: 1, 115–22.

Blaustein, F. and Wolff, H. (1972) Adolescent Group: A Must on a Psychiatric Unit, Problems and Results. In Berkovitz, I.H. (Ed.) *Adolescents Grow in Groups.* New York: Brunner-Mazel.

Box, S. (1978) An Analytic Approach to Work With Families. *Journal of Adolescence.* 1: 1, 110–33.

Briere, J. and Runtz, M. (1986) Suicidal Thoughts and Behaviours in Former Sexual Abuse Victims. *Canadian Journal of Behavioural Science.* 18: 4, 413–23.

Briere, J. and Runtz, M. (1987) Post-sexual Abuse Trauma: Data and Implications for Clinical Practice. *Journal of Interpersonal Violence.* 2: 4, 367–79.

Briere, J. and Runtz, M. (1993) Childhood Sexual Abuse: Long-Term Sequelae and Implications for Psychological Assessment. *Journal of Interpersonal Violence.* 8: 3, 312–30.

Briere, J.N. and Zaidi, L.Y. (1989) Sexual Abuse Histories and Sequelae in Female Psychiatric Emergency Women Patients. *American Journal of Psychiatry.* 146: 12, 1602–6.

Briggs, S. (1998) 'How Does it Work Here? Do We Just Talk?' Therapeutic Work With Young People Who Have Been Sexually Abused. In Anderson, R. and Dartington, A. (Eds.) *Facing it Out. Clinical Perspectives on Adolescent Disturbance.* London: Gerald Duckworth.

Brown, G.R. and Anderson, B. (1991) Psychiatric Morbidity in Adult Inpatients with Childhood Histories of Sexual and Physical Abuse. *American Journal of Psychiatry.* 148: 1, 55–61.

Burck, C. and Speed, B. (Eds.) (1995) *Gender, Power and Relationships.* London: Routledge.

Carr, A. (2000) *Family Therapy Concepts, Process and Practice.* Chichester: Wiley.

Carr, A. (2004) Thematic Review of Family Therapy Journals in 2003. *Journal of Family Therapy.* 26: 4, 430–45.

Carter, B. and McGoldrick, M. (1989) *The Changing Family Life Cycle.* 2nd edn. Boston: Allyn and Bacon.

Cashmore, J. (1997) Systems Abuse. In John, M. (Ed.) *A Charge Against Society: The Child's Right to Protection.* London: Jessica Kingsley.

Cashmore, J., Dolby, R. and Brennan, D. (1994) *Systems Abuse: Problems and Solutions.* Sydney: New South Wales Protection Council.

Coleman, J. Various Audio Tapes for Parents. Brighton: Trust for the Study of Adolescence.

Coleman, J.C. (1974) *Relationships in Adolescence.* London: Routledge & Kegan Paul.

Coll, X. et al. (1998) Child Sexual Abuse in Women who Take Overdoses: A Study of Prevalence and Severity. *Archives of Suicide Research.* 4: 4, 291–306.

Cooke, P. and Standen, P.J. (2002) Abuse and Disabled Children: Hidden Needs? *Child Abuse Review.* 11: 1, 1–18.

Cottrell, D. (2003) Outcome Studies of Family Therapy in Child and Adolescent Depression. *Journal of Family Therapy.* 25: 4, 406–16.

Coverdale, J.H. and Turbott, S.H. (2000) Sexual and Physical Abuse of Clinically Ill Psychiatric Outpatients Compared With a Matched Sample of Medical Outpatients. *Journal of Nervous and Mental Disorders.* 88: 7, 440–5.

Dainow, S. (1994) *How to Survive Your Teenagers.* London: Sheldon Press.

Dale, P. (1999) *Adults Abused as Children. Experiences of Counselling and Psychotherapy.* London: Sage Publications.

Dale, P. et al. (1986) *Dangerous Families: Assessment and Treatment of Child Abuse.* London: Tavistock.

Dallos, R. and Draper, R. (2000) *An Introduction to Family Therapy.* Buckingham: Open University Press.

Dare, C. et al. (1995) The Listening Heart and the Chi Square: Clinical and Empirical Perceptions in the Family Therapy of Anorexia Nervosa. *Journal of Family Therapy.* 17: 1, 31–57.

Department of Health (2003) *Every Child Matters.* London: DoH.

Department of Health (2004) *National Service Framework for Children, Young People and Maternity Services.* London: DoH.

Dong, M. et al. (2004) The Inter-Relatedness of Multiple Forms of Child Abuse, Neglect and Household Dysfunction. *Child Abuse and Neglect.* 28: 7, 771–84.

Donovan, M. (2003) Family Therapy Beyond Postmodernism: Some Considerations on the Ethical Orientation of Contemporary Practice. *Journal of Family Therapy.* 25: 3, 285–306.

Durham, A. (2002) *Young Men Surviving Child Sexual Abuse: Research Stories and Lessons for Therapeutic Practice.* London: Wiley.

Elliott, M., Browne, K. and Kilcoyne, J. (1995) Child Sexual Abuse Prevention: What Offenders Tell us. *Child Abuse and Neglect.* 19: 5, 579–94.

Epps, K. (1999) Causal Explanations: Filling the Theoretical Reservoir. In Calder, M.C. (Ed.) *Working with Young People who Sexually Abuse.* Lyme Regis: Russell House Publishing.

Erikson, E.H. (1968) *Identity Youth and Crisis.* London: Faber & Faber.

Essex, S., Gumbleton, J. and Luger, C. (1996) Resolutions: Working With Families Where Responsibility for Abuse is Denied. *Child Abuse Review.* 5: 3, 191–201.

Etherington, K. (1995) *Adult Male Survivors of Childhood Sexual Abuse.* London: Pitman.

Finkelhor, D. (1984) *Child Sexual Abuse. New Theory and Research.* New York: The Free Press.

Finkelhor, D. and Baron, L. (1986) Risk Factors for Child Sexual Abuse. *Journal of Interpersonal Violence.* 1: 1, 43–71.

Finkelhor, D. and Brown, A. (1985) The Traumatic Impact of Child Sexual Abuse: A Conceptualisation. *American Journal of Orthopsychiatry.* 55, 530–41.

Finkelhor, D. and Brown, A. (1986) Initial and Long-Term Effects: A Conceptual Framework. In Finkelhor, D. et al. *Source book on Child Sexual Abuse.* London: Sage Publications.

Fleming, J. et al. (1999) The Long-Term Impact of Childhood Sexual Abuse in Australian Women. *Child Abuse and Neglect.* 23: 2, 145–59.

Fleming, J., Mullen, P. and Bammer, G. (1997) A Study of Potential Risk Factors for Sexual Abuse in Childhood. *Child Abuse and Neglect.* 21: 1, 49–58.

Frankel, R. (1998) *The Adolescent Psyche. Jungian and Winnicottian Perspectives.* London: Routledge.

Frenken, J. and van Stolk, B. (1990) Incest Victims: Inadequate Help by Professionals. *Child Abuse and Neglect.* 14: 2, 253–63.

Freud, A. (1966) *The Writings of Anna Freud Vol. II: The Ego Mechanisms of Defense.* (revised edition) New York: International Universities Press.

Furniss, T., Bingley-Miller, L. and Van Elburg, A. (1988) Goal-oriented Treatment for Sexually Abused Adolescent Girls. *British Journal of Psychiatry.* 152, 97–106.

Gadd, E.M. (1996) Developing Psychiatric Services for Women. In Abel, K. et al. (Eds.) *Planning Community Mental Health Services for Women.* London: Routledge.

Giaretto, H. (1981) A Comprehensive Child Abuse Treatment Programme. In Mrazek, P.B. and Kempe, H. (Eds.) *Sexually Abused Children and their Families.* Oxford: Pergamon Press.

Glaser, D. (1992) Abuse of Children. In Lane, D.A. and Miller, A. (Eds.) *Child and Adolescent Therapy. A Handbook.* Buckingham: Open University Press.

Glaser, D. (2000) Child Abuse and Neglect and the Brain: A Review. *Journal of Child Psychology and Psychiatry.* 41: 1, 97–116.

Goldner, V. (1998) The Treatment of Violence and Victimization in Intimate Relationships. *Family Process.* 37: 3, 263–86.

Gottleib, B. and Dean, J. (1981) The Co-Therapy Relationship in Group Treatment of Sexually Mistreated Adolescent Girls. In Mrazek, P.B. and Kempe, C.H. (Eds.) *Sexually Abused Children and their Families.* New York: Pergamon Press.

Gunnell, D.J., Brooks J. and Peters T.J. (1996) Epidemiology and Patterns of Hospital Use after Parasuicide in the South West of England. *Journal of Epidemiology and Community Health.* 50: 1, 24–9.

Hagar, T. et al. (Eds.) (1998) *Breaking the Silence. Working with Adult Survivors of Childhood Sexual Abuse.* Brighton: Pavilion Publishing.

Hall, L. and Lloyd, S. (1989) *Surviving Child Sexual Abuse: A Handbook for Helping Women Challenge their Past.* Lewes: Falmer Press.

Hardiker, P., Exton, K. and Barker, M. (1996) A Framework for Analysing Services. In *Childhood Matters: Report of the National Commission of Inquiry into the Prevention of Child Abuse.* London: HMSO.

Harris, M. (1998) Modifications in Services Delivery and Clinical Treatment for Women Diagnosed with Severe Mental Illness who are Survivors of Sexual Abuse Trauma. In Lewis, B.L. et al. (Eds.) *Women's Mental Health Services: A Public Health Perspective.* London: Sage Publications.

Harry Enfield and Chums (1994) BBC Video.

Herman, J. (1981) *Father-Daughter Incest.* Cambridge, MA: Harvard University Press.

Herman, J., Russell, D. and Trocki, K. (1986) Long-term Effects of Incestuous Abuse in Childhood. *American Journal of Psychiatry.* 143: 10, 1293–6.

Hester, M. and Pearson, C. (1998) *From Periphery to Centre. Domestic Violence in Work with Abused Children.* Bristol: The Polity Press and Joseph Rowntree Foundation.

Hester, M., Pearson, C. and Harwin, N. (1998) Domestic Violence and the Abuse of Children. In *Making an Impact: Children and Domestic Violence. A Reader.* Bristol: Barnardo's, NSPCC and University of Bristol.

Horowitz, L. et al. (1996) Factors Affecting the Utilisation of Treatment Services by Sexually Abused Girls. *Child Abuse and Neglect.* 21: 1, 35–48.

Howe, D. (1989) *The Consumers View of Family Therapy.* London: Gower.

Howe, D. (1998) Adoption and Attachment. In Hill, M. and Shaw, M. (Eds.) *Signposts in Adoption.* London: BAAF.

Huffington, C. (1996) Consultation and Service Development. In Jennings, C. and Kennedy, E. (Eds.) *The Reflective Professional in Education.* London: Jessica Kingsley.

Hughes, D. (1998) *Building the Bonds of Attachment: Awakening Love in Deeply Troubled Children.* New Jersey: Jason Aronson Inc.

Hughes, J. (1992) *Participants' Perceptions of the Outcome and Process of a Group for Sexually Abused Young Women.* Unpublished MSc dissertation, University of Exeter.

Hunter, M. (2001) *Psychotherapy with Young People in Care Lost and Found.* Hove: Brunner-Routledge.

Iwaniec, D. and Pinkerton, J. (1998) *Making Research Work: Promoting Child Care Policy and Practice.* Chichester, Wiley and Sons.

Jenkins, A. (1990) *Invitations to Responsibility: The Therapeutic Engagement of Men Who Are Violent and Abusive.* Adelaide: Dulwich.

Jennings, A. (1998) On Being Invisible in the Mental Health System. In Lewis, B.L., Blanch, A.K. and Jennings, A. (Eds.) *Women's Mental Health Services: A Public Health Perspective.* London: Sage.

Jezzard, R. (1994) Adolescent Psychotherapy. In Clarkson, P. and Pokorny, M. (Eds.) *The Handbook of Psychotherapy.* London: Routledge.

John, M. (2003) *Children's Rights and Power: Charging Up for a New Century.* London: Jessica Kingsley.

Jones, E. (1993) *Family Systems Therapy.* Chichester: Wiley and Sons.

Jukes, A. (1999) *Men who Batter Women.* London: Routledge.

Kashani, J. and Allan, W. (1998) *The Impact of Family Violence on Children and Adolescents.* London: Sage.

Kazdin, A. (1994) Psychotherapy for Children and Adolescents. In Bergin, A. and Garfield, S. (Eds.) *Handbook of Psychotherapy and Behavior Change.* New York: John Wiley.

Kendall-Tackett, K.A., Williams, L.M., and Finklehor, D. (1993) The Impact of Sexual Abuse on Children: A Review and Synthesis of Recent Studies. *Psychological Bulletin.* 113: 1, 164–80.

Khantzian, E.J. (1997) The Self-Medication Hypothesis of Substance Abuse Disorders: A Reconstruction and Recent Applications. *Harvard Review of Psychiatry.* 4: 5, 231–44.

Kiesler, D. (1971) Experimental Designs in Psychotherapy Research. In Bergin, A. and Garfield, S. *Handbook of Psychotherapy and Behaviour Change.* Chichester, Wiley and Sons.

Kirk, K. (1998) The Impact on Professional Workers. In Bear, Z. (Ed.) *Good Practice in Counselling People Who Have Been Abused.* London: Jessica Kingsley.

Kitchur, M. and Bell, R. (1989) Group Psychotherapy With Pre-Adolescent Sexual Abuse Victims: Literature Review and Description of an Inner City Group. *International Journal of Psychotherapy.* 39: 3, 285–310.

Kruczek, T. and Vitanza, S. (1999) Treatment Effects With an Adolescent Abuse Survivor's Group. *Child Abuse and Neglect.* 23: 5, 477–85.

Lamb, M.E., Sternberg, K.J. and Esplin, P.W. (1994) Factors Influencing the Reliability and Validity of Statements made by Young Victims of Sexual Maltreatment. *Journal of Applied Developmental Psychology.* 15, 255–80.

Lange, A. et al. (1999) Long-term Effects of Childhood Sexual Abuse: Objective and Subjective Characteristics of the Abuse and Psychopathology in Later Life. *Journal of Nervous and Mental Disorders.* 187: 3, 150–8.

Langs, R. (1976) *The Bipersonal Field.* New York: Jason Aronsom.

Lincoln, Y.S. (1993) 'I and Thou': Method, Voice and Roles in Research With the Silenced. In McLaughlin, D.M. and Tierney, W. (Eds.) *Naming Silences Lives. Personal narratives and Process in Educational Change.* New York: Routledge.

Lindon, J. and Nourse, C.A. (1994) A Multi-Dimensional Model of Groupwork for Adolescent Girls Who Have Been Sexually Abused. *Child Abuse and Neglect.* 18: 4, 341–8.

Lipschitz, D.S. et al. (1996) Prevalence and Characteristics of Physical and Sexual Abuse Among Psychiatric Outpatients. *Psychiatric Services.* 47: 2, 189–91.

Llewelyn, S.P. (1997) Therapeutic Approaches for Survivors of Childhood Sexual Abuse: A Review. *Clinical Psychology and Psychotherapy.* 4: 1, 32–41.

Loftus, E. (1994) Memories of Childhood Sexual Abuse. Remembering and Repressing. *Psychology of Women Quarterly.* 18: 1, 67–84.

Lyons-Ruth, K. and Jacobvitz, D. (1999) Attachment disorganisation. In Cassidy, J. and Shaver, P. (Eds.) *Handbook of Attachment Theory, Research and Clinical Applications.* New York: Guilford Press.

Maclennan, B.W. and Dies, K.R. (1992) *Group Counselling and Psychotherapy with Adolescents.* New York: Columbia University Press.

Madanes, C. (1991) Strategic Family Therapy. In Gurman, A. and Kniskern, D. (Eds.) *Handbook of Family Therapy. Vol. 11.* New York: Brunner/Mazel Inc.

Manion, I.G. et al. (1996) Secondary Traumatization in Parents Following the Disclosure of Extra-Familial Child Sexual Abuse: Initial Effects. *Child Abuse and Neglect.* 20: 11, 1095–109.

Marchant, R. and Page, M. (1992) *Bridging the Gap: Child Protection Work with Children with Multiple Disabilities.* London: NSPCC.

McCarthy, I. and Byrne, N. (1988) Mis-taken Love: Conversations on the Problem of Incest in an Irish Context. *Family Process.* 27: 2, 181–99.

McGee, C. (2000) *Childhood Experiences of Domestic Violence.* London: Jessica Kingsley.

McLeod, J. (1993) *An Introduction to Counselling.* Buckingham: Open University Press.

Mendel, M.P. (1995) *The Male Survivors: The Impact of Sexual Abuse.* London: Sage.

Messman, T.L. and Long, P.J. (1996) Childhood Sexual Abuse and its Relationship to Re-victimisation in Adult Women: A Review. *Clinical Psychology Review.* 16: 5, 397–420.

Minuchin, S. (1974) *Families and Family Therapy.* Cambridge, MA: Harvard University Press.

Monck, E. (1997) Evaluating Therapeutic Intervention with Sexually Abused Children. *Child Abuse Review.* 6: 8, 163–77.

Moon, L.T., Wagner, W.G. and Kazelskis, R. (2000) Counseling Sexually Abused Girls: The Impact of Sex of Counselor. *Child Abuse and Neglect.* 24: 6, 753–65.

Moran, E. et al. (1997) Stranger-Danger: What do Children Know? *Child Abuse Review.* 6: 1, 11–23.

Morrison, T. (1996) Partnership and Collaboration: Rhetoric and Reality. *Child Abuse and Neglect.* 20: 2, 127–40.

Mullen, P.E. (1993) Child Sexual Abuse and Mental Health: The Development of Disorder. *Journal of Interpersonal Violence.* 8: 3, 429–31.

Mullen, P.E. et al. (1994) The Effect of Child Sexual Abuse on Social, Interpersonal and Sexual Function in Adult Life. *British Journal of Psychiatry.* 165: 1, 35–47.

Mullen, P.E. et al. (1996) The Long-Term Impact of the Physical, Emotional and Sexual Abuse of Children: A Community Study. *Child Abuse and Neglect.* 20: 1, 7–21.

Mullen, P.E., Romans-Clarkson, S.E. and Walton, V.A. (1988) Impact of Sexual and Physical Abuse on Women's Mental Health. *Lancet.* 1: 1, 841–5.

Mullender, A. and Morley, R. (Eds.) (1994) *Children Living with Domestic Violence.* London: Whiting and Birch.

Muller, R.T. and Lemieux, K.E. (2000) Social Support, Attachment, and Psychotherapy in High Risk, Formerly Maltreated Adults. *Child Abuse and Neglect.* 24: 7, 883–900.

Muncie, J. and Sapsford, R.J. (1993) Issues in the Study of the Family. In Cochrane, A. and Muncie, J. (Eds.) *Politics, Policy and the Law.* Milton Keynes: Open University Press.

National Commission of Inquiry into the Prevention of Child Abuse (1996) *Childhood Matters.* Vol 2. London: The Stationary Office.

Nelson, E.C., Heath, A.C. and Madden, P.A. (2002) Association Between Self-Reported Childhood Sexual Abuse and Adverse Psychosocial Outcomes: Results From a Twin Study. *Archives of General Psychiatry.* 59: 2, 139–45.

Nicholas, S. (1995) *Society's Child.* Exeter: Outsider Press.

Nishith, P., Mechanic, M.B. and Resick, P.A. (2000) Prior Interpersonal Trauma: The Contribution to Current PTSD Symptoms in Female Rape Victims. *Journal of Abnormal Psychology.* 109: 1, 20–5.

O'Farrell, T. and Fals-Stewart, W. (2003) Alcohol Abuse. *Journal of Marital and Family Therapy.* 29: 1, 121–46.

Obholzer, A. (1996) Working With Institutions. In Jennings, C. and Kennedy, E. (Eds.) *The Reflective Practitioner in Education.* London: Jessica Kingsley.

Oosterhoorn, R. and Kendrick, A. (2001) No Sign of Harm: Issues for Disabled Children Communicating About Abuse. *Child Abuse Review.* 10: 4, 243–53.

Orbach, S. (2000) *The Impossibility of Sex.* London: Penguin.

Palmer, R.L., Chaloner, D.A. and Oppenheimer, R. (1992) Childhood Sexual Experiences with Adults Reported by Female Psychiatric Patients. *British Journal of Psychiatry.* 160: 2, 261–5.

Parker, R. (1999) *Adoption Now. Messages from Research.* Chichester: John Wiley and Sons.

Paul, A. and Cawson, P. (2002) Safeguarding Disabled Children in Residential Settings: What We Know and What We Don't Know. *Child Abuse Review.* 11: 5, 262–81.

Pennant (1992) *The Other Victim.* Luton: Pennant Production (Bedfordshire Sexual Abuse Helpline).

Price, J.L. et al. (2001) A Review of Individual Psychotherapy Outcomes for Adult Survivors of Childhood Sexual Abuse. *Clinical Psychology Review.* 21: 7, 1095–121.

Ray, R. (1998) *A Certain Age.* London: Penguin.

Read, J., Mosher L. and Bentall R. (2004) *Models of Madness.* Hove: Brunner Routledge.

Reder, P. and Duncan, S. (2003) Understanding Communication in Child Protection Networks. *Child Abuse Review.* 12: 2, 82–100.

Rice, A.K. (1963) *The Enterprise and Its Environment.* London: Tavistock Publications.

Roberts, R. et al. (2004) The Effects of Child Sexual Abuse in Later Family Life; Mental Health, Parenting and Adjustment of Offspring. *Child Abuse and Neglect.* 28: 5, 525–45.

Roberts, V.Z. (1994) The Organisation of Work. In Obholzer, A. and Roberts, V.Z. (Eds.) *The Unconscious at Work.* London: Routledge.

Rogers, A. and Pilgrim, D. (1997) The Contribution of Lay Knowledge to the Understanding and Promotion of Mental Health. *Journal of Mental Health.* 6: 1, 23–35.

Ross, G. and O'Carroll, P. (2004) Cognitive Behavioural Psychotherapy Intervention in Childhood Sexual Abuse: Identifying New Directions from the Literature. *Child Abuse Review.* 13: 1, 51–64.

Rowe, C. and Liddle, H. (2003) Substance Abuse. *Journal of Marital and Family Therapy.* 29: 1, 97–120.

Russell, J. (1993) *Out of Bounds. Sexual Exploitation in Counselling and Therapy.* London: Sage.

Rutter, M. (1999) Resilience Concepts and Findings: Implications for Family Therapy. *Journal of Family Therapy.* 21: 2, 119–44.

Sanderson, C. (1995) *Counselling Adult Survivors of Child Sexual Abuse.* London: Jessica Kingsley.
Sayce, L. (1996) Campaigning for Change. In Abel, K. et al. (Eds.) *Planning Community Mental Health Services for Women.* London: Routledge.
Shadish, W. and Baldwin, S. (2003) Meta-analysis of MFT Interventions. *Journal of Marital and Family Therapy.* 29: 4, 547–70.
Sheridan, M.J. (1995) A Proposed Intergenerational Model of Substance Abuse, Family Functioning, and Abuse/Neglect. *Child Abuse and Neglect.* 19: 5, 519–30.
Sinclair, R. and Bullock, R. (2002) *Learning from Past Experience.* London: DoH.
Singh, N. (1987) A Perspective on Therapeutic Work with In-Patient Adolescents. *Journal of Adolescence.* 10: 2, 119–31.
Spencer, M. (2000) Working With Issues of Difference in Supervision of Counselling. *Psychodynamic Counselling.* 6: 44, 505–19.
Street, E. (1994) *Counselling for Family Problems.* London: Sage.
Street, E. and Downey, J. (1996) *Brief Therapeutic Consultations.* Chichester: Wiley and Sons.

The Mental Health Foundation (1999) *Bright Futures: Promoting Children and Young People's Mental Health.* London: Mental Health Foundation.
Trowell, J. (1999) Evaluating the Effectiveness of Psychotherapy for Child Sexual Abuse. In *Research and Policy Briefings from the Mental Health Foundation* 1 (Internet publication).
Trowell, J. (1999) Reported in *Research and Policy Briefings from the Mental Health Foundation,* 1 June.
Truax, C. and Carkhuff, R. (1967) *Toward Effective Counselling and Psychotherapy: Training and Practice.* Chicago: Aldine.

Usher, J.M. and Dewberry, C. (1995) The Nature and Long-Term Effects of Childhood Sexual Abuse: A Survey of Adult Women Survivors in Britain. *British Journal of Clinical Psychology.* 34: 2, 177–92.

Von Bertalanffy, L. (1968) *General Systems Therapy: Formulation, Development and Application.* New York: Brazillier.

Wallen, J. and Berman, K. (1992) Possible Indicators of Child Sexual Abuse for Individuals in Substance Abuse Treatment. *Journal of Child Sexual Abuse.* 1: 3, 63–74.
Watson, G., Scott, C. and Ragalsky, S. (1996) Refusing to be Marginalized: Groupwork in Mental Health Services for Women Survivors of Childhood Sexual Abuse. *Journal of Community and Applied Social Psychology.* 6: 5, 341–54.
Watzlawick, P., Beavin, J. and Jackson, D. (1968) *Pragmatics of Human Communication.* New York: W.W. Norton.
Westbury, E. and Tutty, L.M. (1999) The Efficacy of Group Treatment for Survivors of Childhood Abuse. *Child Abuse and Neglect.* 23: 1, 31–44.
Westcott, H.L. (1993) *Abuse of Children and Adults with Disabilities.* London: NSPCC.

Westcott, H.L. and Jones, D.P.H. (1999) Annotation: The Abuse of Disabled Children. *Journal of Child Psychology and Psychiatry.* 40, 497–506.

Whiffen, J. (1994) *Community Care.* 1008: 14.

White, J., Essex, S. and O'Reilly, P. (1993) Family Therapy, Systemic Thinking and Child Protection. In Carpenter, J. and Treacher, A. (Eds.) *Using Family Therapy in the 90's.* Oxford: Blackwell.

White, M.C. (1995) *Re-Authoring Lives: Interviews and Essays.* Richmond, Australia: Dulwich Centre Publications.

Whitely, A. and Alexander, K. (1990) *A Review of the Work of the Joint Agencies Child Abuse Team.* Devon County Council.

Winnicott, D.W. (1965) *The Family and Individual Development.* Tavistock Publications.

Winnicott, D.W. (1986) *Home is where we Start From. Essays by a Psychoanalyst Compiled and Edited by Claire Winnicott, Ray Shepherd, Madeleine Davis.* London: Penguin.

Wyre, (1991) The Grooming Process in Male Sexual Assault of Children. Paper presented at the conference *Women who Sexually Abuse Children*, Greenwell Clinic, Birmingham.

Yalom, I.D. (1975) *The Theory and Practice of Group Psychotherapy.* New York: Basic Books.

Index